In Pursuit of Radio Mom

In Pursuit of Radio Mom

Searching for the Mother
I Never Had

TERRY CRYLEN

Published 2023
Printed in the United States of America
Print ISBN: 978-1-64742-575-3
E-ISBN: 978-1-64742-576-0
Library of Congress Control Number: 2023906754

For information, address:
She Writes Press
1569 Solano Ave #546
Berkeley, CA 94707

Interior Design by Kiran Spees

She Writes Press is a division of SparkPoint Studio, LLC.

For Grace

*Every woman's path is difficult, and many mothers
were as equipped to raise children as wire monkey mothers.
I say that without judgment. It is, sadly, true.
An unhealthy mother's love is withering.*

—Anne Lamott

Contents

Part One

Part Two

Part Three

Part One

My Radio Family

Thanksgiving comes late

in this museum of childhood,
flower painted at the bottom

of a porcelain teacup:
cracked saucer, no sugar, no milk.

—Joyce Peseroff,
"Museum of Childhood"

"ANYBODY HOME?"

1958. Chicago's south side. I was not quite five years old as I sat there in front of the living room's radio console, attempting to rouse my imaginary family by brushing my pinkie against the glass front. I can see my reflection: an explosion of hair, mouth set in a line. Crouching low, certain this miniature group must be at home nestled together in the rear compartment of our second-hand Zenith, I pressed my ear against the cool surface to listen for any movement coming from the set. "Anybody home?" I called again, telegraphing them with my finger and keeping my voice to a whisper so that my mother wouldn't find me in the living room.

I wasn't looking for a new family because I didn't like my own. A dreamer, I was a girl who lived elbow to toe with nine blood kin—the sixth and next to youngest child. At least for the time being, since baby

1

number eight had yet to arrive. The problem was that my real family was both everywhere and nowhere. A three-ring circus with too many acts performing all at once. A place where I couldn't grab hold of the ringmaster—my mom. Her attention always seemed focused on someone else in the tent or on performing her own magic act. The one where she could make herself disappear for long parts of a day.

We were packed into our six rooms in a house that, at a thousand square feet, was hardly bigger than a box. Perhaps it wasn't all that surprising, then, that when I went out scouting for a fantasy family, my search fell within a similarly small space.

Like the console, most of our furniture was hand-me-down stuff, functional and nicked around the edges. On the mantle stood a ceramic statuette of the Blessed Virgin Mary; a large oil painting of Jesus at Gethsemane hung on one wall. All shadow and gloom, the picture seemed not so much haunting as haunted. Early on, I developed the habit of scurrying past Jesus, no direct contact. If brave enough to do so, I shot him only a sideways glance.

But in the Radio Family's living room there was a luxurious velvet sofa with crocheted doilies stretched across its wide arms. A thick, floral-patterned rug warmed the room, and the polished wooden end tables had lamps that threw light into even the darkest corners. In the kitchen, the table was set, readied for the meal to come. With seating enough for everyone, and chairs that matched.

Every night in bed, I strategized about how I would at last coax Radio Mom out from where she and the others huddled together. My desire for her had grown increasingly intense. I was sure that once Radio Mom saw me, everything else would be easy-peasy—it was getting her attention that was the problem. Now, taking a deep breath, I made up my mind to be more forceful if necessary, even willing to risk discovery. I reminded myself that this tiny clan just out of reach would be the perfect fit to adopt me.

On this day, I'd already planned for the hours when kindergarten had ended for me but the bigger kids hadn't come home yet. I'd waited for the lull in household activity. Still hunching forward on a patch of the worn carpet, I stared for as long as I dared, adjusting the volume on my thoughts and tuning out the static of my younger brother's background clamor, content to be in the company of just the old radio.

As I let my nose kiss the glass, I imagined Radio Mom to be as beautiful as my own mother, with dark eyes, and curly hair that always looked neat even when she was bustling about cooking and cleaning. But unlike Real Mom, she also spent time just sitting with her children, or playing a game. And, being surrounded by her own family who adored her, she loved sticking around the house. If I closed my eyes, I could almost hear Radio Mom humming, her voice silky, warm enough to carry me toward sleep.

Just as much as I was certain that Radio Mom had magical powers to soothe, I could see that my own mother was like a bundle of wires: tangled and frayed. The mother who gave birth to me could light up a room with her high voltage power, but was also prone to bouts of short-circuiting. Good looks aside, the truth was that Real Mom and Radio Mom bore little resemblance to one another, except that they both lived behind a wall and were impossible to find on the dial.

"Yoo-hoo," I sang.

I could hear my mother washing dishes in the kitchen.

On the other side of the console "window," tall numbers marched across the width of the case. If I gazed at them long enough, the numbers began to glow, like a visual doorbell. Now, gazing through the picture window that only moments before had been the radio's glass partition, I sensed something else. Little figures hugging tight on the other side of that rectangular wall.

Listening!

I tapped again, this time with my knuckles. Then harder, my heart beating wildly.

No response.

Time passed and eventually I rocked back on my heels, struggling not to cry. Nothing I did was working. The tiny family dreamed on behind the glass without me.

A bitter taste on my tongue. I shifted my gaze toward the front door.

She wasn't coming out and would always remain just a mom behind glass. I would never sit in her lap and feel her hand untangle my hair. She would never slick a Band-Aid over a cut on my elbow, never make me a peanut butter and grape jelly on white. The realization cut through me. Radio Mom hadn't heard me after all, despite my determination. The fantasy of being a special and cherished child faded.

After that, I spent little time in front of the radio.

By the time I'd begun to withdraw from my relationship with the Zenith, my family and I had lived in our house on Peoria Street for three years. We'd relocated there in 1955, from the two-bedroom apartment in which my parents had lived since their marriage in 1939. Although at three years old I was too young to remember that move across twelve city blocks to the west side of the Englewood neighborhood, in my mind's eye, I can easily imagine Mom behind the wheel of our old Plymouth—with six kids hanging halfway out the car's windows. Arms flailing, everything noise. And my father following behind in a produce truck borrowed from someone in his childhood neighborhood, its bed packed high with tables and mattresses.

The Peoria house grew steadily smaller in the five years we lived there, its shrinkage hastened by kids growing taller and the birth of an eighth child, my fourth brother. Ten people, a snarly cocker spaniel, three tiny bedrooms—one of which was crammed with a bunk bed for my two older brothers and a double-size bed for my next older sister and me. My two oldest sisters shared a room and the youngest brothers slept in small cribs tucked into a corner of Mom and Dad's room. Rough and tumble and always fighting for space, my bedroom-sharing brothers and sister resembled a litter of puppies in a too-crowded crate. I never ever considered calling for Mom to make them stop. Asking her to do even "one more damn thing," as she often put it, would only make her madder.

After staking claim to the people who lived in the console, only to have the whole effort go bust, I stumbled on a new favorite pastime: surveying the world from the perspective of the top step of the front porch. Scuffing my shoes through the occasional flakes of paint that fell from the wood siding to the floor, I watched the neighborhood kids roam the streets like stray cats, hearing Dad's voice in my head.

"Don't wander off—it's not safe," he told me, over and over.

At one point he had rigged one of my brother's toy rifles to the back porch ceiling, its barrel aimed straight at the screen door. In this working-class version of a home alarm system, nighttime prowlers were supposed to think that any attempt to open that door would be met with gunfire. I never knew if this makeshift deterrent was why we were never robbed during our time on Peoria Street, but I took comfort in my father's determination to keep his family out of what he believed was "harm's way." Out front, weeds grew so tall and thick, I thought they were palm trees planted long before we arrived. The narrow windows at the front of the house refused to open, or to welcome a breeze. With fogged glass panes that repelled the sun's rays, no natural light spilled into the rooms inside.

My dad took a summer photo the year I was five, a copy of which I first came across as a teenager, when I could not have fathomed the metaphor it presented to the viewer; in it, my mother was seated on a bottom stair of the front porch, surrounded by two of my brothers, two of my sisters, and me. I had positioned myself close to my mother, and in this sense, the photo is perhaps not surprising.

There was Mom, looking straight ahead—a remote island, surrounded by a wave of activity. One sister was bolting through the screen door and back into the house, another had one foot forward, as if she were about to race down the stairs. A younger brother held tight to what resembled a metal lunch box, his smile wide. An older brother, a book in his hands, wore no expression at all. Each projected a sense of mission—even those not moving about, around or behind my mother—as if absorbed by thoughts of reaching some destination beyond the range of the camera.

I imagined the day to be a sweltering one, because all the days of childhood summers in Chicago were oppressive. In hardscrabble neighborhoods like ours, air conditioning was found only in movie theaters. As members of the underclass and a family without distinction, we knew, as children, not to complain. Because Mom and Dad weren't shy about talking about their childhoods, we knew that they had grown up "with nothing," in "cold-water flats," and that when she was little, Mom often sat in a parlor lit by a single bulb hanging from a low ceiling. The message was clear even for a small kid like me: "Don't gripe. You've got it good."

Still, as evidenced in this black-and-white photo, I was the poster child for what poor looked like: my hair uncombed, unkempt, dressed in clothing tailor-made for children who wore shame. The picture captured something more, as well: the intensity I carried as a young child. Despite my deadpan expression, I looked as if I might spontaneously ignite.

How untethered I appeared—unbound to any member of my family—though my keen desire to be harnessed to my mother's side is palpable. I leaned toward her, straining, but our bodies did not touch. One of my hands gripped the edge of the step, my fingers curled tightly around its lip. It was as if I was working hard to keep myself grounded.

Mom's good looks shone in that Polaroid. Like the Hollywood actresses she and the women of her generation idolized, she always paid attention to her appearance despite a lack of money for frivolities. In the photo, her dark hair waving thick to frame her slender face, she wore a sleeveless square-patterned dress that showed off long slim arms. Her hands stretched gracefully over her knees.

As I examined the photo throughout the years, my mood always determined the expression I saw on her face as she sat there. Sometimes, it seemed to me, she looked preoccupied and other times simply unknowable. But as I looked into her eyes, I could sometimes perceive a dreaminess that made it easy to remember why I had found her enthralling. Her look off into the middle distance captivated me— not only because it made her features more striking, but because it allowed me to bring her close to me. I saw that she had dreams, too. Dreams of escape, of wanting more. Dreams not so different, perhaps, than the ones awakening in me.

Next to Mom, tucked in the folds of her summer dress, was her ever-present handbag. "Where's my purse?" and "Get my purse!" were two of her most frequent questions and commands. "Where's my purse?" signaled that she was headed out the door. Leaving. The photo gave no hint about her arrival or departure status that day, but that get-away bag was there, the reminder that Mom might fly off at a moment's notice.

I hated that she always had her purse nearby.

Like my sisters and brothers, I tried to avoid long hours of separation from Mom by finagling ways to leave with her. Capturing her attention when she was home was difficult enough, but when she was out of the house, the hours stretched long. Most times, she was with her mother, my Grandma Healy, and getting permission to accompany her represented a real coup—the better part of a day in her company, away from the other kids. The way to wheedle an invitation was never to ask to join her, but to wait patiently until she was about to leave. Then I would position myself, like a newly trained puppy, near the door.

My mother's level of enthusiasm for these field trips with Grandma was hard to measure. Was her participation propelled by guilt, or perhaps a desire to keep her own mother close?

"Okay, Ma," she'd say in a subdued tone over the phone. "I'll pick you up and we'll go for a cup of coffee." "Cup of coffee" was code for "we'll window-shop down Halsted Street and have a nice lunch along the way." Taking my mother out to eat was part of my grandmother's ritual. Grandma always slapped her hand over the scribbled slip that the waitress dropped on the table, and I marveled at her skill in snatching the bill.

The rules of these outings were inviolable: Keep still, don't ask for anything, and don't interrupt Mom's conversation with Grandma. For me, the rewards were worth following these directives. As for my mother, who knew? While these trips allowed her time away from taking care of all of us, they didn't seem particularly relaxing.

"Skinny Grandma" could spend hours searching for a cheap, embroidered handkerchief or a plastic rain bonnet. "Skinny Grandma" scoured through long rows of bins filled with clearance items, never tiring of the hunt for some small treasure. A prim and fussy lady, at seventy she resembled the woman in the American Gothic picture, except she wore thick wire glasses. She dressed the way she expected everything to be: "as neat as a pin." On her coffee dates with Mom, she wore a pastel, cotton shirtwaist dress that was as starched as her personality. My job while she was bin-rummaging was to focus on her back and follow her from aisle to aisle.

The highlight of the day came around noon: "Florence," she'd say to my mother, "why don't we stop and have a little something." Once in the diner, I'd wait for Grandma to declare, "I think I should just have the special." Which meant we would all be eating roast beef with a scoop of mashed potatoes, our food drenched in gravy. This was far more exotic fare than what appeared on the dinner table at home. There, ground beef smothered in ketchup and tossed with canned peas was a staple that, due to logistics in our kitchen, we ate in shifts.

As we sat waiting to be served, Grandma held court, presenting a litany of complaints—most of which featured her bad stomach, my bachelor uncle's drinking, and her attempts to prevent this middle-aged son, who still lived with Grandpa and her, from squandering his monthly disability check.

"I have a lousy life," she'd begin, shaking her head.

I didn't doubt that Grandma's life was lousy, not only because I'd heard her declare it as such at least a million times, but because even at a young age I knew some of her sad backstory: how her mother was sickly and died when Grandma was nine, and how Uncle Buddy's twin had been dropped by a nurse attending at the birth and hadn't survived. Also featured was the story of Mary and Robert—Grandma's oldest children—who had contracted tuberculosis in their late teens, and, one after the other, succumbed to the disease. Now, sadly, only Uncle Buddy, my Aunt Dorothy, and Mom, the youngest, were left.

Over time, I would hear my mother reminisce about what she remembered: Robert and Mary's deaths—her brother's when she was twelve and her sister's when she was seventeen. The stories were always about how they had died alone, and dying that way became a fear that obsessed her for the rest of her years. In contrast, when Grandma talked about all the things that proved her life was lousy, including her children's deaths, everything focused on her. Maybe all that illness and all those deaths had been too crushing, making it hard for her to focus on the rest of her family. It was as if she'd called dibs on all the suffering there was to be had. Misery, it seemed, belonged only to her.

According to Grandma, Uncle Buddy, the one other person in Mom's family who'd had his own brush with TB, was "not a bad person, except when he's 'pifficated.'" Grandma never used the word "drunk." But from the way she described it, I knew "pifficated" meant he was eligible for free rides in the back of a paddy wagon.

Except for the talk about Uncle Buddy, which scared me, Grandma's predictable lunchtime recitations mostly bored me, like a white noise that could induce coma. I'd stay alert by watching her fiddle with the creamers: thumb-size glass bottles of half-and-half that usually ended up spilled on the table after her fingers lost their battle with the lids.

Throughout Grandma's litany, Mom looked as if she were listening, her eyes on her mother, her lipstick-stained coffee cup clutched with both hands. Grandma alternated between taking bites of food and speaking her mind; gesturing with her fork held high, she talked until every last morsel on her plate disappeared. And then ordered rice pudding with raisins for all three of us.

After lunch, the browsing down store aisles continued until, finally, my grandmother announced that her feet hurt. It was time to go home. I liked her the best when these outings came to their end, as an afternoon of Mom's entertainment would soften her irritability and she would take notice of me at last. Sometimes Grandma would ask about school, or press a nickel into my hand. I'd hold her arm as we headed back to the car, slowing my pace to accommodate her wobbly gait.

As the car pulled up at the brick building where she lived, Grandma would turn slightly and tilt her head toward me as she got out.

"Goodbye, peaches and cream," she'd say.

Thrilled to hear her liken me to a sweet dessert, my eyes followed her as she moved toward her apartment. When she reached the entrance, she turned back toward my mother and me, her hand extended in a little wave. Her vestibule was dark and I felt a jolt of sadness as she walked into its shadows.

"Stop!" I wanted to yell. "Grandma, get back in the car." I imagined Uncle Buddy peering out at me from behind the window's heavy curtain, his tuberculosis-ravaged lungs rattling like chains.

My uncle became the "Bogeyman" whenever he was in need of drinking money, which was whenever Grandma had confiscated his disability check. She always phoned Mom to let her know he was probably on his way to our house to look for a handout. It wouldn't be long then before the sound of Uncle Bogeyman's cane thumped against the stairs of our front porch.

"Mom, Mom—he's here!" I'd scream, as I dropped to all fours and got away from the windows.

"Did you put the envelope in the mailbox like I told you?" she'd shout from the bedroom, where she'd run to hide.

Placing money in the mailbox seemed the surest way to prevent the Bogeyman from attacking us, but my six-year-old brain always worried that I'd forgotten to lock the front door behind me. What if Uncle Bud jiggled the doorknob, opened the door, and came reeling into our house?

Was he really a harmless drunk or would he kill us all?

If he was harmless, how had he come to know the inside of a paddy wagon so well?

All I could do was freeze in place and pray that whatever was in the mailbox would be enough. Only when metal on metal slammed did I dare to breathe, exhaling with each *thump-thump* of his cane as Uncle Buddy retreated down the stairs.

After a minute or so, with the Bogeyman undoubtedly on his way to the nearest tavern, I'd rush to where Mom was in hiding.

"He's definitely gone, Mom," I'd announce, pride now added to my relief.

I'd protected my mother from her older brother. Instead of worrying about what I would have done if I'd been caught by the hook of my uncle's cane, I focused on the way I'd kept her out of danger.

What a good little girl I was.

If only my mother's disappearing acts were simply running from Uncle Bud or the occasional neighbor who dropped by. Instead, when Mom began using Grandma's phrase to describe her own "lousy" life, a wave of worry swept over me. I was too young to understand why she was so unhappy; all I knew was that Mom was about to grab her purse and leave.

On her bad days, the air crackled with tension. From the pantry where I pretended to be looking for food, I'd watch her. Slouched in a chair at the kitchen table, she'd tap her fingers on its Formica top and stare out the window. Too scared to go near her and too scared to move to another part of the house, I'd wait, hoping for a miracle. Maybe this would be the one time when Mom would rise up out of her chair and say something—anything that might indicate that the mysterious black spell had been broken.

Being alone with her thoughts made her edgy. After a while, she'd stand, throw her coffee spoon into the sink and wander from room to room. Only then would I sneak from my spot in the pantry, and from a distance, track her movements. Picking up speed, she slammed doors, pulled at drawers and then grabbed her purse, which hung on the kitchen doorknob. Without a word or even a glance, she'd fly out of the house.

On those days when my mother bolted out the front door, my anxiety zoomed high. Even when my brothers or sisters had witnessed the same scene, even if my eleven-year-old sister, Flo, stepped in to take care of the younger kids, I felt scared and alone. Shell-shocked. We did not comfort one other. Like strangers at a funeral, we moved slowly past each other, our heads bowed to avoid eye contact, each of us on our own to grapple with our loss.

Waiting for Mom's return, I spent hours worrying. Like a small animal trying to find its way out of a hole, I scrambled to figure out what I should have done to make Mom stay rather than run. Though I was hardly big enough to push a broom, I swept floors and picked up clothes that were scattered around the house. All as a way of demonstrating to my mother that I was her good helper. All as a way of making her life less "lousy."

Mom always returned, having spent those long hours, I later learned, in a darkened movie theater watching double features, but experience soon taught me that when she did reappear, things would not necessarily improve. Rather, a day or more of seclusion in her bedroom was required before she re-emerged and became "normal." Helpless to change the course of events when Mom had one of her "episodes," I swept harder and tried to keep a low profile.

No mention was ever made of my mother's disappearances. It was as if she had become possessed, and afterward no one wanted to revisit what had occurred. By the time she finally climbed out of her bed and rejoined the family, my body would be weak with anxiety and relief. Once Mom began talking to me again, I cared only that she was back, not why or where she'd gone.

I was almost seven, and getting ready to make my first Holy Communion, when Mom chose the Catholic Church's sacrament of the Eucharist as an occasion to become my fantasy mother. For a moment, Radio Mom was within the circle of my arms and my first communion became its own blessed event. The day I accepted the communion wafer—the food of eternal life—was the first time in memory that I'd bathed in Mom's unadulterated attention. I was in communicant heaven.

Days before the celebration, the head of our school, Sister Anastasia, ushered me down to the office and instructed me to wait for my mother. Baffled by the fact that Mom was obviously picking me up from school when I usually walked home, I sat in an uncomfortable chair, nervously eyeing a row of tables where Communion accessories were neatly arranged. There, near the full color pictures of Jesus baring his chest to reveal his Sacred Heart, was a separate door, and in walked Mom, her purse hanging from her forearm as she smiled politely at Sister.

I was shocked. Mom had a strict policy of refusing to be seen anywhere near a nun. It seemed impossible for her ever to be at our school where a flock of them might appear at any moment. Even as a second grader, I knew how much my mother loathed telephone calls from the church office reminding her that her account was overdue.

"Oh! Yes, Sister. Yes, Sister," she'd say then, quickly, groveling. "Tomorrow morning for sure."

After she hung up, she'd swat the air with her free hand. "Why the hell didn't one of you answer the damn phone?" she'd yell.

But on this afternoon in the principal's office, Mom was entranced by the process of buying accessories for my Communion outfit. Without any detectable embarrassment in being around Sister, she thumbed through prayer books, compared different types of rosaries and examined the square cloth of a scapular that was meant to be worn like a necklace. Selecting one of each, she transferred the items into my outstretched hands.

As we moved toward the office secretary to pay for our purchases, Mom paused in front of a stack of child-sized patent leather purses. She worked the clasp on one she'd pulled from the pile. *Click*. Open. *Snap*. Shut. With crossed fingers, I waited to see if the shiny pocketbook passed Mom's sturdiness test. Raising her eyebrows, she asked, "Should we get this, too?" Clutching my bounty to my chest, I floated out of the building.

More was to come. The night before I made my Communion, she had me kneel on a chair in front of the kitchen sink, and measured a capful of White Rain shampoo over the back of my head. Lathering my hair, she slowly worked her fingertips across my scalp until it tingled. I'd never dreamed of such a thing, not even with Radio Mom.

She massaged my temples, the space behind my ears, and finally, the muscles at the nape of my neck. Next, taking a pot from the dish rack, Mom filled it to the top and rinsed my hair clean. Luxurious. Then, just when I thought my time in beauty-shop wonderland had ended, she began untangling my wet hair as if performing a delicate surgery. Each pass of the comb became a show of affection, her breath soft against my neck. With my hair still damp, she twirled strands into circles, then fastened each with two bobby pins, one crisscrossed over the other.

"There," she announced, as she wrapped toilet paper around her handiwork. "You're all set, and it's time for bed."

I moved reluctantly toward the bedroom I shared with three siblings.

In the early morning, sleep still in my eyes, Mom sat on a kitchen chair and pulled me in between her knees. Carefully, she unwound my toilet paper hairnet, and then, the field of bobby pins. Curls cascaded to my shoulders. We moved together to the living room and my hands reached up as Mom let my dress's chiffon drop over my head. As I studied myself in the hall closet mirror, the scratch of crinoline against my legs told me that I was not in a dream. I had been transformed. When Mom finally positioned the rhinestone band of my long communion veil onto my head, I moved onto the center stage of my own coronation. I had as many accessories as the Barbie doll I'd never been given: sheer white gloves, pretty new socks, and patent leather shoes. My little purse rounded out my Holy Day ensemble. Best of all, my clothes were new, unwrinkled, and my hair was shiny and styled. For the very first time, I viewed myself as being like every other girl in my second-grade class.

Rain fell hard as our elated band of communicants prepared to walk from school to the church next door. Concerned that we would dissolve like sugar if we ran across the courtyard in the downpour, nuns in black cloaks moved quickly around the room, placing what looked like bed sheets cut from oilcloth over each of our heads. Once freed from my makeshift umbrella at the church, I walked the long aisle to the communion rail with an expression of piety that I was sure would make Jesus proud.

By the time the service concluded, the deluge had stopped and the afternoon turned warm. Back at our house, as I stood on the front porch, emboldened by having spent so much time in my mother's orbit and filled with pride at my acceptance into the church, a new question floated past. Could I ever have Mom by my side again, the way I had on this special day? In my journey to connect with Radio Mom, I had come up empty and alone. Yet, as much as I had been desperate to know her and crushed when it became obvious to me that she was only imaginary, never having held her hand or felt the warmth of her gaze on my face made it easier to accept the fact that she would be forever unattainable. My mother's presence in the days surrounding my first Communion—physically and emotionally—*was* real. Could I hold her attention from here on out? Over the next few ensuing years, this taste only made me long for her all the more. And, not surprisingly, once Communion was past, life in our household went back to the way it had been before.

My relationship with Mom paralleled hers with Grandma, but I had no way of knowing this as a child. No way of knowing that my devotion toward my mother—and the feelings of responsibility I harbored for her—mirrored how she had responded to her own mother. Or that she might have been seeking something more from Grandma, a mother who had been just as emotionally unavailable to her daughter as Mom was to me.

Devil and The Pitchfork

It's a funny thing, hope.
It's not like love, or fear, or hate.
It's a feeling you don't really know
you had until it's gone.

—Anna Quindlen
Still Life With Breadcrumbs: A Novel

MY FATHER'S WARNINGS NOT to venture beyond the front porch were no match for the allure of the street. From the time I was five, until we moved from Peoria Street two years later, I heard phrases like "changing neighborhood" and "things aren't safe" often. To me, those expressions didn't make sense. Especially the part about the neighborhood changing. As far as I could tell, every day when I went to school, the neighborhood looked the same as it had the day before. The only thing that I was pretty sure was changing was me. I was itching to get out of a house that was cramped and too noisy and where nevertheless I felt alone. I wanted to have what Mom was always praying for: a change of scenery.

Like so much else inside the four walls of the house on Peoria, even the oxygen seemed in short supply. From my perch on the steps of the porch, I could breathe. Outside, I saw how kids played and laughed together, how they ran so fast the soles of their shoes seemed never to touch ground. When I looked up and down the block, my eyes tracked a universe that teemed with possibility. So, the decision to either abide by Dad's instructions or to defy him and sail into another orbit proved to be easy. Out there were my people, who, unlike Radio Mom, were real. Accessible. I wanted to be part of something not only different from my family, but bigger. Part of a larger whole. I wanted to be hugged by the arms of the neighborhood.

I wanted a chance to belong.

During these years, the street along Peoria became my home away from home, a galaxy of sensory delight. My first mission beyond the porch took me to the curb some twenty paces away. I stood there, flushed with pride and self-importance. At my feet, finely ground glass reflected shiny worlds of light. A smile spread across my face. Already, a new discovery. When I looked up, I saw Tommy McCormack standing across the street, pitching a rubber ball against the stairs of his own front porch. Several years older than I, Tommy kept a makeshift pigeon coop in the rafters of his family's garage. *Thump*-pause. *Thump*-pause. It wasn't long before Mrs. McCormack appeared at the window.

"Tommy, quit the racket," Mrs. McCormack yelled, her thick Irish brogue making the command sound almost pleasant—so unlike Mom's response if one of my brothers had been caught doing the same thing. "You're going to punch a hole in the damn screen!" she'd scream. "What the hell are you doing outside, anyway?"

Brushing the image aside, I stood there, mentally mapping the coordinates of possible destinations, and decided a future trip to Pigeon World would be necessary.

Behind me, dandelions dotted the dry lawn. I turned my back on Tommy McCormack and floated along the sidewalk, already feeling a long way away from Daddy's rule about the porch. A flicker of guilt sparked in my chest. I didn't want to worry him. Daddy was like a grizzly who hollered loud when he was mad, even if he was actually all growl and no bite. He'd wave his arms above his head and yell, "Jesus Christ, you're gonna get hurt," when we'd done something that met with his disapproval. Underneath this gruffness, his feelings, like mine, got hurt easily. I knew my show of disrespect would make him sad, mirrored in his gentle brown eyes. Letting my father down was what bothered me most, but I trotted down the street, nevertheless.

Trying to convince myself that I hadn't really done anything so terribly wrong, I heard Mom's voice in my head again, this time joking about what we all knew to be true about Daddy: "That man can tell you how to get anywhere in the country—which roads to take and how long it will take you to get there— even though he's never left his own backyard." Remorse lessened as I moved along the sidewalk. My father didn't like risk; he couldn't possibly know about adventures. He wouldn't be able to understand my mission—places to go and people to know. I pressed onward.

Several doors down, a house similar to ours was in the middle of being torn down. Dad said they were building a school, but as a Catholic kid enrolled at St. Bernard's, I knew the chances that I would go to that school were zero. The house looked as if it had been bombed into rubble. Only a few walls with water-stained wallpaper remained. I stared as older kids, none of whom I recognized, raced like termites around collapsed beams and discarded lumber. No one waved me off and I inched closer, crouched low for balance. Then scooted my way down a narrow plank to what had been the basement.

Boys climbed on all fours over mounds of broken concrete and jagged boards. Stories that my brothers had shared about old nails and lockjaw wormed through my mind. I eyed my shoelaces as I walked around slowly. Worrying that the rubber soles of my sneakers might not be thick enough to protect against rusted metal. Opening and closing my mouth every few minutes, I tested my jaw. I stayed for a long time, ready to run if a dead body were discovered under all the wreckage. But really, I was imagining myself a member of the hunt.

Hanging out with Mr. Newton at his corner mom-and-pop shop turned out to be even more amazing than the search for dead bodies. The success of my first mission to the demolition site the day before had emboldened me to launch another one. This time, I slipped out of the house and hurried to the very end of the block, ready to peek through the smudged glass into Mr. Newton's store and then run away fast. Once there, I decided to take a closer look. Mr. Newton was sitting behind the counter, and waved me inside.

I knew about Mr. Newton, though he knew nothing about me. He'd once driven several of my older brothers and sisters to school in his giant Cadillac—something they'd bragged about for days afterward. How jealous I'd been because I'd been home sick that day. It had been raining when they'd walked past his store, and apparently, he'd stepped outside and offered everybody a lift. Mom remarked that it had been a very nice thing for Mr. Newton to do, which confused me. As far as I knew, neither of my parents had ever met him. Mom shopped only at the A&P and I'd never heard my dad mention the shopkeeper's name. Maybe they'd known that he was the store's owner, as well as a minister. Maybe those facts were enough information to erase suspicions they might have otherwise harbored. Or maybe they'd actually been inside the shop and knew more about him. To me, what mattered most was that the other kids had been lucky enough to be taken to school in a car the size of a battleship. But, at this moment, all that mattered was being the only person in Mr. Newton's store. I had him all to myself.

"And who might you be?" the soft-voiced man inquired. Deep wrinkles lined his face and his skin was as dark as the Folger's coffee that Mom kept near the stove.

"Terry," I announced. "I live at 6625."

Cramped and dusty, the space smelled like old newspapers, with soap flakes, bleach, and all kinds of canned goods arranged neatly on wooden shelves reaching to the ceiling. Some of the cereal boxes looked as if they'd been placed there at the beginning of time.

"Too busy a street out there for a little girl like you, all them trucks flyin' by," Mr. N. said. "Wouldn't nobody see somebody big as a nickel."

He went to a battered metal cooler and reached down to pull an ice-cold bottle. Kayo chocolate milk. My favorite. He flipped the cap off the top, and with a laugh and a wink, held his arm out. We both knew I had no money to give him, but I took the drink anyway. And then hesitated.

"Are you sure?" I said, my words rushing out.

"You're O-KAY with KAY-O," Mr. Newton sang back to me.

I took a long swig of the sweet taste. He was right. I felt absolutely okay.

Mr. Newton's shop soon became an important way station on my travels from one end of the block to the other; it was from him that I first learned the power of small kindnesses.

Until Mom and Dad responded to the "white-flight" that plagued our neighborhood by joining the exodus, my solo expeditions continued, though I strove to fly out of range of their radar. My parents were housing a serial rule-breaker, and that didn't bother me—not on moral grounds, at least—but I knew getting caught would hamper all chances for voyages in the future.

How did I so easily fool them? And, especially Mom? How could it be possible that she didn't see I was missing?

Maybe she just had too many people of whom to keep track. Pictures of Mom when she and Daddy were eight years into their marriage and had only Patty and Jeanie show her smiling, the girls surrounded by toys. But then the avalanche of more kids began. Four more mouths to feed—mine being the fourth—in the space of five years. And then two more hungry birds after that. We'd all started school a year early to give Mom some relief from caring for so many of us together, but perhaps that was hardly enough to provide her any breathing room.

I didn't know the answer as to why she never seemed to be there when I turned to look for her. Other mothers, even those with big families, seemed to know how to hover. But my desire to break free from the feel of walls that closed around me overshadowed any guilt or fear I possessed. Any fear of punishment. The desire to belong to someone or someplace else was greater than any sadness I harbored over my unnoticed absence.

Another premier destination was the Baptist church. With a roof that sagged, and siding in desperate need of a fresh coat of paint, the church could have passed for an abandoned building. But its looks were deceiving. When services were held, yellow light beamed from the windows, and loud pleas to the Lord Almighty competed with a chorus of amens. Even the walls seemed to breathe when the Baptists were at worship.

On Sunday mornings, I'd suffer through Mass, returning to our house with whichever sibling had been dragged by Mom for the 9:00 service, then wait for a chance to slip out undetected. I'd wander past the blaring TV where my brothers sat watching episodes of *Flash Gordon*; so mesmerized by the screen, they never even moved during the commercial breaks. On Sunday mornings especially, the house seemed to shrink and the strident noise of the television jangled my nerves.

The Baptist church wasn't only the place of salvation for its members. Standing on the sidewalk across from the church's entrance, I felt saved, too. Unlike our church, where the organ made you feel as if you had lead weights on your eyelids, the Gospel music at the Baptist church was like sipping on a bottle of 7up. Sweet fizz. I loved the rippling slide of fingers over the keyboard. That organ's music could surely push somebody's soul straight through the gates of heaven.

From my post, I fought the impulse to dash inside and be where joy lived. But Catholics, the nuns warned, were unlike other religions: We were "The One True Church." Some rules I could break. But eternal damnation? That was too steep a price to pay for such impudence. I stayed put, aggrieved that Catholic Mass was like being shot with a tranquilizer gun, while those who prayed at the Baptist church enjoyed a weekly injection of exuberance. Usually, I hung around until services were over, always excited by the parade of stylish ladies in hats worn at an angle. I loved how they lingered on the sidewalk, surrounded by their children, touching one another at the elbow as they talked. They seemed more interested in conversation than their next destination. How different they were from the St. Bernard's mothers I saw, who wore chiffon scarves knotted tightly under their chins—headpieces that were functional, not fashionable. They were women who streamed through the church doors like shoppers hurrying to catch a bus.

My travels to the demolished house, Mr. Newton's store, and the steps of the Baptist church had transported me to the outskirts of belonging. In this other universe, I became energized. I trusted that if I were patient and kept my Sunday vigil, the pretty women in their fancy hats would eventually notice me and welcome me into their arms. I would have my pick of Radio Moms, and in the reflection of their eyes, I would see myself.

"Let me look at you, child," they would say, as I absorbed their warmth.

I knew what I wanted. And I was willing to wait.

The morning Candy and Sissy invited me to Candy's birthday party, I felt like Dorothy when she first opened the door to Oz. It was as if everything changed from black and white to technicolor. Coming up on seven, I'd been traveling to different worlds for quite a while by now, but had not yet snagged a friendship with even one kid, let alone a pair of sisters. The three of us had played Devil and The Pitchfork on a few occasions, but we hadn't engaged in any sort of real conversation. Instead, we'd focused on the game. Since I already knew how to play tag, learning the ropes of Devil and the Pitchfork was a snap.

"Knock knock."

"Who's there?"

"Devil and the Pitchfork flying through the air."

"What do you want?"

"YOOUUU."

Unlike the sisters, who easily outran me when it was my turn to be the Devil, I was slow. Still, I never minded getting caught. Being poked by the imaginary pitchfork, tackled to the ground and then tickled under my ribs meant that I had a real part in the game. To catch me, you had to see me. On the morning I learned about the birthday party, I'd been leaning against the side of Mrs. Tobola's house, struggling to catch my breath after having once again been captured. Candy whispered to her sister.

"Yeah, let's ask her," Sissy shouted, punctuating her answer by hopping from foot to foot.

"Ask me what?"

I laced my fingers through Candy's. Hers were dark and pudgy, their length the same as mine. She squeezed back.

"Come to my party today." She leaned in close, our noses almost touching. "We've got my aunties comin' and we're gonna play pin the tail, for sure. Definitely cake. Definitely ice-cream. Can you come?"

Had I heard correctly? "Sure." I rushed to answer, before she changed her mind. "I can come," I said. No sooner had I blurted out the words, than a flurry of worry rushed through me. How would I get Mom to let me go?

I'd never been allowed to play at anyone's home, unless they were a relative. I'd never been encouraged to have a friend. And these friends? "Colored girls," is how Mom would describe them. I knew that like all the other white parents, mine too didn't like the race changes in the neighborhood. I loved Candy and Sissy. But Mom wouldn't.

The knot in my stomach pulled tight. I could just imagine my mother's quick comeback if I even worked up the nerve to ask permission.

"For Christ's sake, don't be so ridiculous," she'd say.

What would be so ridiculous about wanting to go to another kid's birthday party? I wondered with anger. Why did Mom say things so meanly, and act as if I weren't entitled to have any fun at all?

It was not good to have such thoughts.

Even at almost seven, I'd begun to suspect that my mother resented us having fun when she hadn't had the same opportunity. Her stories about her own childhood had begun to unfold like chapters in a book that eventually I would know line by line. One story in particular stood out: as a young girl, she had cleaned other people's houses and babysat their children. She "worked like a damn dog" and was "treated like dirt." The mention of a friend in any of Mom's tales was rare—certainly not in this one from her childhood, because she worked "morning till night." And she didn't seem to have any friends now. I felt sorry for Mom, and never interrupted her laments about no friends and no fun. Although I hated how this particular recounting made me feel—always sad, and sometimes, as when thinking about it now, mad. But being resentful never felt safe. Anger could make a person explode; I pushed my irritation down.

Saying nothing, I waited for the right moment to disappear out of the house over to Candy's. But then, Mom walked into the room with my three-year-old brother Robby in tow.

"Keep an eye on your brother for a while," she said, as Robby toddled over to me.

I was doomed.

Or maybe not. I coaxed Robby out to the porch where I could more easily keep an eye on Candy and Sissy's apartment. While Robby's small hands guided a metal car over the wood planks of the porch, I counted the number of rolls of his toy. Ten, twenty.

I'd give him one hundred more rolls, I decided.

No Candy and Sissy sightings.

After the extra hundred, I gave him ten more to lessen my guilt.

"Robby, I'm tired. I can't play anymore."

Before he could protest, I hoisted him up by his tiny arms and fast-walked him into the house.

"He's back, Mom," I hollered, and then ran down the front steps.

I waited on the street for some small signal from the girls, ready to bound up the stairs to their apartment. Was I supposed to bring a present? I had nothing to offer. My excitement now mixed with worry. Still, I pictured myself sitting between Candy and Sissy on a comfy couch, all smiles as I nodded at their aunties. I would wear a blindfold and finally be spun in the direction of the donkey picture taped to a wall. I imagined using my fingertips to lift the last crumbs of cake off my plate. And Candy and Sissy's mother offering me "seconds" and how I would say, "Thank you, ma'am."

I knew exactly what I wanted. I wanted to belong.

I positioned myself on the ledge where the grass and the street's edge met, struggling to be patient. Walking atop the curb, I lifted a toe in the air whenever it seemed I might lose my footing. After I'd gone a few yards in one direction, I did a slow pirouette, with my arms extended, and then reversed course. More time passed. A breeze rearranged my hair, and up above, a curtain panel fluttered against the open window that marked where the girls lived. I cupped my hands around my mouth, ready to shout up to the second floor, but then I stopped. It was then I heard the laughter.

On the other side of the window, in another world, happy voices grew louder. The singing of "Happy Birthday" started—but only after the last words of musical celebration had finished and the hoots and clapping stopped, did I drag myself to the sidewalk. I felt myself wobble, and dizzy; I had a sudden urge to pee. I imagined the eyes of the neighborhood watching intently from their windows, and my ears grew warm. Still hoping that Candy might somehow materialize and call out my name, I fidgeted with my hands.

No one came.

My disappointment weighed on my chest. Had I been older, I might have understood that "changing neighborhood" also meant "wary neighborhood"—one where little white girls and little black girls weren't allowed to visit one another's homes. Even on their birthdays.

I raised my head and headed home. My legs moved like wooden blocks, as if they knew I no longer had anyone to chase. And worse, no one to chase me.

I couldn't go to either of my parents for comfort. Abandonment is what I had been taught, and this is what I had done—I'd ditched my baby brother.

Back at the house, I stood behind the screen door, staring at the world outside. The pavement was filled with cracks, all the houses looked drab. The street—just a repository for broken glass. Everything had changed and nothing had changed.

What did I want?

To be wanted.

Sticks and Stones

Decoded, the message etches itself in acid
so every syllable becomes a sore.

—Ruth Stone
"The Wound"

THE DISAPPOINTMENT OF BEING excluded from Candy and Sissy's party lingered. I'd thought if I just kept running, just continued trying, I'd find the place where I belonged—Paradise. It took until the summer of 1960, when our family left Peoria Street, for me to take to running away from my family once again.

The summer we bought the house on Campbell, still on Chicago's south side, I was seven, and looking forward to third grade. Now it seemed our entire family was headed to the land of fresh possibilities. The new neighborhood, four miles from Peoria Street, might as well have been light years away. Towering trees with leafy branches formed canopies over well-paved streets. Streets that were perfect for free-range roaming. Gage Park, as the area was known, was a meat-and-po-tatoes neighborhood: a blue-collar enclave of brick bungalows and large families. Imagining scores of kids on every long block, I vowed to myself that I would make a slew of new friends.

We arrived several days before the fourth of July and were greeted by the gaze of a half dozen immigrant grandmas. Each took one look at the truck piled high with our belongings and stopped pushing her broom across a sidewalk that needed no cleaning. The grandmas wore house dresses and flower-patterned aprons that accentuated their bellies. I was shocked. Every one of them looked like my Fat Grandma Crylen, Daddy's mother. Minus her smile. I raised my arm in a tentative hello and they nodded politely, but these gatekeepers of the block continued to eyeball us warily.

"Off the grass! Go to the park!" the grandma two doors down shouted whenever a bicycle came too close to her lawn. She obviously wasn't impressed by us, but I didn't care. I wanted nothing more than to explore the world beyond her patch of green.

Even the Independence Day fireworks that later exploded over our heads could not match my excitement as I ran from room to room in our new home. This "new" house on Campbell Street wasn't nearly as ancient as the one on Peoria, and at fourteen hundred and sixty square feet, it seemed a palace. Sheer white curtains billowed in the breeze of windows opened wide. In the main floor bedrooms, light filtered through onto polished wood floors. In every room, I crawled through closets in search of hidden treasures, slamming their doors, just to hear them bang. Every square inch was spotless and the full basement had none of the creepiness that characterized the cellar we'd played in at Peoria Street.

The attic sweltered in a blast of heat, snatching the air straight out of my lungs. Once I'd scoped out the one small bedroom and the cavernous area that led up to it, I ran back downstairs and into the yard. The chatter of grackles filled the humid summer air. Thick and green, only grass grew here—not a spiky weed to be found. A red-painted push mower stood near the garage. Lilac bushes ran along a low chain link fence, their blossoms in hiding until the next year's spring. Only then would they would deliver on their promise to paint the yard purple, offering a kind of continuity synonymous with hope.

The improved safety of our new neighborhood meant Dad had lifted the ban on leaving the front porch. On my first Campbell Street journey, less than an hour after our arrival, I ended up at the corner of our block, overwhelmed. I stood at the edge of a park, watching boys in uniforms playing baseball. Separated from the dugout by a row of tall elms, a playground beckoned. Two days later, while on my way to Sunday Mass, I took my inaugural trip through Gage Park. Everywhere I looked, I saw green, tasted freedom, heard laughter. What I didn't see were people who looked like Mr. Newton, or the Baptist ladies, or Candy and Sissy. But I didn't miss them. Not yet.

That first summer, I especially loved the warm evenings when the sky turned a deep orange, streaked with violet. It was then that the neighborhood men, home after a long day in some factory, came out to water their lawns. Sitting on the porch, Daddy would first tap out a cigarette from its cellophane-wrapped pouch, then fish in a pocket for his matches. Brushing past him, I'd catch a whiff of benzene, the solvent he used at his job to clean paint from his skin.

Across the street stood barrel-chested Mr. Shumowsky, who made coffins. Next door was Mr. Doherty, who worked at American Can and whose smile was like a leprechaun's grin. Catty-corner, Mr. Polacek leaned against a tree, and two doors over sat Mr. Hagen, sporting the pea-green sweater he wore even on hot days. Nearly every night, I'd see all of these men and others like them. They were the "father collective:" dads who wore dark, baggy pants and white tees and steadied long black hoses in their working-man hands. Streams of water arced high, then fell across neat squares of grass. All along the street, nozzles sputtered and hissed.

I knew little about my own father's actual work days, but I did get a peek into his world not long after we'd arrived on Campbell. One afternoon, I tagged along with my mother as she drove to Standard T Chemical, better known as "the plant," to give him a ride home. A paint manufacturing company, Standard T was a dreary-looking complex where my father would spend forty-six of his working years. There, he coaxed room-sized boilers to life and oversaw the development of all manner of pigments and stains. Like my uncles—Dad's three brothers who worked in the trades—my father did not talk about life on the job. As a young man, according to Mom, he'd turned down promotions because he "didn't want the stress of managing other people." But when I was seven, nothing about how much worry he carried permeated my small world. He never spoke about aging machinery or his fear that even with his best efforts at maintenance, a boiler might malfunction and cause an entire building to explode.

On this day, Dad crossed a large fenced-in lot to where Mom and I waited in the car. In his mechanic's jumpsuit, someone else might have mistaken my father for a prison inmate. To me, he looked like a matinee idol. With his dark curly hair and chocolate eyes, Daddy radiated star power. When he reached into his pocket and handed me a package of M&Ms, happiness was mine.

This first summer on Campbell was also when Dad converted some of the attic space into two extra bedrooms, which meant that my sister and I no longer had to share a bedroom with our two brothers. The days of coed rooming were over at last.

Five years older than I, Flo had turned twelve the summer we set up space in our new quarters. A master of the squinty-eyed stare, she gave me "the look" whenever she felt the need to remind me of what an awful roommate I made.

"Dirty socks," she'd say, pointing at my feet. "Disgusting."

Flo never soiled her socks. Nor her sneakers, thanks to regular coats of white shoe polish. Once, I snuck a look at her nursery school report card I found buried in a drawer: "Florence is organized and likes to take a leadership role with the other children." Apparently, my sister had been "Bossy Flossy" long before I officially awarded her the nickname.

During those initial months after the move, Mom seemed emotionally calmer, and more physically present. I wondered if perhaps she'd found a sliver of hope for her "lousy life" because she was in a house that was bigger, cleaner, and brighter inside. Sometimes, I'd find her sitting on a kitchen chair in the back yard, her eyes closed, her face tilted toward the sun. Behind her, freshly laundered sheets that ran the length of the clothesline moved back and forth in the breeze. Those afternoons when my mother looked almost relaxed made it safer to approach her and to be near.

It was about this time that I became a good audience for her stories, including the one about the "good times" in her life. What I soon discovered was that my mother's happiest days were not then, or anytime recent. According to her, her best days were long past.

Mom's storytelling usually began with how, at seventeen, she would sneak out of the house and spend Saturday evenings at White City, a popular ballroom not far from her family's home in Chicago's Canaryville neighborhood.

"I'd scour the sidewalks looking for coins and if I found ten cents, I'd ride the streetcar," she'd say. "But if I didn't have a dime, I'd take off my shoes and walk."

It was not clear how Grandma Healy didn't know her daughter had an escape routine, but the details didn't matter to me. I couldn't see then that this mirrored my own absences and the way Mom never paid attention to the fact that I was missing. Nevertheless, I enjoyed knowing that Mom had found ways to ditch her dreary home situation; that she'd been a rule-breaker, too. Listening to her stories of escape made me feel that she had taken notice of me in some way, after all. As if she didn't mind having me around. So, I wasn't too bothered that she didn't experience Gage Park as the paradise I was finding it to be. We were connecting. And more family outings came along, as well.

Some Sundays, usually in the late afternoon, my parents would take us younger kids for a drive to the cookie factory—an old warehouse in an industrial park several miles from the house. The trip there, where broken cookies were sold at discounted prices, instilled the same thrill I felt on Saturday morning trips with my father to the nearby lumber yard. Both excursions involved acquiring bargains: cookie seconds from the warehouse, and odd lots of materials from Gee Lumber, which my father used to replace stairs and railings, flooring, faulty wiring, and old plumbing. From the lumber yard, we hoped there would be the small bags of wood pieces that were free for the taking and perfect for sinking nails into. Building miniature wooden boats that failed to float became our specialty.

When Mom announced a cookie run, my brothers and I would race toward the old blue station wagon, shouting our predictions: which ones would be for sale? I always hoped the Sandwich Cremes—an Oreo knock-off—would be the cookie of the day. Filing into the gloomy factory with Dad, we'd watch the ceiling fans rotate slowly; small windows cast narrow rays of sun. Cardboard boxes were stacked high, each box labeled with the initial of the type of cookie that was inside.

"Anything except the *G*s," the boys and I would remind Dad. We hated the ginger snaps.

Visiting the cookie factory offered something more than a sugar fix. These were trips when Mom and Dad enjoyed one another's company. They spoke in easy tones, carrying on conversations that had no sharp edges. Maybe it was the aroma of cookies still baking in the factory's ovens that made it possible for me to relax. Or, maybe it was the sensory mix of the cookies and the low buzz of my parents' voices. I didn't feel jittery on these trips, and because I didn't, I was able to take note of the small things, like Mom's perfectly-styled French twist.

One of the few luxuries my mother allowed herself was a weekly wash and set at Mr. Anthony's local beauty school. Since Mom was a regular, Mr. Anthony usually did the comb out on her hair, which probably explained why the results were so good. And why Mom had recently allowed Mr. Anthony to dye her hair a white-blond. With my feet propped against the back of the passenger's seat during these expeditions, my eyes fixed on the swirl of curl planted at the top of the twist—a finishing touch that reminded me of a Dairy Queen cone. Trips like these, when the air wasn't fogged with tension, were as delicious as the Sandwich Cremes.

But, despite her weekly appointments at the beauty shop, money remained tight after we'd settled into life on Campbell, and that fall, Mom took on a part-time sales clerk position at a clothing store. Dad left for "the job" each morning at five-fifteen sharp. Occasionally, I'd wake to hear the scrape of his chair against the kitchen tile, which meant that he'd finished his coffee and was getting ready to light another cigarette before heading out the door.

Several days each week, Mom left for work shortly after the four of us middle kids arrived home from school. By this time, my two oldest sisters had finished high school and had jobs as secretaries, which meant that until Dad arrived, it was Pauly and Mike's job to take care of themselves, while I—with Bossy Flossy in charge—helped out with little Robby, and Tommy, the baby.

Home from his day job at the paint factory, Dad would sit at the table and eat whatever Mom had prepared for him before beginning her work shift. Meals were now strictly buffet style, meaning everyone helped themselves in the crowded kitchen. After napping for an hour, Dad would leave again to clean offices at a nearby home mortgage company. Sometimes, a couple of us traipsed along with him, whiling away the time twirling in a secretary's chair or sucking on sugar cubes stolen from a lunchroom bowl. Once everyone was finally home around nine, my mother would take out her change purse and count out the exact amount Dad would need to cover the cost of his next day's bus fare, a newspaper, and a pack of Pall Malls. Then she'd line up the coins up on top of the television. No one dared pilfer even a penny, knowing as we did that Dad likely had no other money in reserve.

At the end of my father's shift at the paint factory, I sometimes waited for him at the corner of our street, excited when I saw his figure. Walking an easy pace in the distance, his hands usually deep in his pockets, he carried a copy of the *Chicago Daily News* tucked under his arm.

"What's new, Terry?" he'd ask as my hand reached for his.

"Nothing, Dad."

He'd nod his head, as if to acknowledge that I'd said just the right thing. I didn't have to guess whether my father thought I was a good girl. I knew that this, the briefest of exchanges, was my father's version of a hug. A handful of words that I treasured, they would become the greeting we used whenever we spoke to one another.

༃

For reasons I did not understand, things changed dramatically as that first year on Campbell stretched onward. Gage Park was a clean place, the alleyways safe—and our home a definite upgrade. The move should have afforded Mom pride about which she could shout: pride in the strides she and my father had made to provide a better life for themselves; and pride in all their efforts to ensure their children would prosper. But, if Mom felt satisfaction, or pleasure, or a renewed sense of hope during these years on Campbell, she kept those feelings hidden.

By the time I turned eight, I saw that while she still had good days, my mother's memory of them could vanish in a second under a dark cloud of resentment. The excitement that the move to Campbell had sparked in me—of belonging and of being wanted—had dimmed. I faced a bigger problem now: words gave me trouble. Especially the ones my mother would string together when she was in a downward-spiraling mood and direct at me. No longer a mother who just slammed out the door, I began to see how skillfully she used her words as weapons. And unlike the old rhyme about sticks and stones, where names supposedly never hurt you, my own experience told me otherwise. The impact of my mother's words was more brutal than being struck with any stick.

Maybe the added burden of working low-paying jobs to help make ends meet had factored into what was her obvious discouragement. Or perhaps my oldest sister's hospitalization earlier that year for a thyroid problem—along with what seemed like Baby Tommy's constant crying—contributed to Mom's distress. However, too young to piece together why she seemed so restless and dissatisfied, I knew only the importance of treading around her with care.

Believing that good girls did not become the target of their mothers' razor-edged put-downs, how desperately I wanted to be recognized by Mom as such. But this became tricky. My mother was hardly easy to please, and now, her behavior became even harder to predict.

Often, my mind spun faster than a Tilt-A-Whirl trying to determine whether I was a good girl or a bad girl—and how I might become a better one.

Now, Mom's ability to maintain the house and keep us younger kids on a schedule also began to falter. Baskets of fresh laundry competed with piles and piles of dirty clothes. She still shopped for groceries almost daily, but food disappeared faster than she could fill the pantry. Floors were mopped, but the sink was never empty. Counter tops remained sticky and cluttered. Mom still cleaned, but nothing had a shine.

Color Polaroids from the Easter holiday that year showed all of us lined up in front of the house. We are holding colorful wicker baskets, wearing outfits from Robert Hall, the clothing store where Mom worked. Perhaps she was trying to pass us off as the Kennedys. I see these snapshots as the evidence that Mom hadn't yet totally given up trying to create some sense of normalcy in the midst of her discontent. But not long after that photo was taken—by the end of third grade—I worried all the time. The lights in paradise didn't just flicker. They went out.

When the really dark years hit, Operation Help Mom began in earnest. Eventually, Mom left the job at Robert Hall and took a new one at Walgreens. Tommy, six years younger than I, had reached toddlerhood by then. A real challenge, he screamed a lot and threw tantrums.

"Don't upset Tommy," Mom would warn in a weary voice. "He's high strung."

Tommy heard everything in stereo—louder than most people did. The constant noise in our house made him cover his ears and wail. When not upset, my little brother was sweet and curious. Unfortunately, that curiosity meant he sometimes got into trouble: he drank furniture polish that had been left on a table; he sat alone in front of the gas oven and turned it on when the pilot light wasn't lit, creating a boom as loud as a jet breaking the sound barrier. When we all rushed into the kitchen, Tommy was still sitting on the floor, stunned.

Structure helped keep him calm. Art projects helped, too. During the years of Operation Help Mom, I played school with Tommy, generally as a way of giving Mom a much needed break. Had I been a baby sitter who was paid, I would have been rich.

My efforts, however, weren't always successful. Tommy continued to struggle and Mom's dark moods showed up regularly. She'd stare blankly into her coffee cup—a signal it was beginning. Anxiety skittered through my mind like a mouse trying to outrun a broom. The urge to do *something* hit fast. As I tended to Tommy's bad temper, hope flared: there must be some way to avoid Mom's silence turning from smoke to fire.

Stay alert. Distract her. Don't get burned.

"Do you want me to make you a piece of toast? You look tired, Mom."

"Why the hell wouldn't I be tired?"

Uh-oh. Mom had pulled the match from its box.

"My goddamn soul is in Hell because of all of you! There's not a one of you that gives a good goddamn how exhausted I am."

Why hadn't I picked up on her mood sooner and set out the coffee and toast without even asking if she wanted some? Or been quick enough simply to apologize and then dart from the kitchen, so that I might have saved myself? But I usually froze instead, ensuring that I would have to spend the rest of the day trying to put out the brush fire I'd fanned rather than quenched.

I grew confused often. Wired. Since Tommy had already cornered the market on being "high-strung," giving my own anxiety a voice was impossible.

Mom's cursing came to be the hardest to bear, as she'd use profanity in a way that other mothers never did. I was terrified that she'd swear in front of my friends and this fear became reality. At the words, "get in the goddamned house," I wanted to disappear.

Being alone with my mother after her rage had spilled out in public felt dangerous, her words like stones to bones.

"You're out all the time," she'd scream. "So damn shiftless. I can't count on a one of you to lift a finger to help around here."

Mom's eyes never met mine when she carried on in her rages. I didn't want her to look at me, petrified as I was. The way she stared past me hit like another kind of punch: I wasn't even worth noticing.

Don't say anything, was all I could muster to myself. This became a regular internal mantra. In a blur, I would slink out of the room— guilty, confused, and defeated.

I wasn't the only target during the Operation Help Mom period. Rather than feeling any relief when Mom turned her sights on another family member, however, I felt physically ill. In 1963, when I was ten, and shortly after my oldest sisters married, Mom's litany of resentments grew harsher.

"That husband of Jeanie's has his hooks in her, and she's just happy to go along with the show," she said one day, in a fury of paranoia. "And that Patty. She's so nervous, she wouldn't be able to make a decision on her own if her life depended on it."

Pots and pans clanged to the floor as she opened a door under the sink. I wanted to cry and find a way to defend my sisters but I didn't dare. When Mom's rants circled around brainwashing and betrayal, I knew we had moved into dangerous territory, her mood rapidly turning black—and vicious.

With my older sisters moving on to create lives of their own, it was clear they had failed Mom's loyalty test. Tensions in the house escalated. The pressure to participate in Operation Help Mom had always been considerable, but with two sisters married and Flo working long hours after her high school day ended, I felt pressed to steer this ship.

Increasingly, when Mom arrived home from Walgreens, she looked exhausted. I was jumpy and worried until I knew which mood she had brought home with her. Sometimes her mood was positive and I would have to adjust my reactions. It all kept me on the knife's edge of anxiety. On unlucky nights when Mom returned home from her job at Walgreens, the homecoming could turn ugly fast.

"What a rotten life I have," she'd mutter, kicking her shoes across the room. "Day after day, year after year, and I'm in the same goddamn Hell."

If he hadn't already slipped into the kitchen by this time, Dad would whisper in a resigned tone, "Help your mother out, will you?"

Help Mom out? Of course I would. Even if I couldn't make Mom feel better, surely I'd gain points for being *Dad's* good girl.

I made the choice to stay, to sit quietly in a chair across from her. Willing to risk a verbal smack. If I absorbed the sting, at least Dad would feel sorry for me and I could bask in the feeling that, in a small but perhaps important way, I had rescued him—though never her.

Operation Help Mom also meant continuing to listen to Mom's travels down memory lane, although my motivations became less about wanting to bask in her presence and more about wanting to please and support her. Always hoping I could deflect some of the tension I sensed building inside her, I'd wait until she referenced something about her past and then settle in to hear more. White City always featured prominently, but when I could, I'd remind her of important facts she glossed over.

"That's where you met Daddy," I'd coach her when she focused too much on the music and how she never sat out a dance.

"Yeah, your father was pushy," she'd respond. "I could have had my pick of nice-looking fellas, but he made sure nobody else had a chance."

"But Daddy was crazy about you. And he got you away from Grandma! You said you hated it at home!"

"Ma thought he was pushy, too." But then she conceded that Dad was the only one who'd never been intimidated by Grandma Healy. That he had made it possible for her to escape.

I always wished my mother could have left the story there, sticking with the Prince Charming part. But too often, she added the punchline that smacked of her bitterness: "Little did I know I was trading one prison cell for another." Then, she'd launch into her tale of thwarted stardom.

Newly married, she'd been on a shopping excursion when a man who claimed to be a casting agent approached her. Enchanted by all things Hollywood, especially stories of glamorous actresses and how they became famous, her idol was Lana Turner, whom, it was rumored, had been discovered in a Los Angeles drugstore. Unlike the White City stories, Daddy figured largely in this drama. Unfortunately, Mom cast him as the spoiler.

"I had a contract and everything and your father took one look at it and tore it up."

On cue, I delivered the line I knew Mom wanted to hear. "Oh, Mama, you missed your chance!"

Daddy just rolled his eyes at these stories, insisting Mom had been under the spell of a con man. "Your mother's nuts," he'd say.

A part of me wished the story were true. Mom deserved to be happy. I'd seen scads of pictures of her that Daddy had taken when they were younger, and she'd been a beautiful girl. Yet, another part of me recoiled as she talked about how she had been cheated out of her dream. Nauseated, I couldn't bear the prospect that the Hollywood spotlight had more appeal to my mother than her life with us.

Mom's "Happy Time" tales collapsed under the weight of her disappointment. Her theme of having been "robbed" so colored her world view that I hated even those moments she described with pleasure. I hated the way she talked about Daddy with derision. Much as I did when Mom criticized my older sisters, I was trapped between wanting to defend him or them—but not daring to challenge her, I remained silent and guilty, wrestling between loyalty and fear simultaneously.

But then, remembering my purpose—to be there for Mom—I would rebuke myself: after all, what did I know about a hard life of cold-water flats, rooms with single lightbulbs, and family members succumbing to tuberculosis? Unlike Mom, I hadn't experienced any of the loss and deprivation that she had. What right did I have to judge? I could hear her voice in my head, confirming that she'd read my mind and knew what an ingrate I was. *You have some nerve*, it said, echoing hers.

Unlike the lilacs, Mom didn't blossom in the springtime. Still, I couldn't figure out if things were as bad as I believed, or whether I was simply a bad daughter.

Did other families live this way?

And then I'd brush away the questions. Mom was the one who'd never had a chance. Mom was the one with too many crosses to bear.

"Help Mom out." My father's familiar words reverberated in my mind.

One night when I was eleven, an unnamed worry wrapped its arms around me, and I tossed and turned, the sheets as tangled as my feelings. Finally, I abandoned my bed. Uncertain why I felt such anxiety, I tiptoed downstairs and across the linoleum floor of the kitchen, aware only of the need to escape my distress. Awake then, I stepped into the living room doorway, and as I did, I saw something move. I froze.

Gradually, the shadowy figure slumped on the couch became recognizable. Mom.

I blinked several times, willing my eyes to adjust to the dark. With her arms crossed over her chest and her head lowered, she looked asleep. But then she lifted her chin and stared right at me.

She made no sign of greeting. No acknowledgement of my presence.

I took a step closer, but still she said nothing. The relief I'd felt began to slip away. What's going on? Is she okay? Maybe she's sick. Or maybe something bad has happened.

What are you going to do? the voice inside me demanded.

"Mom?" I finally whispered, worry paralyzing the words. "Mom, are you okay?"

And then her words slithered across the room.

"I wish to Christ you were all dead."

In the cold silence that followed, I struggled for breath. And then backed out the doorway. Stumbling up the attic stairs, I crawled into my bed. Flo slept on. Hard knots formed at the base of my neck. I lay there staring at the ceiling, panicked that I couldn't slow the bleed of hurt that spread through my body.

Maybe she's right—maybe it would be better if you were dead. I put all my thoughts on pause, knowing what needed to follow if I had any hope of holding myself together in the middle of this hideous dream. I must take responsibility for what had happened: *Why were you so stupid to leave your bed in the middle of the night? Why did you barge in on her when she needed to be alone? What kind of idiot are you?* I asked myself. *Thinking you can be the sort of person who can help her?*

A horrible possibility, one I didn't want to believe and hoped wasn't true, pushed its way forward: *What if she's really crazy and this never stops?*

I just lay there then, hyper-aware of each time my sister rolled over in her sleep and of the shifting pattern of the moon on the floor. No matter how hard I tried, I couldn't ease the throb of my pain.

At last I slept, but I woke early, feeling bruised. I dressed slowly, stalling for time. I dreaded facing my mother over the kitchen table. I really had only two choices. The first: to accept that she did indeed wish her very own children dead, and then bury those blinding words in a hole so deep they could never be unearthed. The second: to admit that I, as one of those children, had somehow failed her yet again— and then strive to redeem myself by becoming an even better, more dutiful daughter. One who would take her mother's burden and carry it on her back.

I chose both, vowing to kill my mother's words and promising also to atone for my failing. I would bear, like a sack filled with bricks, the weight of her misery.

Liar, Liar, Pants on Fire

To me a lie is a dream that might come true.

—Malachy McCourt
Death Be Not Fatal

HAD THE CIA BEEN looking to recruit a young girl as a double agent, I would have been an excellent candidate. By the time I'd turned twelve, I had established a good track record in my efforts to be a more dutiful daughter. But, poised on the threshold of adolescence and high on the idea of running with a pack of fun-loving girls, I began to resurrect my formerly clandestine life as the girl who not only broke the rules, but fraternized with kids my mother considered to be the enemy. My need for this new girl-world had awakened a part of me that wanted nothing more than to ditch my responsibility to Mom and defect to the other side.

That need had actually made itself felt three years earlier, when I'd first tasted what adolescence held in store. I'd been ripe for what my mother would have called "corruption." It was a hot Sunday morning in August when Ruthie Valynas, a next-door neighbor my own age, rang our doorbell an hour before she and her parents were due to depart on a forty-seven-mile road trip. Had it not been for Ruthie, along with some help from Marilyn Monroe, my introduction to vamp education at age nine might never have happened.

"Find your bathing suit! See if you can come to the Dunes!" Ruthie called through the screen. "Hurry!"

The Dunes? Who were the Dunes? But in the end, it didn't matter who, what, or where. I'd hungered after any invitation to play the way a toddler craves a lollipop. Stepping backward from the door, I begged her not to leave without me. What luck! There, in the back hallway—still damp, rolled in the towel I'd used after my last visit to our neighborhood pool—was my Sears-issued, one-piece wonder.

"Mom!"

Darting through the kitchen, I searched for her, needing permission for liftoff.

"Whaaat?" The annoyed wail came from her bedroom—the room she no longer shared with Daddy, but instead with Tommy-the-insomniac, my three-year-old brother.

Watching her pull a sponge curler from her bangs, I took a breath and slowed myself down.

"Ruthie needs me to go to the Dunes with her. They're leaving right now, and Mrs. Valynas said I should come if you'll let me go. So, can I?"

Framing any request to have fun as if I had a duty to perform—in this case as if I were responding to Ruthie and her mother's *needs*—was just one more way in which I was inclined to bend the truth. Demonstrating too much excitement about the Dunes wasn't going to help me gain permission to get out of the house. My mother still did not subscribe to wanting her children to have fun.

Mom paused, the tick of her wind-up alarm clock keeping beat with my heart. I waited. Finally, tossing the curler into a shoe box, she shrugged her shoulders. "Don't go in the water past your knees." She shook her finger. "You could get caught in a damn undertow."

I had been handed a get-out-of-jail-free card. I raced to the front door, wanting to be long gone before she realized that going to the Dunes meant I would miss Sunday Mass. It took me only a minute to discover how much fun it was to be a guest. Mr. and Mrs. Valynas treated me as a model kid—seeming to ignore the fact that I belonged to a family that screamed and shouted a lot, the family that owned Sandy, the annoying dog who barked continuously and who was constantly told to "shut the hell up!"

Smiling at one another as they drove along, Mr. and Mrs. Valynas were like an Eastern European version of Ozzie and Harriet. Dazzled by my hosts, I reveled in how lucky I was. Next to me, the usually serious "Ruta"—as her parents called Ruthie—cracked jokes and plied me with comic books.

As the car headed through Gary, Indiana, the rotten egg stench of its steel mills punched us square in the face, but Ruthie and I barely blinked. Living so close to the Chicago stockyards had made us connoisseurs of industrial stink. Pinching our noses, we agreed that this was no worse than the dirty-sock smell that permeated our city's "back of the yards" neighborhood.

For the next two hours, Ruthie and I whispered about school, our favorite books, the kids in the neighborhood—and ourselves. Ruthie was stick thin, in contrast to my more average size—though I felt like a blimp and walked with a hunch, trying to disguise the fact that I was taller than nearly every other girl in our class. We compared the size of our feet (mine were larger), the length of our hair (hers was styled in a smart "pixie cut" while mine was long and perpetually tangled), and compared answers to the question about what you would do if you had three wishes. Answer: wish for an unlimited number. Then, we debated who could run the fastest.

Our bond grew stronger as each milepost along the highway passed. I inhaled the pleasure of this perfect day and the fact that I had no responsibilities. No little brothers to look after. No household chores. My sole responsibility was to keep from drowning in Lake Michigan.

Marilyn Monroe's contribution to shaping the girl I would become arrived just as Mr. Valynas's car pulled away from The Dog 'n' Suds, where we had stopped for mugs of frosty root beer. As he turned on the radio, Mr. Z leaned in toward the dial, then shook his head. Ruthie and I then eavesdropped on her parents' conversation, hoping to learn more about Marilyn Monroe, whose death was storming through the news. Apparently, Marilyn was dead in her bed. Naked. Mrs. Valynas leaned toward her husband, her whisper branding the movie star with the label "floozy." Then she repeated one word over again and over again. "Sexpot." Trying unsuccessfully to stifle our giggles, Ruthie and I compared notes on exactly what "sexpot" meant.

It seemed sad that someone so pretty and famous had died, and to demonstrate that we knew how to be sexpots, too, Ruthie and I took turns posing on the sand for glamour photos. One hand behind an ear and the other on a hip jutting to the side—pin-up style—we smiled at an invisible camera, and egged one another on with shouts of "ooh-la-la" and "va-va-va-voom."

Marilyn Monroe's death sparked my curiosity about sex, my body, and the art of flirtatiousness. Suddenly, all this was at the forefront of every serious question I had about my own future as a young woman. Mrs. Valynas's whispers about "bumbshells" and sexpots, my image of a hypersexualized Marilyn with cotton candy hair, as well as the buzz among the other beachgoers who were hearing the news for the first time—all of it had coalesced and intensified my sense that I was about to embark on a strange new voyage. I was happy I had someone to share it with, like Ruthie, my trusted friend and play twin, because it was both frightening and exhilarating. But perhaps most tantalizing of all, even if I couldn't articulate it as such just then, was the fact that this new threshold upon which I stood did not have mothers front and center stage.

My friendship with Ruthie slowly faded away as circumstances pushed us apart, however the memory of the day we frolicked at the Dunes imitating Marilyn Monroe stayed fresh. In seventh grade I made a new friend who would be my guide deeper into the girl-world I so longed to enter. She took me by the hand and I waded in knee deep.

Unlike me, Susie was both pretty and self-possessed, so I posed no threat to her, especially when it came to getting attention from boys. What we shared was a sarcastic sense of humor and a fondness for small gestures of rebellion against authority figures that were likely to go undetected. Penny-ante stuff, like telling our mothers we were going to confession on a Saturday afternoon and walking instead to the Sears store to poke around the record section. As Susie's sidekick, I practiced ways to cultivate friendships with the cool girls, and tried to copy her fashion style. The results were underwhelming. When I whined about my failed "look," Susie reassured me with a casual "you're fine." Not hard for her to say, with her willowy shape already firmly in place. I winced, wishing I hadn't opened my mouth.

Through the rest of grade school, listening more and sharing less worked better. Not just with Susie, but with the other girls, too. Sometimes, this proved quite easy, as when cryptic references about sexual facts and desirability became part of the group speak. More naive than the others, I didn't have anything to contribute to the conversation, anyway. But I listened, both shocked and mesmerized by the new language I was learning. Playing hard to get, playing the field, playing with yourself—all were topics about which I knew zilch.

I snagged a copy of *Sex and the Single Girl* in a stroke of luck one day while snooping through my sister's bedroom drawers; reading this little training manual augmented the tutorials provided by my circle of friends. Although the book's intended audience was adult women, its title called to me the way I imagined *Playboy* magazine called to every boy in my seventh-grade class.

Because so many conversations with my friends had by this time begun to revolve around the opposite sex, I'd finally figured out that ogling sexpots was compulsory for nearly every teenage boy. Secretly, I wanted to be a sexpot, too. Not that I understood the particulars of the job. I just wished some boy, any boy, would think of me that way. I wanted to be noticed, but I also wanted to have someone real to fantasize about when I felt tingles of excitement in the place I called "down there."

Compared with the other girls, however, my chances of fueling any young boy's sexual fantasies were nil. My dull brown hair, still frizzy, was now made worse by the way I teased it into a poorly executed bouffant, or—as Mom called it—a "rat's nest." Stealing my sister's prized can of Aqua Net to spray the mess into submission did nothing to improve my looks—or the way I felt about myself. With a lacquered helmet for hair, eyebrows that ran wild across my forehead, and no sense of style, I was neither "perky" nor "pretty." Tall as I was, I felt like a Great Dane. What I wanted to be was the equivalent of a toy poodle, pink bows and painted nails included. Stuck with a body without curves and breasts hardly bigger than mosquito bites, I knew no boy would look at me and be reminded of the voluptuous Marilyn.

Having no breasts, however, would be the least of my problems. By the time I was nearing thirteen and headed toward high school, figuring out how to be a good daughter became one more pressing problem. When I'd first assumed the dutiful role, I'd been eight, and at that time, my efforts were driven by compassion and a desire to please. Following the "I wish you were all dead" nightmare when I was eleven, I'd made an unconscious pact with myself: if Mom was not happy, then I should have no claim on happiness, either. I'd bumped up my effort then to forgo asking for things, believing my role was to babysit my mother's mood. But now, on the cusp of becoming a young woman, it became apparent that empathy could never be enough. I had to reconfigure how to be the "good girl" she needed.

Something else shifted then, too. Mom *expected* me to be the daughter taking care of her, just as she had once had to take care of her own mother. "Ma kept me a prisoner in that shit hole of a house," Mom often told us. "I loved school. But she was looking for company and that's all that mattered." I'd been shocked when I heard that Grandma Healy had permanently pulled Mom out of school after she'd finished the eighth grade. But by the time I was old enough to understand better, the emotion was different: I was conflicted by a sudden wash of empathy. All Mom had was Grandma, and now, as I was hitting adolescence, it did indeed seem as if she'd had a sorrowful, "lousy" life. Sometimes, in fact, it seemed she'd had no life at all.

Not sophisticated enough to understand what was happening and aware only of how much occupied my every thought, neverthe-less, I plotted ways around her possessiveness of me: worry about her rode side by side with schemes about how to put distance between us. Because Mom viewed my friendships as threats, we were wary of one another. Perhaps she could smell my desire to spend time with girls my own age. I had to mask the scent, and became even more dutiful to reassure her that I was still her champion. Like the meat-cutter at the A&P who had his thumb on the scale, I tried to make it seem as if I were giving her all she demanded, willing to shortchange her if I had to—but only if I didn't get caught. And so, to throw her off when I wanted to sneak out with my pals, I pressed down hard on Mom's side of the scale, ready to become a cheater. And a world-class liar.

Whenever I needed to protect myself from feelings of not being worthy—an emotion I dreaded but which plagued me most of the time—I just twisted the truth. But the lies I spun as a budding teen were not limited to the ones I told my mother. As her long-time caretaker, I lied to protect her, as well.

When Mom was too exhausted to go to work, I was the one who fielded the calls to and from her employer at Walgreens, asking her boss to okay yet another sick day. My inventions about why she couldn't come always involved some crisis requiring her attention—and her attention only. Grandpa fell in the tub. Grandma was having trouble breathing. Robby almost sliced his arm off. One benefit of being a kid from a large family was that there was no shortage of characters to be conjured up for imaginary rescues by Mom.

But being a gatekeeper was hard work. No matter how clever I considered my fabrications, I worried about getting caught. This was especially true when the phone call came from school.

"I'm sorry, Sister. My mother isn't here at the moment," I'd say as Mom put her finger to her lips and then bolted from the room.

"You're in the eighth grade now, aren't you, Therese?" Sister asked, after I'd identified myself. "Your tuition is past due again. Does your mother understand that you won't receive your graduation ribbons at the end of the year if your bill is not paid in full?" Her voice grew cold. "Does your father know that you will be the only one not allowed to wear them pinned on your uniform?"

The next day, Mom invariably gave me an envelope to take to the school office with a five-dollar payment toward the outstanding bill. I suspected those phone calls reminded my mother of her own days as Grandma's gatekeeper, when her job as a ten-year-old was to fend off an irate landlord demanding the rent. But for me, being the steward of my mother's evasions with the nuns was not the only issue: having to manage Sister's phone calls also taught me a lesson in the dance of shame. Shame at being so strapped that my parents couldn't pay my tuition. Over the phone, I was forced to take on Mom's shame, and so I made it my own. And there was more to come.

The St. Clare's clothes drive at church began just after such a phone call. Known as "The Bishop's Relief Fund," the charity event was part of an all-parish effort for the diocese's poor.

"How would you like to have some new things to wear?" Sister Ann Christopher's stern voice echoed down the church aisle. Confused, and horrified at being singled out, I stared at the length of rosary that hung from Sister's waist as a way of avoiding her eyes.

"We think it would be good to have your family benefit from the clothes drive this year."

My mouth went dry. Benefit? What did that mean? It seemed that Sister expected Mom and me, later that morning, to come back to the school's makeshift gymnasium and select clothes for the family—before the cast-offs were transported to a central clearing house for the underprivileged. As a teen who desperately wanted to be seen as cool, I was mortified by Sister's words. What if Sister showed up to supervise and picked out something that had belonged to one of the popular kids in my class? What if one of them overheard her and spread the word that I was a poor kid who needed church charity? I prayed that a parishioner leaving Mass would interrupt us.

My stomach tightened as I stood there without a word. Sister's expectation that Mom would forage through somebody else's sweat-stained rejects was wildly off base. Mom would never show up for such a thing. Even mentioning that Sister Ann Christopher had approached me would cause a problem. My mother would simply assume that Sister intended to make her look bad in front of others rather than to have made a kind gesture.

Knowing that she would spout off in private to me, but never risk crossing Sister face to face—her shame greater than her courage to challenge clergy authority—I readied myself to put on "the grateful act." I donned my best fake smile and took a deep breath.

"Gosh, Sister. That's so nice of you to think of us, except I know my Mom won't be around—some Sundays she works and the others she helps out my Grandma. I don't expect she'll be home today till late."

Sister eyeballed me.

I looked down at my shoes.

"Well," she said, tucking her plain handkerchief back up her sleeve. "Why don't you go over to the gym right now, by yourself?" It wasn't a question. It was a command. "You've got strong arms. Carry a load home with you."

There was no escaping her directive, and as I stepped inside the dim makeshift gym a few minutes later, I was greeted by the chill of the unheated space. How long did I have to pretend I was searching for something to wear before I could sneak out the back door? Staring at the mountain of second-hand clothing leaning precariously against the wall, I stepped back. Sister's voice echoed in my head: *How would you like to have some new things to wear?* "What a bunch of crap," I muttered, referring to Sister's words, as well as the mound of discards in front of me—nothing more than a giant-sized replica of the dirty laundry back at home.

New things to wear? The voice inside me laughed. *Like the skirt with the torn hem? Or the sweat stained blouse with the wrinkled collar?* Maybe Sister meant the sweaters that smelled like old Mrs. Patterson, our addled neighbor who, in the fall, picked up the leaves from her front lawn one by one. These were *poor* people's clothes. Garments for the lesser-thans. Unable to muster the disdain I imagined my mother would have shown, my face grew hot. Beneath my fury lay fear: wasn't I really just as soiled and unattractive as the discards I was supposed to claim?

Desperate to flee, I crept toward the rear exit and just stood there, estimating how many more minutes I'd have to wait to be certain Sister wasn't nearby. When the church bells announced the start of another Mass, I fumbled with the door knob and bolted.

The next day, Sister Ann Christopher caught sight of me after science class and inquired about my finds.

"Oh, I brought home so many nice things, Sister," I responded politely, stepping to the beat the dance of shame required. "I wanted to thank you for thinking of me."

Two lies.

On a growing pile of lies.

The biggest kick to my confidence that year, however, came when I was reassigned from "the smart kids' class" to the one reserved for the ordinaries. Academics had always been easy for me; I'd even started kindergarten a year ahead of my peers. To be demoted was devastating, as believing I was smart had been the armor I wore to ward off my perceived inadequacies—my one mark of distinction among my friends. Now, as an ungainly, budding adolescent with crooked teeth and bad hair, I struggled to find a way to cope with this latest blow. With no time to understand why I'd been reassigned, I pushed my disappointment down as far as I could, and concentrated on getting to Mom before she heard the news from Robby or Tommy. Naturally, to minimize my humiliation, I intended to create a solid lie.

"What do you mean you're not in the split class this year?" Mom snapped before I could unfurl my fabricated story.

"It's not bad," I quickly interjected. "Sister said she put me there so that I could help the other kids. Because she wanted to choose somebody really smart."

The words floated out of my mouth with such ease that I would have sworn it was true.

"What the hell is wrong with you?"

I flinched, regretting that I'd said anything at all. Why had I thought I could get away with this?

Now Mom had caught me in my prevarication.

"You get yourself back in that class where you belong," she demanded. "Tell that damned nun that you're not there to help the other kids. You're there to help yourself!"

Relieved that she hadn't been angry with me, per se, I nevertheless felt stupid and scared. Stupid ever to have believed I belonged with the high achievers. Scared to realize that Mom would eventually discover the truth. Even if we never learned why the switch had been made, when she discovered how I'd lied, she'd lash out and insist that my demotion was proof that I'd slacked off, that I hadn't "given a damn" about doing well. And then out would come her favorite refrain: "You're running around too much with those *tramps* while I'm here busting my ass!" Her finger poked at the air between us. "They don't have any brains in their heads, and they're going to pull you down with them!"

And find out she eventually did and her reaction was just as I'd known it would be: Too much time with Tramps. Bums. Out flippin' around.

Mom denigrating my friends was the handy whip she used to punish me—not, it seemed, because she cared so much that I excel academically, but because she'd caught the scent of my desire to be with my friends and perhaps felt betrayed and abandoned. Her hurtful words were intended to keep me lashed to her side through a prolonged childhood. But who was I to argue? Every time I finagled a way to flee to girl-world, I was breaking the implicit promise I'd made to be her keeper. And so I continued to lead an increasingly double life.

Nothing stopped me—not even the nuns. When I got kicked out of the Young Ladies Sodality in eighth grade because I'd been overheard mouthing off about the sisters, I made sure Mom never learned about it by simply pretending to attend meetings of this lame organization at St. Clare's—the one charged with instilling morals and enforcing the laws of sexual purity, and the only "club" that met with Mom's approval. When I wanted to go on a Friday night sleep-over with girls of whom she might have disapproved, I invented meetings of Sodality that would supposedly take place Saturday morning, just when she would be at work—when, I explained, the other mother would be able to drive us all to church.

By eighth grade graduation, this kind of double life had begun to wear me down. I still worked hard to be a good daughter, but I was hungry, too, creating all my elaborate lies with the hope that at last I'd be able to grab the small slice of pleasure I so craved. How I wanted to be like the other girls, to have a mother who would welcome my friends into our home. How I wanted to have a mother who encouraged her daughter to enjoy new experiences and to have dreams. How I wanted to have a mother who embraced her daughter's desires to discover herself. But instead, my mother wanted, with ferocity, to keep me bound to her side. Still, a young woman now inhabited my body. And she had a voracious appetite, too.

She wanted more. This time, for herself.

Odd Girl Out

Helen of Troy didn't launch a thousand ships because she was a hard worker. Juliet wasn't loved for her math ability.

— Mary Pipher
Reviving Ophelia

GRANDMA HEALY TALKED ABOUT her bad eyes, sour stomach, and weak ticker as if she was playing a damaged record, and I'd listened to it all my life. It was a tricky business to ask, "How are you, Grandma?" as that question guaranteed her a stage from which to hold forth on the state of her bowels.

"Jesus, Mary, and Joseph," she'd sigh, assuming a tone worthy of Sarah Bernhardt. "I've got so many troubles, I'll be dead before you know it."

I couldn't escape until she delivered her grim prediction about her imminent death. The forecast that never changed.

As I set my sights on high school what did change, however, was how much more Grandma seemed to be getting on Mom's nerves. When I was still little, before Mom began working so many hours at Robert Hall's and then at Walgreens, Grandma's visits to our house had been different—ones that my mother appeared to appreciate and enjoy. Many afternoons, Grandma kept her company and helped with the laundry. She wore a cotton apron tied around her dress, with a peek of her slip visible below its hem, while manning her station in the kitchen. Watching Grandma glide the iron over a pair of Dad's work pants—hearing it hiss as it produced small clouds of steam—was like witnessing a magician perform a trick. Her hands moved with a flourish. Presto chango. The wrinkles disappeared.

"Ma, sit down and have a cup of coffee," Mom would insist after a while, pulling a chair out from the table. "All that work is going to take the starch right out of you." Their voices low, the two sat huddled together, talking, sipping, until Grandma leaned forward and tapped the dial on her wristwatch.

"Time to get me home, Florence. Back to my prison," she'd eventually say with a sigh. But as I hit ninth grade, those moments of pleasure between them grew increasingly scarce. No longer did Grandma dabble in the art of vanishing wrinkles, but instead demanded far more from Mom than she gave. She became less sturdy on her feet and more shrill in her complaints, which made her visits to our house vibrate with tension. She had little interest in her grandchildren. She wanted only Mom. And whatever my mother provided seemed to be insufficient.

My mother's days were cramped with work at Walgreens, Grandma's needs—and bitterness. On her time off, she often took Grandma to Dr. Schimmel's office for whatever ailed her just then, or to the local grocery store, duties that consumed inordinate amounts of her time, and her energy. When she barreled through the front door after an afternoon spent carting Grandma around, she didn't say hello, or give me the chance to offer a greeting of my own, or to express a thought, a need—or to say a single word.

"Take that goddamn phone off the hook and don't let anyone bother me," she'd shout as she stormed through the door, tossed her coat on the hook and headed in to start a bath. "I'm about to have a heart attack."

"Relax. I can do the tub for you, Mom," I blurted out. Uneasy. She was too far over the edge to hear my words of support.

"Ah, cut out the shit," she snapped, pointing in the direction of the bathroom. "I could die in there—I can't count on any of you to lift so much as a finger."

Mom's litany about how caring for Grandma was doing her in,

and how she couldn't count on her family to help her, tore at me. One part of me knew she was overwhelmed, while another part of me wanted just to run and escape her reach. Just as it had when I'd been younger, her tone terrified me. As did my inability to calm her down. Home had become a chronically miserable place and all the signs pointed to an idea that both depressed and frightened me: my mother had given up on trying to grow a family. Saddest of all, although I was not yet able to articulate it clearly, one simple fact was fast becoming obvious: just as Mom, despite all her efforts, was unable to soothe Grandma, nothing and no one could soothe Mom. And so it seemed inevitable that Mom would be unable to soothe me when I had difficulty with homework, with the nuns, or even with a friend.

Other problems beyond the turmoil that plagued me at home were outright teenage problems. Problems that might appear minor in retrospect, but were major at the time. I was carrying my troubles with me as I moved beyond St. Clare's and into a much bigger social world that I wanted to join but which also frightened me.

Mom, and Dad, perhaps, had decided to send me to the public high school—a move likely dictated by financial constraints—but I feared it was really a result of my demotion the year before to the "regular" class. Perhaps being one of the "ordinaries" didn't warrant paying good money to send me to an all-girls parochial institution. In any case, going to Gage Park High School represented a break with Crylen tradition. All five of my older brothers and sisters had graduated from or were attending Catholic secondary schools. Which meant that I had no context for understanding how different school would become once I "went public."

What a shock to be launched from the cloistered confines of St. Clare's into an environment that had none of the structure provided by the nuns. I was now part of a freshman student body ten times greater than what I'd known before; additionally, I entered in a new period in the history of Gage Park High. A highly controversial pilot program aimed at desegregation began gaining traction: kids from other parts of the city—some of whom reminded me of the children I'd played with on Peoria Street—were bused in for class each day.

With this mandatory integration in the classroom came my first real exposure to the racial tensions that permeated the city, the neighborhood, and the school community. As in every family around us, my parents opposed the idea of black kids being inserted in our local high school without their consent. The code word for all this protest around the kitchen table was concern over "property values"—but the truth was that racial tensions ran deep in other ways, as well. The unspoken message, undoubtedly fueled by fear, was "watch your back" and "stick with your own kind."

Against this backdrop of change, I walked through the front doors of Gage for the first time and was met with a sensory overload. The class bell clanged loudly. Kids pushed and shoved. Lockers banged like firecrackers. Moving through the hallways was like stumbling through the dark, hoping to happen upon something that I recognized as familiar. Beyond the noise and confusion, I soon realized that my choice of a heavy, quilted skirt and jacket, with its splashes of orange on hot pink, did not bode well. Soaked with perspiration, I looked like an over-sized oven mitt. Had I known to pay attention not only to the weather—which was often warm in September—but also to my clothing—which always plays such an important role in the life of a teenager—perhaps I would have found a way to acclimate to the communal atmosphere that governs so much of what happens behind the walls of any high school. But I was too unprepared. And too overwhelmed.

My mother had not helped me get ready for the new kind of life such a different school required. Or what to expect as I moved into adolescence. There was no conversation about making friends, or boys or dating—or my changing body. Not then, nor a few weeks later when I stood in the basement of our house checking my underwear, bewildered by the arrival of my first period.

Mom had never discussed menstruation or cramps with me; nor had she taken me shopping for bra or underpants—garments which

I secured initially by rummaging through her drawers, a practice that persisted until much later when I began sneaking a few dollars from the cash envelope I received for my work at a local bakery (and was expected to hand over to my mother), and buying underwear of my own. Most problematic that particular afternoon, however, was that no instructions on Kotex pads or belts had been forthcoming. Unfortunately, my sisters were of no help—the oldest ones were gone, and Flo and I had grown apart. In separate bedrooms now, my sister had walled herself off from the family by immersing herself in her college studies and multiple jobs, and I didn't dare approach her with my questions. Having no idea what to do, and unable to even imagine telling my mother that I'd gotten my period, I spent a long time that day—alone—hidden behind the hot water heater, trying to figure out what to do.

Finally, I resorted to using strips of toilet paper fashioned like a cigar. I took my homemade creation and stuck it between what Mary Lou Jakowski—the only girl among us who could speak with authority about what it took to become a slut—had called my "pussy lips." That do-it-yourself tampon was every bit as uncomfortable as the perceptions I had about my body. Eventually, I would begin swiping what I needed from the box of sanitary pads I discovered Mom kept on the shelf in her closet, resorting to tissue stogies when the box was empty. But this first week, until I could get advice from my friends, I winged it.

Many forces were at play in those early weeks of high school— chief among them my sexual naivete, as well as the sense of alienation which cemented my long-held conviction that I didn't belong anywhere at all anymore. All of this dominated my mood from the minute I entered ninth grade at Gage, when the several girls I'd known from St. Clare's began to gravitate toward much older boys. Sadly, Susie, my "go-to," had moved on to a Catholic high school, and so was not by my side.

The boys these girls were attracted to were on the verge of manhood, including a few who had dropped out of high school and planned to sign up for the military unless Uncle Sam drafted them first. Boys who hung out in the adjoining park with girls after classes ended. Boys who found trouble without even looking for it.

In the early fall of freshman year, I got an invitation to join just such an entourage when, heading out the heavy, windowless doors after my last class, I heard a familiar voice call out my name. "Terry! Come with us! We're on our way to the benches."

It was Justine, a sweet girl whose voluptuous body ensured her the attention of nearly everyone—male and female. Initially, I was thrilled to be included. Walking through the park took me in the direction of home, requiring barely a zigzag from my usual route. However, I'd heard the reputations of these boys toward whom we were flocking, and I began to feel uneasy. The desires of these boys were way beyond my skill set. The age difference between me and the other girls mattered in ways it hadn't before. I still had none of their sophistication, or their allure. They'd thought I was funny, a person who didn't get into quarrels. I knew how to be a good friend when given the chance. But now, I felt like a baby.

As I drifted across the grass with the others, I realized I wasn't getting excited the way the other girls were, as they patted their sophisticated beehives and straightened their tight-fitting sweaters over substantial bustlines. I had hoped that by some process of osmosis I might absorb the desirability exuded by each. But by the time the testosterone-charged bad boys came into view, my wish to fit in with the crowd had turned to dread. Perched along the top of a row of park benches like magpies scavenging for scraps, the tough boys who were almost men stared at us. Recognizing Justine, whoops and catcalls soon followed.

"Baby!" a dark-eyed John Muller exclaimed, as he reached for Jackie. She brushed her blond bangs from her eyes as she snuggled up under his arm, her smile bracketed with a wave of dimples.

Muscled Frankie Pella, leered at Nancy, the reputed "fast" older sister of two girls I had known from St. Clare's. "Hey, Nancy no-pants," he cackled. "You sit right here on my lap, little girl. I'm gonna give you some candy."

Demonstrating their approval of Frankie's moves, the boys took turns slapping one another's palms. Still laughing, several reached for packs of cigarettes kept tucked in the rolled-up sleeves of their T-shirts. Lighters appeared from pants that fit so tightly they outlined the wearer's crotch. Every one of them wore "cockroach" shoes— whose sharp points could nail the quickest of vermin. The after-school ritual had begun.

As the girls rolled their heavily made-up eyes, several slick-haired rebels crooned a Motown lyric: "Ain't too proud to beg and you know it." Standing on the sidelines, I watched the mating dance with a fake smile pasted on my face, wondering why I had responded to that call to go to the park, why I had chosen to subject myself to fear and embarrassment.

"Gotta go," I said, knowing that no one heard me, or even cared if I left. Used to feeling invisible, I rationalized—despite my anxiety and sense of isolation—that it was good to have friends who wanted me to tag along. And then, my arms folded over my chest, I hurried out of the park and headed home, eager to forget how much of a loser I was. Until the next invitation came to make a foray to the park and I accepted. And then I would remember all of my emotions once again as I fled only minutes later.

It was not until eighteen-year-old Donny O'Mara introduced himself to me—by trying to force his tongue down my throat—that I decided "a walk through the park" was anything but. And not worth it.

High school was unsettling in other ways, too. For the first time, I lost interest in doing well in my studies. Before the cold winds blew that first year, I mimicked—albeit unconsciously—what Mom had already done on the home front: I gave up. And no one except my teachers seemed to notice.

I discovered quickly that they had little patience with what looked like disinterest—I stopped going to class on time and my academic performance deteriorated. Even my freshman honors English teacher—whose class I loved—didn't understand what was happening to me.

"You're just choosing not to do the work, Terry. It's a shame you enjoy messing up so much."

His words stung, but I could not tell him that each day I was struggling to keep myself from drowning. I couldn't explain it to anyone. Especially not to my parents. Mom would have ranted on, accusing me of being brainwashed by my friends to pay no attention to my grades.

I had lost my way. And my voice. Rather than feeling happy about the companionship offered, I took no pleasure in cutting classes to join fellow escapees on the school's front steps. Instead, my anxiety skyrocketed. Each misstep I took compounded the sensation that I was being sucked down a pipe. I seemed incapable of turning things around. Or of finding my way back.

Homework? I didn't do it. At least not with any regularity. And yet, I was very responsible in other ways. I never missed a single day at the bakery, where I'd had a job since the eighth grade. A hard worker, I waited on customers, took my turn scouring hundreds of dirty trays, and scrubbed the floors clean. It was a relief to do something simple, something that required no forethought or afterthought. At school, an emotional swirl had caused a power outage in my ability to complete tasks. I worried about what Mom, had she known, would have called my "shiftlessness." But my worry did not motivate me to press harder academically.

Extracurricular activities? The lights were off there, too. Having any desire to engage in the larger world had always been risky, and expressing interest about things happening in high school was no less perilous.

Had I found the courage to express an interest in after-school activities, I imagined Mom would say, scornfully, "What a waste of time." And had I acknowledged that sense of longing to myself, I would have been subjected to my own disdain—the disdain of the dutiful daughter, whose voice lived on in my head. Whose voice I often heard on those afternoons when I sprinted out of the park, away from the mating dances: *Mom's killing herself. You're gone from the house enough as it is. Get your ass home.* Succeeding in school, making new friends and, especially, having more than Mom had ever had—all this tapped down into the same fear that I'd struggled with for years. Succeeding. Failing. Wanting. Denying that I did. A revolving door of confusion and distress.

I understood none of this consciously, although it persisted as a powerful torment, coexisting with other problems, such as the right tools to make good decisions not being accessible to me. I had none of what I needed to pull myself out of the darkness that began to descend, and did not stop. The curiosity and resilience I had possessed earlier in my life—whether it was the ability to dream up an imaginary family for myself or to explore life on Peoria Street on my own—had all but been extinguished. How many times now was I unable to tap an ability to stretch and grow inside myself. It just seemed so far beyond me. Why did I always find the solutions to my difficulties to be just beyond my reach?

Snuffing out my remaining resolve were the combined forces of being unprepared for the challenges I had faced as I grew into adolescence and my guilt about having more opportunities than Mom had ever had offered to her. Mine was a different long-playing record than Grandma's, but like hers, it was scratched and the stylus was stuck in a groove. Repeating and repeating. How tired I was of hearing the same old song.

Late August, 1968. Another sweltering first day of high school. Junior year this time. And with it—amazingly enough—came the opportunity for a fresh start in a new school. Mom's decision to enroll me at Queen of Peace was impulsive, coming as it did only a week before school began. Had she at last sensed I was foundering? That throughout yet another year—my sophomore—I'd thrashed even more wildly than the one before?

Transferring schools did not guarantee that I'd be able to right all that had gone wrong at Gage, but Mom's new plan suggested she'd known something was amiss. While I'd rarely talked about school with her, and never about anything of substance, perhaps she had decided that my silence, in and of itself, was odd. Or, maybe she had at last begun to wonder why she'd never seen one of my report cards.

Although surprised by her announcement, the two depressing years I'd spent at Gage left me desperate to try something new. Anything at all. I couldn't have cared less where Mom sent me. Back to the nuns would do. Being awarded this new beginning was like being handed a roll of shiny black electrical tape. I finally had an opportunity to use a tool that just might work—a tool to patch up things that were hot and dangerous.

As Mom negotiated the thirty-five-minute drive from our house in Gage Park to suburban Burbank, where Queen of Peace High School for Girls awaited me, I began peeling off my regulation blazer. I needed air. But then I stopped. *"No. Put it back on,"* the voice in my head corrected me. *"You'll feel less jittery."* Never before worn, and despite its now damp lining, the chocolate brown jacket had already morphed into an emotional security blanket. Wearing it meant I could avoid revealing my drenched armpits.

I was also grateful to be able to return to the lack of choice a uniform represented. A uniform meant just that: uniformity. Initially, all of us would be on the same safe footing as far as a sense of style went. Once again, I was back within the arms, and the rules, of the nuns. And unlike my freshman year at Gage—when I'd worn the quilted number that screamed "out of place" and was equally as hot as today's uniform—I desperately wanted to arrive at my new high school looking like every other student.

Fantasies tumbled through my mind. All the girls would be smart. And with clean-cut, committed boyfriends. I imagined myself wearing the class ring of the Catholic boy I would certainly meet at my first dance. As did all the girls, I would wind threads of angora around it to make it fit my finger, no matter its size. The ring would testify to the fact that someone wanted to "go steady." That someone loved me; connecting the dots was all I needed to create my own portrait of what belonging would look like, or of how happiness would appear. Follow the rules. I was ready to conform.

Just like navigating our way south on busy Cicero Avenue, finding my way around a new Catholic school was something I'd done several times before, but because nothing about this transfer had been mapped out in advance, I knew little about the school itself. Mom didn't know much either, except that Burbank, where Queen of Peace had opened several years before, was considered a half-step up from the neighborhood in which we lived. Farther away than the other Catholic girls' high schools, we knew of no other family whose daughters attended. But I'd decided to be undeterred in making new friends, even though I did not have a single friend there. I would do whatever it took to fit in. And my lack of familiarity might just be a plus, because in the same way I knew no one, no one knew me either.

Damp ringlets sprung up around my hairline as new beads of sweat dotted my forehead. A question occurred to me then, one that might threaten my future at Queen of Peace. I looked over at my mother, who was sucking on a lifesaver as she waited for a red light to turn green.

"Mom, what if I get there and they ask me about Flo?"

"What about her?"

"The twenty-five dollars she never paid back to the nuns at her high school after she promised she would? What should I say?"

"The tuition at this place already costs a fortune. I can't worry about what they might do, Terry." Sounding exasperated as she tugged on the steering wheel, she directed our car into the next lane, then added: "Those nuns are eating better than I am."

With this evasive answer, Mom did not address, much less quell, my fears about walking into a new school. Gave me nothing about how to handle the situation if the sister in charge confronted me.

As we made our final approach to my new school, the last thing I expected to see was an open field where tall wildflowers bent like ballerinas. Or to hear the whirr of a thousand katydids. How different it all was from Gage, with a rural, rather than citified, atmosphere.

This was fairyland. I pulled the sun visor down and practiced smiling in the mirror. Crooked teeth. *Keep your mouth closed.*

Ahead of us, a caravan of yellow buses snaked around a freshly-paved parking lot before finally coming to a stop. Girls in plaid skirts skipped down the bus steps—some unrolling the waistbands of their uniforms in a hurry. The school's dress code dictated that hems had to kiss the knee. All around me, I heard laughter. Not the deep, raucous kind so common at Gage, but a happy tinkle, like wind-chimes.

Mom had parked behind the row of buses and was just sitting there, her hands tapping the steering wheel. She was calm, with a dreamy look in her eyes when she turned to face me. She seemed present—but was not, I knew, really there with me. And then she smiled, with the same expression that she'd had the only other time I could recall being the recipient of her undivided attention: that day she'd helped me get dressed for my first communion.

That dreamy quality didn't last long. She shook it off. "You know how to get home?"

"The number eight bus, if I can find it. Or the CTA Cicero bus if I can't. I can walk to the stop if I have to. Probably that way." I turned and pointed. "I'd better go, Mom. Thanks for the ride," I said, pleased that Mom had driven me to school on this day which might turn out to be so different for me.

But as I pushed myself out of the car, a new wave of apprehension broke over me. I was unsteady. Dizzy from the heat, and dizzy with the fear of the unknown. A group of girls were clustered a few yards away. Each of them wore the blazers that identified us all as fellow citizens. Here were potential compatriots and friends.

"Who's that?" asked one of them in a low voice.

Slowing my pace, I lowered my head. Maybe one of them would call out to me. Invite me to join them.

"No clue," another answered. Their conversation turned to the comparing of class schedules.

My feet moved faster, slowing only when I entered an enormous foyer where voices echoed. Unsure of where to go, I stood still for a minute, clutching my manila admissions envelope as if it contained every secret desire I'd ever had. My dream to do well here. The hope that I would make friends.

I found the main office and dropped off my papers, holding tight to another wish: that my arrival would present no surprises. No recriminations for the sins of my sister. And I got lucky: good fortune prevailed.

Other things to celebrate bobbed to the surface as I began a new school year. My grades soared and so did my confidence. In history class, I learned how to debate. In English, we read Shakespeare and modern classics. I dabbled in science experiments and stayed afloat in math. To appease my mother—whose long-range goal was for me to become a secretary—I took typing and shorthand. While the idea of secretarial work held all the appeal of a jail sentence, I took pride in my ability to click-clack fast and to quickly transcribe dictated words into squiggled code. My long-fogged brain had fired up and I could think again.

Despite all this, however, friendships with other girls eluded me. My job at the bakery continued to preclude my joining clubs or meeting up with classmates after school, but something more than this was at play. Even with work, I'd had friends at Gage, including some who were *not* "fast girls." But at Queen of Peace I was isolated—unlike I'd ever been before in all my fifteen years. And worse, I now attracted the attention of an enemy. Just one. But as "Queen of the Mean Girls," Joanie Randall was more than enough. The sole inflictor of adolescent schoolgirl torture, she wasted no opportunity to make the new girl's days more than miserable.

Only a few weeks after school started, the taunts began in earnest.

"What are you *doing?*" she goaded me one day in Religion class, as I clumsily made my way to my assigned seat next to hers—a seat that she undoubtedly wished belonged to one of her friends. She glared at me as if I'd farted.

It was behavior typical of a bully, but new territory for me. Never the most popular kid, at Gage I had nonetheless been a personable sort, someone adept at mingling from clique to clique without getting dragged into drama. A skill I'd probably learned just by being the sixth child in a sibship of eight—as well as being a daughter accustomed to handling a volatile mother. I was someone who did *not* offend.

"And what's with your eyebrows?" she went on in a loud voice, as we all waited for class to begin. Other girls began to titter. This question would be only one of a hundred designed to bait me, perhaps one that might have made another girl laugh. But the disdain in her voice crushed me. "Haven't you ever heard of tweezers?"

And later there was this. While feigning graciousness as she talked about me to her minions as if I weren't within earshot, as if I were invisible: "No, I don't think she's fat. I think she's just *big-boned.*"

"Joanie Randall just thinks she's better than girls like us," agreed Stella and Sophie—two immigrant classmates who generously made room for me at lunchtime.

Nodding their heads with excitement at having discovered another unfortunate victim of Joanie in their midst, my lunchmates had offered up their consolation for Queen Mean's vicious commentary as if, voiced aloud, their support would solve all my problems. What did I really want to hear from them? "She's a bitch. Let's go tear her hair out."

But the fact that they'd said "girls like us" troubled me. I didn't want to be included in their group, because Stella and Sophie clung together like new arrivals at Ellis Island. They were "old country" girls, who, under their big smiles, seemed wary of others. Even me. And as grateful as I was for their companionship, I carried a knowledge that made me ashamed. In another context, I would not have spent time with them because Stella and Sophie looked like younger versions of Grandma Crylen. I wanted to be "cool," and no one who resembled my grandmother—a Croatian immigrant—had a prayer of being "cool," or of being tagged as my friend, either. And so I used them.

Perhaps because they sensed how shallow I was—even if that quality was the product of my adolescent insecurity—Stella and Sophie sometimes drifted into talking in their native Polish as we ate at the lunch table together. I doubted that they were actually saying "maybe Terry thinks she's better than us," but I couldn't be certain.

Not everyone was mean toward me like Joanie Randall. But as the Queen, she carried a lot of influence among her friends in the hive. And she had many. While most of the girls in our junior class were polite, none of them went out of their way to include me. What they had in common with one another further set me apart. I was an outsider.

These girls were better dressed, their uniforms crisp, their blouses whiter than mine. Their saddle shoes—though surely a clunkier style had never been created—somehow looked bizarrely cute on their feet. Saddle shoes on someone who wore a size ten, as did I, could only look like row boats. And unlike my shoes, theirs didn't look so cheaply made. Or scuffed. Their knee socks graced tight calves and well-turned ankles. On me, knee-highs looked more like casings stretched over sausages.

Small worries perhaps, unless you were a fifteen-year-old girl who'd never felt she belonged. Or been told she was pretty. Who'd never heard her mother say, "You're great. I love you, honey." The Queen of Peace girls had class. They had boys asking them for dates and I didn't even know any boys. Getting good grades wasn't enough. Once again, I was miserable.

Unable to talk with Mom about this alienation from my peers, about my state of friendlessness, about not knowing how to win anyone over to my side, I began soothing myself the only way I knew how: with sweets. Joanie Randall had been wrong when she'd implied that I was fat early on in the semester. Unfortunately, with the weight I'd put on by June, she was no longer so far from the mark. I couldn't button my skirt. Afraid of Mom's anger when she found out we'd need a new uniform for the following year, I left its button undone and the zipper at half-mast so that I didn't have to tell her.

The year ended and my efforts to conform had failed. I hadn't fit in. At all. And while I'd demonstrated that I could put my brain to good use, I'd sugared up my body until it had rebelled against me. Not only had I not been able to patch together the new life I'd planned, I didn't recognize myself in the mirror. It wasn't just my clothes that did not fit. I had no idea of who I was.

The summer passed, with long hours clocked at the bakery.

Only days before it was time to return to Queen of Peace for my senior year, plans for me shifted again. The prospect of another year there depressed me: once again I would be an ungainly girl lumbering through the school halls alone, and lonely, and the butt of cruel jokes. When Mom began grousing about the $225 price tag for the privilege of my attending parochial school—though the tuition that my paychecks, which I turned over to her each week, would easily have covered it—I seized upon her ambivalence to use the money this way and lobbied to return to Gage.

If she had other reasons for wanting not to send me back to the Catholics, or if money was far tighter than I realized, these issues remained invisible to me. I cared only that Mom put up no fight to my return to a school filled with boys. It didn't matter then that it would be to a place where I had previously failed. Rather than think it odd that Dad had not weighed in at all on the issue—or of how absent he always was when it came to making important decisions—I was glad to deal only with my mother. Wasting no time lest she change her mind, I hurried over to Gage and brought home the paperwork to reenroll.

The geographical cure hadn't taken—the same cure I'd sought for my loneliness back when I'd first discovered Mr. Newton's pop shop. At sixteen, I was odd girl out and already tired. Circling back to the world I knew, desperate for old friends, and still wishing to belong to something and someone, I convinced myself that this time, things would be different. And they were. Where there had once been only smoke, soon there was fire.

Outside the Lines

Guilt and grief go hand in hand.

—Ann Hood
The Obituary Writer

FOR THE FIRST FEW days after my return to Gage in the fall of 1969, I was something of a celebrity. A rumor made the rounds that I'd been gone for a year because I'd gotten pregnant and then had to give my baby up for adoption. Absurd though the gossip seemed, I pushed back by scoffing that I wasn't *that* kind of girl. Weeks later, after the talk about me died down on its own, new word spread that I'd been involved in another scandal. However, this time my disgrace was not something to joke about. There was nothing funny about it at all.

Much had changed in the year that I was absent from Gage Park High. The demographics of the student population had continued to shift, and the racial hatred rooted in fear had only increased. By the time I returned there for my senior year, fistfights between blacks and whites erupted regularly during the change of classes, sometimes spilling out onto the street. The rules of engagement were clear: stick with your own kind. The rumor this time was that I had gone rogue in following that edict. The confrontation about my social transgression came fast.

"Don't think we don't know what *you've* been up to." It was a voice that boomed over the noise of students heading to their classes. Startled, I turned to see my PE teacher rumbling down the high school's second floor corridor like an armored tank headed into battle.

Straight toward me.

I was confused to see Miss Kraus in this part of the building, so far from the gym, where she routinely tortured girls like me, who didn't excel at athletics. But then her words registered—and the message became clear. Millicent Kraus already knew the details of what I'd been "up to," and in a minute, many of my classmates would know, as well.

She was referring, I was certain, to the field trip for inner city children I'd attended as a camp counselor the weekend before. The field trip had been sponsored by the YMCA—and I hadn't shared the particulars with my parents. The angry flash in Miss Kraus's eyes made it clear that she knew all about the hours I'd spent "mixing" with a boy who sported an Afro. I had colored outside the lines.

As she closed in, I froze, unable to step out of her path. Dozens of kids who, like me, had been headed to eighth period, edged toward the walls. Only when Kraus had barreled past them did they creep closer toward the action. Eager to tune in. Listening. Waiting.

A smile spread across the gym teacher's face. She stopped, inches from where I stood riveted by fear—and shook her head slowly. "Look at you," she hissed.

My classmates stared. The change-of-class bell clanged. No one moved.

Frightened by what Miss Kraus might say next, and how the crowd would judge me—a crowd now emboldened by a few hecklers—I averted my eyes. Kraus, perhaps able to smell my fear, pressed forward. Grabbing my shoulder, she pushed. Hard enough that I was forced to take a step back.

"What the . . ." I protested, but stopped short as her stare pinned me down. Looking every bit like the drill sergeant she was in the gym, Miss Kraus folded her arms across her chest.

"You better watch yourself," she warned, through teeth that were clenched. Pivoting, she started back down the hallway, barking orders to the gawkers to clear the halls. Over her shoulder, she yelled at me. "Crylen, if you know what's good for you, you won't be making any more trouble here!"

Behind me, a locker door slammed. Jarred by the sound, I fought to keep in check the emotions I'd always stored deep down in the recesses of my mind: fury and despair. One part of me wanted to chase Miss Kraus down the hall and pummel her, while another wanted only to cry. Angry, scared, humiliated, I was too caught up in an inner swirl to make my way to class and pushed out the doorway into the stairwell.

Sitting on a step, I began to breathe again, and so stayed for a while. Memories of the weekend at the YMCA camp resurfaced. Good memories. But there was also the current stab of frustration. What had I done that was so goddamned bad? What stupid school prohibitions had I broken? I hadn't challenged the unspoken edict that said white kids ate lunch with other white kids and black kids with other blacks. I hadn't yelled support for the black kids when racially charged fights broke out in the school's hallways daily. I hadn't gone out of my way to befriend anyone at school who was not "my kind." I'd only tried to maintain friendships I'd previously forged on both sides of the racial divide. The proscriptions of the Millie Krauses at Gage made little sense to me, but on school premises, I'd tried to stay under the radar.

Pulling a stick of gum out of my pocket, I considered something new. Maybe it took breaking the rules to create good things. Hadn't that always been true for me? From wandering the streets of Peoria to cadging change from my mother's purse, I had discovered the joy of liberating myself from other peoples' restrictions. Maybe the problem was not really in *breaking* the rules but instead having to deal with the fallout if one was *caught*.

My claustrophobia began to ease. Fueled by anger that tussled with fear, I hurried down the flight of stairs and out into the sun. Bright red and yellow leaves swirled in the autumn breeze. Shoving another piece of gum in my mouth for good measure, I decided to be consciously willful from this minute on. Rebellious. Millicent Kraus wasn't going to tell me how to live my life. It was 1969: blacks were rioting in Chicago and women were burning their bras around the nation. I was ready to join the revolution.

∾

By Christmas, I was wholly invested in recreating myself. I had shed the twenty pounds I'd gained at Queen of Peace and five more for good measure. While not a Skinny Minnie, my body was just north of slender. Broiled hot dogs, cottage cheese, and the different flavors of Diet Rite cola made losing the weight as easy as it was unhealthy. I adopted the uniform worn by every flower child in the country—a pair of hip-hugger blue jeans and a gauzy blouse—a move that was transformative. If she had any inkling that I hoped to attract a boyfriend, my mother gave no indication. All I knew about her views about dating was what she'd advised my older sisters about only wanting somebody with something to offer. If Mom had known how low my standards were, she would have been steamed. For me, "something to offer" meant that I should exclude guys in prison and those who were too nice.

Soon, someone noticed.

"Lookin' good," commented a star athlete on one of Gage's teams. He was a senior. Eighteen to my four months shy of seventeen. Tall. Smooth. And dark as the blazer I'd worn at Queen of Peace. "How about walking me to the bus?"

To the bus? I would have walked across four lanes of super-highway with him.

And that, metaphorically speaking, is what I did for the next several months. Cocky and short-tempered, alternately charming and dismissive, this first boyfriend was nothing like the gawky but amiable males I'd hung out with at the YMCA weekend. Or like any boy I'd ever known. But his interest in me was all I needed to plaster myself to his side.

To spend time together, I traveled by bus—alone—to meet him in places closer to his family's apartment. Rough neighborhoods. Before long, I had lost my virginity to him, engaging in unprotected sex on a bare wooden floor in the unchaperoned home of one of his friends. This kind of sex carried with it far more anxiety than any pleasure; yet taking steps to prevent a pregnancy seemed too much to face. Scared by how in over my head I already was, I wanted only to close my eyes to what might happen. Condom, diaphragm, IUD, the Pill—I knew next to nothing about these forms of birth control and couldn't imagine asking friends or any adult for advice. Doing so, I reasoned, would only stoke the rumors at school that were already flying and be met with widespread recrimination.

Engaging in sex was similar to every other new situation I faced then: without the resources that might have enabled me to use better judgment, I had no way to protect myself. Mom and Dad would be horrified should they discover what I was doing; I imagined his silence and her fury. Still, despite my fear that they would find out, my desperation to feel "special" to someone was exponentially greater. Terrified of becoming pregnant, worried that my boyfriend would lose interest in me, I used my anxiety as a method of birth control. "I'm really nervous," I'd say, looking for his usual response.

"I'll pull out," he'd respond each time, a "plan" that, even as a naive sixteen-year-old, I knew, based on what I'd heard other girls' say, was no plan at all. My sexual encounters became more and more dominated by jangled nerves, compliance, and silence. And sometimes, even as we were having sex, thoughts of New York intruded—the place where, according to what I'd gleaned from the news, abortions were legal. There was no pleasure for me in what we were doing. Miss Kruse would have been furious to discover I was once again mixing with a boy of a different race, despite the status he'd achieved as a superior athlete. She might even come after me again. But I was deep in the grip of my rebellion, not even caring where it took me—rendered both scared and reckless when I was with him and wanting to believe that his interest in me would move beyond his casual, almost indifferent attitude toward the deeper relationship I craved. Surely this was possible—if I just stuck around long enough.

"Do you love me?" I found the courage to ask him one afternoon, as I lay next to him, naked.

"Ask me no questions and I'll tell you no lies," he answered, with a sly look.

Another girl—perhaps one who had an ounce of self-confidence, or a teaspoon of self-worth—might have been appalled by his response. But I had neither. I'd allowed myself to become vulnerable. As vulnerable as an adolescent girl could possibly be. Someone who was so insecure she could not look at herself in the mirror and enjoy who she saw reflected at her.

Instead of allowing myself to be offended, I simply tried my hardest not to appear devastated. Feigning a smile, I told myself that he'd only been joking or trying to be clever—but a hollow ache had already settled under my skin. Unable to tolerate my grief, I fought to bury it. I kept right on having sex with him, usually sneaking out of the house on Saturday nights after I'd finished my shift at the bakery.

The first Saturday in April, we spent the better part of the evening cruising in his friend's old Dodge beater; with me sandwiched between the two boys, the three of us wound our way without purpose around Chicago's deteriorated Woodlawn neighborhood, several miles from my home. Motown hits played loud on the radio and the air was electric. Excited as I was to be hanging with a boyfriend on a Saturday night, and relieved to be far enough away from where I lived to avoid detection by family, friends, or neighbors—I could not shake my worry that I'd later be caught in my lie about where I'd been. I lied so easily now, sometimes it was hard to remember at which friend's house I'd told my mother I'd be. Or whether I'd reminded that friend not to call me at home during the hours I'd be gone.

Each time we hit a well-lit street, I slunk lower in my seat, worried that my presence in the car would attract the attention of people who were passing by. The harsh voices of my parents, Winifred Kruse, and a chorus of adults from Chicago's southwest side echoed in my head: "What in the name of God were you thinking, going into a bad area? Being in a place filled with *those* people?" Their message was absolutely clear: don't cross the line and go where you don't belong. People who cross the lines wind up dead.

Unable to silence the voices, my anxiety intensified. Suddenly, the more familiar meeting places—in the shadows of a park or a badly lit apartment vestibule in a sketchy part of town—seemed far safer than what we were doing. Reaching to turn down the radio, I sighed. "It's late. If I don't get home soon, my father's gonna be out looking for me." This was a lie, as Dad, whose routine, even on weekends, was work, eat, and sleep, had likely gone to bed hours earlier, exhausted. "Just drop me at the Ashland bus stop and I'll catch the bus the rest of the way." Ashland divided black housing from white.

"That's cool," our driver replied. I exhaled with relief.

As he drove toward the drop-off point, I began to wonder if he was worried, too. *Maybe he's thinking how bad this could be if a white cop in a police cruiser spotted you right now. You'd both be hassled. Or maybe even arrested—no questions asked. Whatever were you thinking when you got into the car?*

Whatever concerns the guy behind the wheel might have had, they did not seem to be bothering my boyfriend, whom I'd been so eager to see just a few hours earlier.

"Take care of me before you go," the star athlete whispered in my ear, taking my hand and shoving it down inside his pants.

Caught off guard and speechless, I prayed that the other boy had not noticed the crude gesture. I was mortified.

Ignoring my furtive glance, my boyfriend—who no longer seemed like a boyfriend at all—slouched back in his seat. He gripped my wrist like a vise. I stared out the front windshield, pretending that he wasn't growing stiff against my fingers. Even as I allowed him to push my hand up and down in the rhythm he demanded, I reached for the radio's knob with the other. A reflex. I turned up the sound. I was building a protective wall around myself. And my humiliation.

As we approached the CTA stop, he groaned and pulled my hand out from his pants. Fumbling under the car's dashboard for my purse, I acted as if nothing had happened. And so did he. But when I got out of the car and watched them drive off, I let the mask drop. Rubbing my sticky fingers against the fabric of my jeans to wipe him off my palm, I felt used, plain and simple. That emotion could not be wiped away. Tears welled up.

The bus arrived soon, and smiling weakly at the driver, I threw coins in the fare box. Passing row after row of vacant seats, I quickly sank into one. In a blur, numb, I was working hard to bury any emotion at all.

Three weeks later, the house was empty. Grandma Healy had died alone in the hospital, her coronary heart disease having at last triumphed; my mother, lost in a grief so powerful it seemed unstoppable, was trying to escape her emotions by taking a cross country road trip with my oldest sister, Patty, and her husband, Jim. Shortly after the funeral, a getaway for Mom was hastily patched together, leaving Dad to look after my younger brothers and me. Even before she departed, my mother's impending absence seemed oppressive. As accustomed as I was to her distraction and inability to notice me, since Grandma's death she'd paid even less attention. In those days following her mother's death, Mom was not present emotionally, and now—once again lonely and alone—for the first time, I was coming close to admitting to the feelings that pressed down on me. Dark ones.

With Mom on the West Coast, the house remained unoccupied during the day, until my two brothers or I returned from school. After classes ended, I would come home to watch them, except on those afternoons I was scheduled to work. I must have told my boyfriend that my mother was gone, but for many years I would work hard to block out any memory of enlightening him in this way. Just as I would also block out everything that happened afterward.

One afternoon near April's end, a week before Mom's scheduled return, I went home for lunch in between classes, as I sometimes did. A few minutes later, the doorbell rang. Hands stuffed in the pockets of their leather jackets, my boyfriend and his sidekick lounged against the railing that ran along the front porch. Smiling and joking with one another, they looked as if they owned the place. I panicked, terrified that a neighbor might see them. *Didn't you really give him an invitation to come over when you told him everything that was going on in your family? Wasn't it all your fault?* Guilt, then—regardless of my intention.

Here, only two blocks from school, a black face stood out like a stop sign. Walking down the halls together at school was provocative enough, and going with him to the bus stop even more so. But on this day, the two of them had wandered with impunity past many houses on my street before they came, at last, to my front porch.

"Are you nuts?" I implored. "You'll get hit with a brick if you don't get out of here. And I'll get killed, too, if someone sees you!"

"Well, let us in then." My boyfriend laughed. "Before some crazy ass honky comes swingin' his bat."

Stepping back, I hurried them into the house.

"Come here," he teased, reaching for my hand and trying to pull me close. Out of my peripheral vision, I could just see the other boy slipping through the door leading to the dining room. The kitchen and bedrooms were only a few steps away. As he looked around, he ran his fingers over a patterned bowl that sat on a buffet. Touched the handles on the drawer that held Mom's tablecloths and a chest of silverware—wedding gifts she used only at Christmas and Easter.

Then, like a roaming cat, he disappeared through the dining room door and into the kitchen. He closed the door. Then, *click-click.* The sound of the key that had rested, unused, in the keyhole for as long as I could remember. In that quick minute, he had shut me out of the back half of my house.

"Come here," my boyfriend repeated in a more forceful voice.

Looking up at him, I was sure he could see fear registering on my face.

He laughed.

"What's the matter with you?" I demanded, angry, despite my racing anxiety.

"You say, what's the matter with *me*?" He grabbed my elbows. "I say, what's the matter with *you*?" *Slap.* Left cheek. *Slap.* Right cheek. He moved like a boxer, but he was hitting me with his open palms rather than his fists.

Okay, he's not punching you. It's just some kind of slap. As I talked to myself, I kept hoping I could reason my way out of this nightmare.

"You need to get the hell out of here right now," I said, attempting to sound firm, but only coming up with desperation. "My brother is going to walk through the door any minute." A lie. I squirmed away, trying to get around him.

He squeezed my arm, his enormous hand so powerful I thought a bone would break. With his other hand, he began to unbuckle his belt.

"Hold on! Just hold on, now. We're gonna do this." He laughed as he spoke, but in his eyes there was only rage.

Overpowered and pinned against the wall, I detached myself from what was happening. I couldn't shout. I couldn't fight back. *This is trouble. This is trouble.* I didn't make a sound even when he started to bang my head against a family photo hanging behind me.

The key on the kitchen side of the door turned in the lock, and his friend swaggered back into the room, a half-dozen steps from where I was shoved up against the wall.

"Oh, my man," the friend laughed. "You're too much."

"Out of the way, bro." He smiled. "I need a few minutes with my woman here." He shoved me through the doorway of my mother's room and onto the bed.

"Your old girl sleep here?" His eyes roamed over my mother's bathrobe and the jars of cream on her dresser.

I didn't answer. Too scared. Too ashamed.

"Lie down! Take off them pants!"

I did. My hands shaking so hard I could barely unzip my jeans.

He let his jeans fall on the floor and dropped his weight down on top of me. Crushing me. It was hard to breathe.

"I told you I wasn't leaving till we did this." His voice, rough. Devoid of any concern at all beyond the determination to get what he wanted: to subjugate this nice white girl.

I floated up to the ceiling and looked down on the two of us from some distance high above, as if I were totally disembodied.

After a while of shoving in and out of me, he pushed himself off and pulled out with a violent wrench of his body. It hurt. Then he stood and slapped me across the mouth with the back of his hand. Raising my hands to protect my head, I rolled away, and then pulled my clothes over my half-naked body as if they could protect me. I pushed myself up on the other side of the bed. He stared at me from only a few feet away, his body blocking the door, no barrier between us.

"Dang." His eyes roamed the room. "I didn't know y'all was so damn poor." He laughed and looked pleased. Poor: the word that had chased me all my life. The contempt in his tone hit like another swat across the face. What I heard: "your family's worth nothing and neither are you."

Afraid to look at him but more afraid not to, I stared at his zipper as he pulled it up and threw his shoulders back. Then he refastened his belt—slowly, deliberately—and laughed again. The sound was so unbearable I wanted to throw up.

He strutted out of the bedroom; the way he walked showed just how much pleasure he had taken in being brutal, in having owned me.

I could hear him talking to his friend and they laughed again. "Let's move," he said finally, and after what seemed like hours, the back door slammed. Running through the kitchen, my hands shaking as I locked the door behind them, trying to grasp why he had turned on me so violently. Was it my initial resistance? Had he wanted to act all macho—to show off to his friend? My mind came up empty as I pulled back the edge of the curtain, and watched them saunter through the yard and into the back alley. In no hurry at all.

In a daze, I never even thought of showering or changing my clothes before heading the two blocks back to campus, determined to make it to my next class before the bell rang. I began to convince myself that what I'd been forced to do wasn't so terrible. Perhaps everything could even be normal again. My mind, my memory, my heart—all of me felt as if I were tiptoeing over a field of fractured glass. I continued to reassure myself it had only been sex with the boy to whom I'd made love willingly nearly a dozen times before. *What right did you have to refuse him this time?* the voice inside me pointed out with a sneer. Yes, he had mocked me. Yes, he had hit me. But getting back to school on time seemed like an omen: if I could slip unnoticed into my next class then what he had done to me could pass unnoticed, as well. His scorn wouldn't really be so shocking. So terrible.

That afternoon, as the clock moved from one to two to three, I told no one about what had happened. Not a teacher or the principal or a friend. Feeling worthless and ashamed, I did not let myself even think of the word I knew was the truth for what had happened to me. I would not tell anyone later, either. Especially not my mother.

It seemed a long time before she returned—the days passed instead like weeks. My emotions had short-circuited into a permanent numbness. But even if they hadn't, I would not have confided in her, anticipating how disgusted she would be with me—and how furious that I had allowed strangers in her home. Telling her would require a litany of lies to make my story a credible and sympathetic one. I focused instead on making her homecoming pleasant, one which would comfort her in her grief of losing her mother, which she surely wouldn't have put behind her yet: a clean house, a prepared meal—the same things I'd always done to try to soothe her. Hoping, as I had countless times before, that by comforting my mother, I would find comfort, too.

I moved through each day as if nothing had happened: I was at school; he was at school; at times our paths intersected. Once I even smiled at him, an old reflex, as we passed one another in the hall between classes. For a moment he looked suspicious. Wary. But then he just walked on, indifferent. I had been erased. Confused, I did not miss him, aware only of another surge of humiliation at having been so discarded, still wondering what had I done to deserve his disdain. Had he only been using me for sex the whole time?

His charm did not stop: he put his head together with the head of the biology department—the woman who was championing his

academic bid for a list of impressive colleges. More than once, he huddled at lunchtime with Coach, undoubtedly discussing his bid for an
athletic scholarship; Coach always gave him a pat on the back as he
headed off to class. To everyone else he was a big deal. To me, he was
heartless. Someone who made me afraid.

And it seemed he was everywhere. When we passed by each other
without speaking, it was not anger that ripped through me. Or even a
ripple of resentment. Instead, I experienced once more my own stu-
pidity. And ugliness. As if I had no right to be in the same building.
As if I had no right to exist.

*After all, Terry, aren't you responsible for everything's that's
happened?*

My mother walked back into the house with a tired smile. Her travel
companions—my oldest sister and her husband, a police officer—followed close behind. A short time later, with a second pot of coffee per-
colating on the kitchen counter and the sound of easy bantering filling
the space, I relaxed for the first time in a week. Family members glided
in and out of the room, and my brother-in-law left for a moment—but
in a second he returned.

"Paul, I can't find my service revolver." He looked confused, then
alarmed when my father shook his head.

"What do you mean you can't find it? I don't understand." Dad's
voice grew loud. "I watched you put it on the shelf in the bedroom!"

"I just went to get it. It's not there—I thought maybe you moved
it."

My heart stopped.

Moments later, the room seemed to explode. "Who could have
taken it? Did someone break in?" The voices rose in pitch until they
became a cacophony. Not surprisingly, in all the commotion, no one
took notice of me. Frightened by everyone's panic, I moved over to
Mom's side, as slowly as if my legs were slogging through quicksand.
Pulling her by the sleeve, I guided her toward the back porch. It took

a few minutes but eventually I got the words out: I had let people into the house without permission, boys I knew. And I told her the truth about not knowing there was ever a gun in the house until just now, when Jim couldn't find it.

She hurried back into the kitchen, and through the open window I heard their low voices quickening. Then the whirring sound of the telephone's dial. My brother-in-law was calling his commander to inform him that his weapon was missing—and explaining that he'd thought it was safer for him to leave it in our home, as his own was standing empty during the trip.

The detective from the Chicago Police Department's eighth district interviewed me an hour later as I sat hunched next to my mother on the front steps of our porch. My eyes stung and my body trembled.

"So, you let a couple of colored guys in? Without your parents' permission?" He frowned. "Why?"

A cool wind brushed my cheeks, which felt as if they were on fire.

"Why?" he repeated, before I could answer. "And then into your mother's bedroom of all places?"

My stomach flipped at his mention of the word bedroom. "I let them into the house because I was scared, that's why." I aimed for a tone that would sound matter-of-fact and then tried to stick to the surface of the truth. "The neighborhood isn't exactly open-minded, you know, and I was afraid someone would see them on the porch and start something. Or that a neighbor would call the police." I swiped at my eyes. "And I felt bad, too, like I should be nice. That's why I let them in but I didn't say it was okay to go into my Mom's *bedroom*!"

"Well, how do you suppose they got in there?"

"One of them was just walking around while I was talking to the other guy." I stumbled over my words. "I wasn't worried because I knew them from school. I guess that was stupid . . ." I trailed off aimlessly. "But I thought they were my friends."

Friends? What the hell is wrong with you?

"How could you think those kind of people were friends?" Mom interrupted.

I didn't answer her, just looked as if I were concerned with answering the cop's questions, which came one after the other, each posed slowly. His voice was very quiet. Which undoubtedly helped him get me to talk. But then he circled back, reframing questions he'd already asked, and my dread only deepened.

"So, the one guy's just walking around and you don't see him go into your mom's bedroom? Into her closet?

Great. He probably thinks you were in on it.

"I told you I didn't know!" I choked on the words as I repeated what I'd already said. "I didn't *know* he'd gone in there. And I never knew there *was* a gun." Even as I spoke, the voice in my head wouldn't let up. *Yeah, but before you got yourself pinned to the wall you should have known the other one was casing the house. How could you be so naive, so stupid to think he was just putting distance between what was about to happen—the sex?* "It wasn't until my mom came home and everyone started yelling that I realized it. Can't you see?" I was pleading with the detective now. And silently praying he wouldn't continue his probing.

Why couldn't I tell the detective what had really happened to me?

Or my mother?

Or a friend?

Why couldn't I tell anyone at all?

Because everything was your own fault.

For months, in defiance of Miss Kruse's warning "not to cause any more trouble," I had courted it recklessly. And now, with a gun missing—a police-issued weapon, at that—I had swept my family into a potentially dangerous situation. What if my boyfriend and the other guy were planning to use that gun in a stick-up? What if they already had? The questions washed over me like cold rain, pelting down on my shoulders.

I had no way to understand, and therefore no way to describe to the detective, or to anyone else, the other theft—the much worse theft—that occurred that day, a week ago: my girlhood; my womanhood. That I had been easy prey. That what had happened to me was a terrible sexual violation. I was light years away from being able to voice that violation as a truth.

"Okay, Miss." At last he stood. "Mrs. Crylen, we're finished here. We've got some work to do on this."

Work to do. They had to find a stolen gun.

After the officer left, Mom and I sat on the steps of the porch, still as statues. Not touching, just staring at the empty street, the way we had once done on Peoria when I was a young girl—so well-captured by that old photo. It reminded me of that different time in my life. A time of innocence and the small rebellions that now seemed so insignificant.

Mom looked drained. Turmoil raged inside me, and yet I could see, with a detached sort of clarity, that her trip to California had not brought her peace over Grandma's passing.

The sky was blanketed by clouds, the wind too chill to provide warmth. But we stayed there anyway, for a long time, without speaking. We were both lost in our own sorrow. Both numb from grief and wishing for the impossible. Both desperate to find some way back to our mothers.

I'd been coloring outside the lines. She hadn't even known. And I wasn't about to tell her.

Part Two

Flying at Low Altitude

It is joy to be hidden, but disaster not to be found.

—D.W. Winnicott. *1963*

I SPENT MY FIRST day as an office clerk at the Harry Alter Company plotting how to quit. Landing a full-time job just days after high school graduation had seemed promising—a new start and a way to distance myself from the frenzy of the robbery and the ache of humiliation. But I had no idea how miserable working in a warehouse could be when I accepted the position through a secretarial agency—especially the dark, musty place I entered, filled with nothing but walls of refrigeration parts awaiting distribution, and a military issue metal desk piled high with invoices waiting for me.

Squirreled away in a corner of the building with no one to talk with, I waited for the door to be sealed behind me. Nevertheless, for the first several hours, I worked hard—typing dozens of billing statements and filing stacks of old folders covered in dust—but by lunchtime I'd lost all interest in the task and wanted only to cry.

At lunchtime, carrying the brown bag that I'd packed that morning, I was invited by several women to join them in the break area. As relieved as I was not to have to eat alone, all hope of meeting someone my own age evaporated when we arrived at the table. Everyone there looked old.

The women chattered on about recipes and S&H green stamps, and initially I was grateful that I didn't have to talk. But then I began to wonder how they could be so excited to gab ad infinitum about meal planning and shopper bonus points and how many stamps it took to purchase a blender. I wanted to laugh—to make light of how silly it all seemed, but inside me, something else was at play, something deadening. *Don't laugh, smart ass. This could be your future.*

At day's end, I pushed my card into the time clock and asked myself how I would explain to Mom that I planned to quit a job I'd held for only eight hours. How could I tell her that, from the minute I'd walked through the door, it had seemed as if I were wrapped in a shroud? A moment of relief filled me as I placed the card back in its slot—*Goodbye Harry Alter Company!*—but it was followed by a wave of uneasiness. I imagined my mother telling me that I was leaving behind "a swell opportunity for no good reason." That I thought I was "too good for the job."

Unable to bear the idea that Mom would force me to return to the mausoleum, I mapped out a different course. I would leave the house the next morning, as if I were headed back here, then spend the day looking for something else. After that? Register for classes at the local community college, as well. And after that, confront the reality of my situation. *Right. You just want to get the hell out of the house and run as fast as your feet will carry you.*

Days later, having scored a waitressing job at the Ford City mall, I enrolled in summer classes at Southwest Junior College. Buoyed by these successes, I pushed myself to tell Mom. I walked in the house and found her in the pantry with the dust pan. "How's that going to work?" She poked the broom into a corner and swept out cornflakes from some long-ago spill. "Flossy had three secretarial jobs when she went to college." She turned to look at me. "Good jobs."

"I can work as many shifts as I need to," I insisted. "Plus, they told me I can make a lot in tips, Mom."

"You know shorthand and you know how to type." She bent to sweep the spilled cereal into the pan and shook her head, a look of resignation in her eyes. "Why would you want to waste your skills?"

I waited to disclose the third secret I'd been carrying, the one harder to admit to than the others, until weeks later when I'd found a place to live. Finally, one late evening, as Mom slathered cold cream over her cheeks before bed, I stood at the door of her bedroom, my arms folded like a shield across my chest.

"Mom," I began, talking as fast as I could. "I just found out about this cool thing. There are two other girls I know—one from the neighborhood and one from my biology class—and I can live with them in an apartment they're renting."

"What are you talking about?" She lifted her chin to smear a glob from the jar onto her neck. "You've got a home right here."

"It'll be easier for me to get to work and to school." I pulled my arms tighter. "I can put in more hours at the restaurant every day."

"You're talking like a lunatic." She turned to look at me, her face lathered white. "You must be on drugs."

Relieved that I had gotten the words out, I ran upstairs to my room before she could say anything more.

The beginning of our Cold War had begun. It would be nearly another week before I could move in with my friends, and nervously, I spent every waking hour trying to avoid Mom. Early one morning, however, having fallen asleep on the couch the night before, I woke to a hand squeezing my shoulder. Startled, I looked up to see my father standing over me. The light coming through the windows had paled; it was early and he was leaving for work.

"Terry."

"I'm going up," I mumbled, assuming Dad was about to grouse about my having sacked out there overnight. "Just a sec."

"We don't want you to leave, you know," he whispered.

Caught off guard, I lay with my eyes closed, pretending I hadn't heard him.

But he persisted. "Your mother and I . . . listen. If you stay, Terry, we'll buy you a new bedroom set."

Coming from anyone else, such an offer would have sent me into spasms of laughter. But hearing it from Dad, in words spoken so softly and so sincerely, only sadness swamped me: how he misunderstood me. For Mom and him to buy me new furniture for my room was an extravagance. I had no way of knowing if they had discussed it together, or if this was solely Dad's way of inducing me to stay, but in that moment, it didn't matter. Struck by how his suggestion didn't touch the real problem, I was moved nevertheless: he was trying to be helpful the best he knew how.

"I can't Dad." I couldn't find any other words but these.

He waited a few moments, and then, as quietly as he'd awakened me, he left for "the job."

Once I heard the screen door close behind him, I went to the window and watched him cross to the other side of the street, where he paused and turned to look back at the house. Dressed in navy blue work pants and a white dress shirt with sleeves rolled to his elbows, he was the man for whom I'd waited when I was the little girl standing at the corner of the block. He reached into his shirt pocket and pulled out a book of matches. One strike and a small flame appeared. Cupping his hands around the glow, he raised it to meet the cigarette in his mouth. And then did not move. My eyes watered.

Unable to pull myself away, I just stood there with the curtain still stretched in my hand and watched him. After a minute, he tossed the butt to the sidewalk and ground it out with the toe of his shoe. And then, with one last glance at his castle, he headed for the bus. Pushing my hair from my face, I remained at the window until I could not see him any longer. The day was so young, the street so empty, that I wondered if I'd only dreamed my father had ever been there.

Once I left home to be on my own that summer of 1970, I discovered that many of my new friends lived the same way I now did and this, too, was a relief: to be something of a vagabond, to live poor and wear frayed clothes—the two things I'd most abhorred while growing up—no longer seemed shameful. Instead, looking scruffy had become a fashion statement. No one told me to go home from the parties I loved, and I could hang out with glassy-eyed "pad" crashers and drink as much cheap wine as I wanted without a curfew. Without money and on my own meant it was easier to secure student loans for tuition and books.

Taking classes during the day, I worked the late shift at the restaurant and earned just enough in pay and tips to make my share of the rent and travel from place to place. Luckily, one of the perks of the job was a free meal. I scrambled to make it all work, but, actually, most of my days were not so very different than that of kids who lived on college campuses. Or so I imagined. Like them, I felt confused and unsure of where I belonged.

"Each of you can choose the grade you'll get in this class," my English professor announced the first day of freshman year. Having migrated from a top university, he loved to challenge the academic status-quo. "You may think that what you've got to do is to please me, but what I really want to see is that you know how to *think*." Chewing on the top of my pen, I wondered if he were joking. I imagined giving myself an *F*: I had no idea what "how to think" even meant. However, despite my anxiety, I didn't drop the course, and over the span of that first summer semester, I did something I'd failed to do through most of high school. I paid attention. And did the work.

By that summer of 1970, political unrest had spread to a more generalized chaos. The deaths at Kent State symbolized living in a world dominated by the unanticipated. I sat out the sit-ins that cropped up now on a regular basis, however, because I was conflicted. Could I protest a war that did seem crazy when blue-collar neighborhood boys had eagerly enlisted without waiting to be drafted? A number of them were still overseas, and two had never made it home. I also wasn't sure about my identity as a woman: though there were groups of women who were torching their bras, all those I knew at that time were still toeing the traditional line, one defined by dominant men. #MeToo was five decades away.

The pervasive anxiety and guilt I'd carried from the minute I left home did not lessen during these first few months at college. I avoided visits with my parents, phoning instead—as if checking in daily made me a better daughter than one who called infrequently, or maybe not

TERRY CRYLEN

94

at all. In my head, I heard Mom's voice chastising me for having "run off." For not contributing to the family either emotionally or financially. Afraid to confront her, I waited until I got settled in my classes before going back home the first time. One rainy Sunday afternoon, I finally showed up. Unannounced.

She let the newspaper she'd been reading fall into her lap. "You look like a freak." She shook her head, her expression hardening. Dad was nowhere to be seen.

"Gee. Thanks, Mom." I lingered at the edge of the room and feigned amusement. Pretending to straighten the red bandanna taming my wild, dark curls, aware of the pull of my shiny hoop earrings on my earlobes, I looked away.

We both knew she was not just commenting on my clothing, or my earrings: she was commenting on me. Her rejection of the young woman I was fast becoming hurt. Nevertheless, instead of flying out of the room, I forced myself to sit down—knowing that if I listened to the inevitable criticism and tolerated her explosion our afternoon would go better. After all, I still wanted a mother. Despite myself. And, as always, to capture her love meant I must convince her that I had not abandoned her.

"Just look at you!" she exclaimed, before I could get out a response. "You've been brainwashed, like all those goddamn hippies you're hanging around with!"

I stared at the lamp, determined not to dissolve into tears. At one time, the operative word had been "dummies," or "tramps," and now it was "hippies."

"Think of all the money you could be saving if you lived at home!" she barked, as she grabbed at the paper and tossed it onto the coffee table. "You're just wasting it on other people!" After a minute, during which neither of us spoke, she pushed herself up from the couch. "Sometimes I wonder if you're just subnormal."

I was certainly back home, in the world where words could wound.

Had anyone else been around that day, I might have stayed longer.

But when Mom decided she was done with me and stomped off to the kitchen, I seized the chance to leave, relieved that I didn't have to listen to her unload more hostility or exact a punishment because I'd broken her rules. After all, in absorbing her anger and disappointment, I'd once again done penance for the sin of satisfying my own need. Maybe I'd even short-circuited a bout of depression for her, as my silence during her eruption had allowed her to discharge her rage. Perhaps she'd be able to function for a while and wouldn't spend days in her room. In exchange for all that, she might someday tell me she loved me.

As I pushed through classes, visits home continued to make me jumpy. Even confining my contact to telephone calls kept me on edge. I could never predict which mother would pick up the phone—the one who berated or the one who was benign. All my worry and stress had an upside, though: they were excellent weight loss tools. Unlike the year when Joanie Randall had slammed me for my weight and I had nervously eaten my way to a larger size for comfort, this time I ate less to alleviate emotional pain: when I dropped under 125 pounds, I was thrilled. Believing this was a perfect number for my 5'8" frame, I loved it when people called me "willowy," or asked me if I modeled. Not once did I consider myself to be too thin or unhealthy. Finally, I had something I could control. My looks. And what I was losing in body fat, I was gaining in attention, just as had happened in high school with my "star" athlete.

Boys—and men—were noticing me. Except now I sought validation that I was pretty; my main challenge was to figure out how to flirt. I really wanted to be noticed more than I wanted to be part of a couple, as being linked with a guy in a serious way would bring up the inevitable question of sex. I imagined myself as a traffic light that only blinked yellow: I wanted men to slow down, pause long enough to see me, and then move right along. In reality, the signals I sent were confusing—perhaps best described as short green/quick red.

I frustrated more than a handful of potential suitors, but I myself, did not understand the cause of my skittish reaction. Connecting the dots with the attack in high school turned out to be impossible; in my mind, I still believed that what had happened then was "just sex." Or sometimes, I wondered, was I only a tease? That question left me worried and depressed.

The next summer, I made the jump to a four-year school, downstate, the next stop on my journey away from Mom and home. There, I became involved with a man, who, like me, loved taking classes in the theater department. Five years older than I, he *did* know how to "think" and he helped me both academically and socially. Soon we were having sex, my decision to succumb made possible by his warm, non-threatening manner—and by numbing myself out. Passive and detached, I preferred quick intercourse in the dark while remaining partially clothed. Before long, unbeknownst to my parents, we began living together. Another big step away from home. Another big secret to keep.

Despite the emotional growth I *did* make during this period, I woke each day feeling both edgy and sad—grateful that I no longer lived with my parents, but mentally frayed. I worried about money and chafed at the idea that my boyfriend and I were too reliant on one another. Around this time, too, I learned that my older sister, Jeanie, now a mother of three young children and living in Los Angeles, had been hospitalized after a psychotic break. The news distressed me more than I admitted, and my upset was exacerbated further with the discovery that my mother had no plans to visit her. Her voice on the phone was hard with a resentment that over-shadowed her concern: she claimed she'd been instructed by Jeanie's husband not to come.

I was flying at low altitude, with just enough drive and tenacity to stay aloft and propel myself forward but with too much emotional drag to safely ascend. I'd left home but brought heavy baggage with me. And though I had yet to understand my irritability as another manifestation of my anxiety, and my "funks" as part of a low-grade depression that hung like a permanent cloud, I recognized clearly the worry that I harbored. Believing, as I always did, that I had left my mother behind.

Once again, I became dissatisfied with where I was, and in the summer of 1973, I moved back to Chicago to pursue a more practical academic plan. If I could earn enough education credits from a local university in the city, I'd be able to supplement my theater degree with a teaching certificate in language arts. And so I enrolled. Excited to have a goal and a path, I was still with my live-in—but not for much longer. It only took the attention of a professor who was directing shows in the theater's summer stock season to set me flying off in a new direction. A charmer in a brooding sort of way, John was twice my age and well-respected in the university's performing arts department.

His personal life, on the other hand, was a mess—but this did not deter me. I jumped right into a liaison that made about as much sense as walking into oncoming traffic. I was delusional: committing myself to a forty-year-old man who looked every bit his age, drank heavily, and had already been married twice. One of his marriages had lasted for a dozen years, the other only a half-dozen months. Did that stop me?

Not for a second.

I fantasized that I would save him—a tortured artist fighting off demons. I would understand him as no one else did and become the devoted caregiver who tolerated his drunken binges and rendered him whole again. Though I didn't really recognize it, hadn't I done something similar with my mother? I'd taken care of her at her lowest—and placated her rages. John posed a similar challenge, perhaps an equally difficult one. But maybe *he* would be grateful and loving in all the ways Mom hadn't been.

By the following spring, about to graduate and move from my basement level hellhole to John's apartment in the suburbs, I finally confided in my mother. Like directions down a dark trail, I'd been providing hints that I was serious about someone—but I'd been careful not to share anything troubling or negative about John or his history.

"We're thinking about getting married," I blurted out one warm afternoon, as we sat together in the backyard. She'd go crazy if she knew too much about him—what mother wouldn't, if they heard the entire story—but I nevertheless hoped that, if I sprinkled in enough tasty tidbits, she might see him as someone who "had something to offer." And so, I acknowledged that John was divorced but omitted the parts about his having been married *twice*, his heavy drinking, and his two young sons—who were being raised by their mother, wife number one. Emphasizing his impressive academic pedigree in the performing arts—filled as it was with earlier stints at Ivy League colleges, both as a student and as a professor seeking tenure—I assured her that my education wouldn't go to waste and that I was engaged in an intense hunt for a local teaching job.

Finally, I worked up the courage to ask my mother if she wanted to come to one of his plays and meet him. My anxiety escalated as she eyed me with suspicion. Then, surprisingly—or maybe not so, given that my mother was a sucker for all things dramatic—she agreed.

My hope that the meet-and-greet would go well died at intermission.

"What do you want with an old duck like that?" she said with a roll of her eyes, once she'd shaken John's hand and watched him disappear backstage. My Aunt Dorothy, who'd come along for the unveiling rather than my father, shrugged her shoulders.

"Mom," I whispered, my voice tight. "I'm trying my best here." Then I added the ultimate in defiance: "And just so you know, I'm not looking for your permission."

"You're ruining your life, hitching yourself to somebody else's wagon." Pushing her hands into her coat pocket, she bent closer. "What the hell's wrong with your brain that you can't see that?"

What she didn't understand was that I *did* know what I was doing. I *was* hitching myself to trouble—just I had back in high school. But this time it would be of a different and permanent sort.

Days before, I'd stood looking out my grimy "garden apartment" window for the last time, and—in a rare moment of honesty—assessed my dubious situation. *This is a mistake. But you've already made your bed. Now lie in it.*

I was tired. And depressed. But still, I didn't have the ability to name these emotions or the insight that would have allowed me to pull myself out of the tight mental crawl space I inhabited. Instead, this man had professed his love for me and even told me I could have become a fashion model: our relationship was a quid pro quo. Something for something. Just as I had in all my years as a daughter, I wanted to be my own person—but without abandoning the person whose needs were greater than mine. Without the benefit of someone to shine a light on the trap I had set for myself, I was getting ready to marry my mother.

In the several months that led up to my late summer wedding, I put on an award-winning performance, acting as if everything were normal—even after my mother expressed horror when I finally told her that John was not only divorced, but Protestant. Already adamant that he was far too old for me, she now had to contend with the fact that a wedding in a Catholic church was impermissible. Dad remained a shadow in the background, just as he had throughout my years at college. Neither condemning my choice, nor challenging Mom's criticisms, he was as neutral as war-time Sweden. Our plans were for a low-key affair at a nondenominational church that would include only immediate family and a few close friends. My wedding dress, however, remained a mystery.

Despite my mother's threats to boycott the day, I tried to cajole her to come with me as I looked for my all-important gown. I assured her that our search would last for just one afternoon. In only one store. I had no real expectation that she would, in fact, come, so when she actually agreed to accompany me, shock and relief overcame me. Maybe she was going to be supportive, after all.

In a small bridal shop at the mall, assisted by a stocky, heavily rouged saleswoman who tactfully ignored our awkward silence, I raced through the process, pulling one beaded gown after another over my head. The fact that each dress was more lovely than the one before only increased the tension between us. Hugging her purse as she sat in a corner of the fitting area, the mother of the bride looked like a woman waiting for a train in the subway—on high alert, lest someone try to mug her. I held up a finger and asked the woman to bring just one more gown, and she smiled broadly. Then she came back with a stunning, silhouette number.

I stepped up to the mirror.

"How much is that one?" Mom asked, at last, with a serious tone.

"A hundred twenty-five," I replied, looking at the ticket nervously.

"Oh. Not cheap," she said. Quietly. "It fits you beautifully, though." And then, as if she were trying hard to let down her guard, she offered something more. "It's a gorgeous dress, Terry. But, of course, they all look terrific on you."

Despite her compliment, crazy thoughts ran through my mind. Did she think I was fishing for her admiration? Why did she want to know what this dress cost? Had she only remarked on how good I looked in order appear supportive—to show the saleswoman that she knew how a mother of the bride should act to be appropriate? Or did Mom secretly think I was being sneaky—convincing her to come along on this most important of days with the hope that she'd feel guilty enough to pay for the dress? *Well, isn't that what you really wanted but just couldn't admit?* the voice in my mind asked, in a sardonic tone.

I wanted to flee. I was marrying a man who had not even bothered to give me an engagement ring. A difficult, complicated man. We had no plans for a honeymoon or even an overnight stay at a hotel. My father remained silent whenever there was any discussion of our wedding plans. None of my family had offered a word of congratulations, however token such might have been. *Why are you even shopping for a dress when there is nothing at all that is celebratory about this wedding?*

I looked over at the saleswoman.

"It's way too much money." I shook my head, quickly. Mom shifted in her chair. "And way too fancy for a small church wedding." Staring at my mother in the full-length mirror, unable to read the look on her face, I forced a smile and exhaled for what seemed like the first time that afternoon. "Let's just go. I'm going to pay the costume designer in John's department to make something for me." I spoke with conviction, cajoling myself into believing what I had said. "I only wanted to come here to get some ideas."

I was lying—to both of us: I *did* want that dress, and I *did* wish my mother would want it for me. But to admit as much would be like opening my mouth to breathe, forgetting I was under water. Our brief silence had been too overwhelming, and I couldn't risk any more disappointment. I had to take control.

The charade hadn't worked. We'd been play-acting, pretending to be an ordinary mother and daughter visiting a bridal shop. Neither of us, however, had pulled off a convincing performance. On the ride back to the house, neither of us spoke of the gowns I'd tried on. We talked about other things, but what they were is lost. What I couldn't forget was the dismissive tone in my mother's voice each time I phoned her afterward. Her threats that she wouldn't come to the wedding continued in the weeks before the ceremony. Only days before did she finally announce to my sisters that she planned to attend. But having relented on her plan to boycott, the chill emanating from her only grew worse. Meaning there was still time for her to do what she'd done so many times before in my life. Disappear.

On the appointed day, my parents arrived last.

"Nice, Terry, Very, very nice!" my father enthused. Which was his way of saying I looked pretty in the dress I'd had made.

An ivory, floor length sheath, it appeared elegant due to its simplicity. And it fit me perfectly. However, upon closer examination it looked, indeed, like a dress made by a costumer and intended for a play: a gown with no lining, a hastily-stitched hem, and a few for-gotten straight pins that pinched at my skin. Had I bothered to try the "finished" dress on earlier, I would have discovered that it felt as insubstantial as did I.

Across the room, my sisters Flo and Patty stood next to Mom, complimenting her on her coiffed hair and the deep pink, sleeveless dress she wore. As I started in her direction, she froze. Nevertheless, I bent forward to kiss her on the cheek, but missed when she moved and nodded without a word. No kiss then. And no words in the restaurant where everyone congregated after the ceremony, either. No words for the entire day. Afterward, Mom walked out looking as if she'd just swallowed a vial of poison.

If only that had been the worst part, perhaps it would not have ranked as the saddest and most stressful in my whole life up to that point. Instead, surprisingly, in the competition for who and what made it hardest, the honors went to my new husband. All afternoon, with my nerves afire, I kept a watch on how much John drank. He was headed toward full intoxication. But no one appeared to notice and my relief was palpable. During our vows, his eyes were watery and red and I became grateful that the ceremony was short. A Mass would have lasted far longer, and John's chances of swaying until he fell off the altar that much greater. A brief service saved us from that humiliation.

Later that night, lying in bed, my head fuzzy from too much champagne and my body aching with fatigue, I was finally alone with my new husband. I'd survived the stress of my wedding and recep-tion, and now, even though John lay drunk at my side, everything nevertheless seemed romantic. I had discovered early on that alcohol made him more amorous, not less. This night I learned that it was important to him that I respond to his sexual overtures with enthusi-asm. I had vowed to comply. Afterward, sweaty and still naked except for our wedding bands, we lay without speaking and just held hands. Breathed the heavy fragrance of a dozen candles I'd placed around the room. I was sleepy, and my body relaxed for the first time all day.

"Your bridesmaid. Susan." John slurred. "That girl sure has a great body."

My eyes shot open. "What did you say?" I choked. As blood rushed up my neck and to my ears, he went on about how much "fun" he imagined my childhood friend would be in bed. Words and more words slipped out of his mouth, each sentence wounding me more than the last.

I got out of bed and hurried into the bathroom—too shocked and humiliated to even cry. Then I turned on the taps and let the water run as I just stood there. Numb inside, I finally went back into the dark of the other room. How this reminded me of still another time, another bedroom, where I had numbed myself to deal with pain.

John lay sprawled across the sheets, passed out. Convinced that I had no longer had any choices at all, I blew out the candles, and slipped back into bed unnoticed.

A little more than four years had passed since I'd left home with the hope I could create a new life for myself. I'd hoped to fly far. Fly high.

Instead, I was moving only faster and faster, at ground level. Out of control. And bracing for the crash.

Show Time

If you have a deep scar, that is a door; if you
have an old, old story, that is a door . . .
If you yearn for a deeper life, a full life, a
sane life, that is a door.

—Clarissa Pinkola Estes
Women Who Run With the Wolves

MY FIRST YEAR OF marriage was like a stage production that should have closed on opening night. In the annals of marital bliss, it bombed. I was working as a teacher in a private school, while John continued as an associate professor in theater arts at Northeastern. Our warmly lit Chicago suburb apartment was the set for our dramatic production. Act One could have been called "Straight Up, No Twist," while Acts Two and Three devolved into "Stupor" and "Post-stupor." Mine was a small, supporting role: the long suffering wife. No understudy. John was the star.

Ours was an eight o'clock curtain, although delays sometimes occurred if my husband was teaching an evening class or directing a show on campus. Or, when he arrived home on time, only to discover that he'd miscalculated how much McCallan was still stored under the kitchen sink. A fifth of Scotch was not just a prop in our homey production. Alcohol drove every scene. So, when caught up short by the sight of a nearly empty bottle next to the sponges, with his surprise that confirmed the night before existed only as a giant black hole in his memory, John would grab his keys from the counter and take off to the neighborhood liquor joint.

By this time, my world had shrunk to the size of the small class of five-year-olds I was teaching. Exhausted by the demands of my first professional job, I raced home each afternoon to nap for an hour, and then starting prep work for the next school day, all the while readying a simple dinner in anticipation of John's arrival. Embarrassed by his unpredictable behavior, I cut myself off from friends. On weekends, I tackled cleaning the house—my need for order standing in stark contrast to John's penchant for creating clutter—and made goodwill visits to my parents, by myself. Despite the stress we had endured prior to the wedding, I now wanted to demonstrate to Mom that I remained the good daughter she always had expected and demanded. I talked to no one about the way John's alcoholism was consuming our lives. As had always been the case, I used lies of omission to cover our tracks.

Each day, I woke trying to convince myself things weren't *so* bad, just as I still tried to convince myself that the "rough" sex with my old boyfriend—as I now categorized it in my mind—had really been some kind of lovemaking. At one point, I attempted to allay my ballooning anxiety by drinking along with John, but doing that had really only heightened my sense of fear. With abstinence came some sort of control. Or so I believed.

But about six months into the marriage, the curtain of denial disintegrated. All that I had tried so hard to believe wasn't horrible, suddenly became harrowing. One particular night began with the usual *clink-clink-clink* of ice cubes dropping into John's glass in the kitchen. Not a highball glass, a tumbler-sized water glass.

When he finally appeared in the living room, I'd already retreated to the couch with a paperback. As always, he was stirring his tall-boy scotch with a swizzle stick. Reminding me of a twelve-year-old who'd just heated up a cup of hot cocoa.

Neither of us spoke. The affable John existed only in the classroom, or when we were out in public. At home, especially before he'd start his drinking ritual, he typically remained silent unless spoken to. He preferred to settle in a chair and lose himself in a book. Without a

television or stereo in the apartment—another oddity that I chose to
see as normal—"library hour" began.

With his drink at his elbow on the side table, he thumbed the
pages of an old *National Geographic*. An edgy vibe overtook the room.
I glanced up. He appeared preoccupied with his magazine, and so I
pretended to read, as well. But I couldn't concentrate. Nevertheless, as
usual, I didn't say a word.

Eight ounces later, John rose from his chair. My chest grew tight
as he headed back toward the kitchen. I steeled myself. *Here we go.*

"What is it?" he said, when he finally returned. Glassy-eyed, he
raised his refilled glass and gestured with it in my direction.

"Nothing." I looked down at the carpet.

"No, really. What're you looking at?"

"What are we even talking about?" I mumbled.

"Terry—you were *staring* at me." Condescension flooded his
voice. "Exactly what'd you want to say?"

"Look, it's been a long day. I'll bet you're tired."

Sounding submissive sometimes prevented things from developing further. From going from scary to terrifying. But the sneer I saw
before I averted my eyes again told me I would not get off so lightly
this time.

"Das macht nichts." Translation: It doesn't matter. Reaching for
the arm of his chair with his free hand, he sat.

Oh, God. When the sober John threw around phrases in German,
it only seemed pretentious. But in a drunken state, such talk—especially *this* phrase—sounded anything but showy. Spoken in a flat tone,
the words were filled with menace. Tonight, everything was happening so much faster than usual. The tenor of his emotions and words
had changed. Fast. Where previously there had been only detachment,
tension now shimmered between us.

"Listen. John," I said gently, hoping to appease him. "You haven't
had anything to eat since you got home. Let me fix you something."
Suddenly, it was as if I were ten years old again, sitting with Mom after
her shift at Walgreens—hoping her mood wouldn't shift from slate to

black. Closing my eyes, I pushed the image away. *Keep talking. Make him a sandwich. Do anything to distract him.*

But he didn't answer and his cold silence shut me out. Too frightened to say anything further, I went back to my book again and pretended to be absorbed. Prayed that he would pass out.

God, who became real for me only when I was desperate, ignored my plea. My persecutor remained mute, staring at nothing, sipping his monster-sized cocktail. When his glass was empty again, he got up and went back to the kitchen. But this time, instead of the clink of ice cubes in a glass, cabinet doors began to bang. Drawers slid open and slammed closed. The disposal whirred, and before long, a screech and whine indicated that it was grinding away without any water.

I scrambled off the couch and bolted into the kitchen, no longer cowed, but rather ready to attack. My mood had changed in a flash. "What the hell are you doing?" I yelled, incensed about an inanimate object in a way I couldn't be about his behavior. "You'll burn out the motor!" Within seconds I was no longer a member of the audience. No longer a bystander in my own life. I was talking back.

"Don't bother me," John answered, his teeth clenched. More banging. The empty water glass broke as it tipped onto the stove. Suddenly, fear rose once again, pushing my fierceness aside. His rage had stopped me cold—just as had Mom's abuse of our kitchen's pots and pans when I was little. The noise of them being shoved in and out of cabinets took me back in an instant.

"John, it's late," I implored, reaching for the switch to silence the disposal.

For a moment, everything stopped and the room grew eerily quiet. But then he wrenched open a drawer and it crashed to the floor, wood splintering, utensils spilling everywhere.

"Happy now?" His lips wet with spit; his face was contorted.

Before I could find the words to respond—and before I could stop him—he grabbed a butcher's knife from the floor.

"God almighty!" I grabbed his arm as he cut the air with the knife's sharp edges.

He pulled away from me and pressed the blade against his wrist. "This's what you want? Isn't it?" His eyes gleamed with fury and hatred.

"Stop it! Stop it!" I shouted. Hysterical.

A staccato sound of metal against metal interrupted our screaming at each other.

It was the door knocker. *Is it a neighbor? The police?* My body shook. But John shape-shifted as fast as a blink, placing the knife into the sink as if he were simply intending to wash it. He staggered toward the front door. A barely audible exchange began, one I strained to hear.

"Sorry." "Yes." "Long day." Reasoned words were sprinkled into whatever explanation he was giving to whomever stood there in the apartment hallway; he employed a tone similar to the one he used on his students. Even. Reassuring.

Who is here? Not the police—they would have been inside the apartment by now. Isn't it too late for anyone to come knocking? Why did you aggravate him? Isn't this just what you wanted? Just what you deserved? From where I stood amidst the scatter of spoons and forks cluttering the floor, I began to panic. He must be talking with a neighbor who had been disturbed by the noise. How would I face any of the people who lived around us tomorrow?

"Right-o. And good night now." The door closed. He sounded normal again. As if none of the violence had ever occurred.

My head pounded. My body ached. It felt as if I had been in a car accident and suffered whiplash. John had moved now into another part of the apartment. I sank down onto the floor. On hands and knees, piece by piece, I gathered up the contents of the drawer and placed them on the counter. Soon, only shattered wood remained at my feet. And then, just as I always did, I began the mechanism of denial: it took only a second for me to imagine that if I hid the collection of knives in the back of the broom closet, I would erase all the danger. Make the horror of what was happening to me disappear.

∽

After the episode with the knife, and as the nights of turmoil continued, playing the role of passive participant was no longer effective. I was trapped in a marriage that I had entered willingly. About this time, a stranger began calling late in the evening—a woman my husband airily dismissed as "nobody." Finally unable to contain the rage about which I had been silent before, I now veered toward the opposite side and became increasingly out of control, grabbing my purse when the evening's show had gone on too long, and using it to push every object off the hall table as I swept out the door.

A game of cat and mouse followed. Sitting in the parked car outside our building, I'd wait to see whether John would stagger to the lot to search for me. If he did, I'd turn on the car's engine, counting on the noise to lure him close. Then, just when he was near enough to hear me—but out of easy earshot of the neighbors—I'd pounce. "Don't come near me, you bastard! You asshole!" Stabbing him with words, I called him every horrible name I could think of. "You rotten son-of-a-bitch who doesn't care if I live or die." I used my mother's language to hurt him in the same way she had once devastated and wounded me. Knowing that he was oblivious because he was drunk only escalated my fury, making me want to hurt him all the more. Would he remember any of it come morning?

In the instant that my rage felt as if it might finally ignite, I put the car in gear and drove off into the night, spending aimless hours on the road until my anger finally dissipated. Exhausted, I'd pull into the twenty-four-hour Denny's, sit in the car and sob with desperation. Hollowed out, I knew deep down how horrible and vicious I had become. *You're a real piece of shit*, I said to myself. *How could you have screamed such terrible stuff at him?*

This cycle of rampage repeated itself many times over. Whenever he became drunk and confrontational, a tsunami of anger propelled me out the door—and then my own guilt and wretchedness dragged me back home again. Even though I couldn't see it, I hadn't just married my mother. I had become her.

A year and a half after John and I had exchanged our vows, I turned twenty-three and gave my forty-three-year-old husband an ultimatum I never intended to enforce: I would not stay with him any longer if he continued to drink. However, to my shock, John then joined AA and got sober.

As part of my role as a repentant spouse, I guarded the pedestal on which my husband now stood with his sobriety tucked neatly beneath one arm. I judged my value as a wife the way I'd once measured my value as a daughter, and my self-image hinged on creating happiness for him. I wrote love notes and left them on the counter each morning. They were filled with superlatives about how wonderful he was. And how lucky I was to have him.

Once again, I began to obsess about my looks—was I pretty and skinny enough for him? My weight hovered around 118 pounds, but what I saw in the mirror was the girl I'd been at the end of my junior year at Queen of Peace. An overweight mess. With small breasts. And then came the memory of my wedding night, the one I couldn't forget. I remembered the sense of being garbage. To hide that hurt and a continuing sense of shame about my body, I wore fake eyelashes to bed. Stripped off my make-up only after sex, and when I was certain John had fallen asleep. Desirability required wearing a mask. Soon, time to rest became elusive.

For John, sex created only the desire for more sex. Unlike me, who was exhausted after a long day at work, he needed and wanted to keep the party going. "Let's go outside," he'd whisper, often just as I was finally sinking into sleep. Other times, he would nudge me in the middle of the night. It was a call to duty, and I always complied.

Down the back stairs, blankets wrapped around our naked bodies, we scurried to a field across the road, where our sex was all about performance and not about intimacy. Each time, our union was empty, as cold as the grass under my back. Usually, I'd look up at the sky with my teeth chattering and count the minutes until I could hurry back to bed. I froze under John's pushy and strange ideas. He wasn't reading me at all. And for my part, in every area of my life, I was pretending—to be happy, to be confident, to project the right image. Sex was just part of the show. A new kind of drama this time around.

The bonus for all my pretense came from John's contentment. And then, too, Mom and I were getting along—I'd figured out various ways to soften her stance on our marriage. Mom loved stage plays and musical theater and I invited her to all of John's productions. His talent at the piano also earned him her favor. "He never has anything to say, but he sure knows how to entertain," she'd say, after he'd played all her favorite tunes. Eager for her to see that I could be a good daughter even if married to someone of whom she had previously disapproved, I called her every day. Each Sunday, I drove the two-hour round trip back home. Just as Mom had done with Grandma Healy, I created visits centered on shopping or lunches out. Regularly, I took her to the beauty shop and sat beside her as she got her hair washed and set.

Being back in Mom's favor also made it possible to risk what I hadn't dared tell her before: some of John's backstory. Not about his drinking—which remained a topic too shameful for me to discuss—but instead about his previous family.

I waited until a day when she was enjoying a "good mood" afternoon. When I brought up the subject, we were at Cameo's, a neighborhood drug store with a lunch counter, picking at egg salad sandwiches.

"What do you mean he has a couple of kids?" Her eyes went wide, as if I'd just announced I had smallpox. She folded and refolded her paper napkin. "You knew he had kids this whole time? From before the wedding?"

"You were already ticked off that I was getting married." I decided to try a joke. "I didn't want to give you a heart attack. Or have you kill me."

"Does he have to pay child support?" Leaning into the table, it was clear she disapproved of my attempt to deliver the news in a humorous way.

"Yeah. No alimony, though."

"Does he go visit?"

"He sees them when they visit their grandparents. Her parents live here."

"How old?"

"Teenagers. Two sons."

This was good. Short questions. Brief answers. Maybe we could keep the air temperature from rising. A pause. And then a shift in the winds. "I don't understand you." Annoyance in her tone. I fidgeted in my seat. "Why in God's name would you want to raise somebody else's kids?"

"I'm not raising them. They have a mother."

"But he pays child support." Folding her arms across her chest, she shook her head. "You'll be working your whole life to get ahead of all that."

"Ma. So what. I like my job." Using the word "Ma" had been a slip. Grandma Healy had been "Ma." The comparison bothered me and I shook it off.

"I think that's crap! I've been working all *my* life *and* raising kids and look what it got me!"

I hesitated. What to say? The impact of her words hit me. Working hadn't gotten her anything. Her children hadn't gotten her anything. It made me feel sad—and rejected. I reverted to the familiar.

"You've had a rough life, Mom."

"I hope to Jesus all my suffering gets me into Heaven."

With my confession came relief. Maybe it made everything I had done less sneaky. And now, by saying something empathetic, I'd turned the conversation back to her and to a place she found comfortable. I'd skirted any potential questions about children of my own, as well. Not that Mom was itching for information about my family plans. With ten grandchildren already—and though they were kids she enjoyed more than she'd enjoyed the children she'd actually raised—she obviously saw no need to be presented with more little ones.

And, really, I had no plans in that regard. The idea had quietly slipped into the not-going-to-happen category when I'd first met John—which should have surprised me, given how I'd been surrounded by kids my entire life. Having looked after two younger brothers, babysat for neighborhood kids, and taken care of all my nieces and nephews, I'd long been told by others that I was "a natural." With so much familiarity and ease around those who were young, I'd assumed that one day I would have a brood of my own. And even at work, every young, new teacher like me seemed to look forward to becoming pregnant. Now it wasn't a topic I even wanted to discuss.

John and I had had only one conversation about starting a family back at the beginning of our relationship. "I have two boys," he'd said. Which surely meant: "Don't have any expectations." Okay, then. I was a girl who'd been well-schooled in the department of no expectations. I'd also seen the envelopes that arrived periodically in the mail from his ex-wife. John would toss them on the table and I would read them on the sly; they were always about late child support payments, neatly drafted reminders that said things like "first of the month, not end" and "the boys are sick of eating cereal . . ." Those messages made me nervous and sad—and embarrassed for John. Most importantly, they closed off the possibility of starting a family together. To have more kids dependent on him just didn't seem possible financially, and in any case, would not make him happy.

And I was a modern girl anyway. It was the mid-seventies; if anyone had asked, I would have claimed that I had no interest in being tied down, that I wanted to do what many women my age were beginning to do more and more at that time. Expand our horizons beyond the worlds of homemaker, teacher and secretary. I was getting ready to think in a broader way—and one that was supported, at least, by my education-driven spouse.

I had a knack for drawing people out and was curious about why they behaved as they did. Being able to tune into the needs of others became a passion I just didn't have for a classroom of young children. And, even more than that, listening to other people's stories seemed so much safer than talking about myself. I toyed with the idea of going to grad school and becoming a professional listener. As a therapist,

I could do more than save my mother and a husband twice my age. Maybe I could save the world.

∾

And so it was that in the fall of 1976, I returned to school and discovered a new world for myself. Delving into research on human behavior fascinated me. As I pursued an advanced degree in counseling, I marveled at the courage others had, sharing their worries and their wounds—and even though I could not yet do the same, I began to look inward for the first time. I began to see how crazy it was to try to be someone else's savior. I traded in my hubris and focused on learning. Professors told me I had promise.

Two years later, in 1978, and still married to John, I had earned my master's degree from Northeastern. At twenty-five, I'd found a purpose—a new direction that I'd consciously picked for myself and then worked hard to achieve. Although still caught up in idealizing my husband and trying to please my mother, for perhaps the first time I was no longer play-acting my way through life.

I came into the profession working as a coordinator and therapist; my most ardent professional supporters turned out to be older women. Women with feminist zeal. Women willing to offer me opportunities. Women eager to take a chance on someone in whom they recognized their own earlier beginnings as young therapists. I absorbed it all like someone walking along a magical hallway, where fairy godmothers popped out from every doorway to wave their wands in my direction. These mentors were smart, savvy, and credentialed women who had made their way up the ranks in educational institutions and community organizations to positions of power. And so it seemed as if I'd found the people that I'd imagined back in the house on Peoria Street. My Radio Moms.

For the next several years, under their guidance as bosses, I began to work with divorced and widowed women; I took a part-time position counseling teens and young adults in a community center. I wrote grants and developed training programs for teachers who were guiding students not bound for college. Usually, I held two posts at a time, which created long commutes and sixty hour work weeks. I made what my father called "good money" and even though I was anxious all the time—worried that everything would disappear if I slowed my pace—I experienced yet another first in my life. I was thriving.

My marriage continued to hold steady despite all this, and I was proud that I was succeeding in an arena—the work world—where my mother had once accused me of failing. And my salary enabled me to do more than simply feel positive about myself. For once, I was making a contribution. I paid for new furniture for my parents, gave them nice gifts. In 1981, John and I bought our first home, leaving the world of rentals behind. Still, although I was thrilled by this burgeoning sense of accomplishment, a new emotion began to gnaw inside me. That familiar voice was speaking even more loudly now: I want more.

The "more" took the form of planning to transition from the work world and return to graduate school, this time in pursuit of a Ph.D. In January 1982, I applied to two psychology programs in the Chicago area: Loyola and Northwestern. Completing a doctorate not only meant gaining more expertise, but it would demonstrate that in reaching the apex in my field, I wasn't the inferior person I'd always believed myself to be—either as a student or a wife.

After submitting my paperwork and test scores, I focused all my energies on Loyola, which I thought was the safer bet. Still, despite having aced the student-at-large class taught by the psychology department's chair, I was wary. I'd watched how students clustered around her before and after class, seeking counsel and approval. But after learning that I had nabbed a personal interview with her, my confidence rose.

Her first question was a pertinent one, but it caught me off guard nevertheless—a description of my research for the master's thesis I'd completed four long years ago. I shifted focus fast, talking up areas of research that held my interest: female development; addictions; the psychology of families and organizations. I outlined the questions that warranted further investigation in each, but still did not see that the topics I had identified so clearly represented the key issues in my own life. But at last, a smile rewarded my efforts. A warm one.

After nearly an hour of animated conversation, I grew convinced that this woman would not have spent so much time with me if I were not a viable candidate: My hopes for admission soared when she favored me with a thousand-watt grin. "We'll be getting our letters out in the next few days," she assured me, placing her hand on my shoulder as she walked me to the door. I practically glided out of the room. By the time the Metra pulled into the station near home, I was relishing the trip upon which John and I were about to embark. An extravagant vacation—at least by our standards. How ready I was to relax in the lushness and heat of Jamaica, tucked away in a posh resort, enjoying fine meals and island entertainment.

Nearly a week later, as I carried my suitcase to the taxi waiting in our driveway to take us to the airport, the mailman met me half-way. There among the bills and advertisements nestled the letter from the Chair. Perfect timing. Ripping open the envelope, I pulled out the single page of stationery and took a deep breath. Here it was, in black and white:

"We regret to inform you . . ."

I bent in two, as if I'd been struck in the stomach with a bat, then straightened up and walked back into the house, where I threw the letter at the bottom of the kitchen trash can. Shame flooded through me.

John came downstairs with his bags.

"I didn't get in." I was numb.

"Well." John carefully lowered the suitcases to the floor and then just stared at me. "That's really too bad."

I waited. But nothing else came from him. Perhaps had I stood there longer, he would have surprised me and pulled me into an embrace meant to console. But John only displayed emotion when he was drinking and always shut down in a crisis. The puzzled look on his face told me that *he* was waiting for *me,* completely ignorant of what direction he should take or how he should react. The silence stretched between us. Feeling as if I were sinking into a very dark place, unable to handle his lack of words and his impotence, I forced myself to move around him. Dazed, I headed toward the waiting cab.

The ten days in the Caribbean were more than miserable. Even in the tropical sun, I shivered. Reggae music played so loudly I couldn't bear it. Each morning, I sat at the water's green-blue edge, listless and alone, injured and small. I worried that other people were staring at me. Could they could see right through to my failure? My Walkman held a single cassette tape of classical music that had been set on play-and-repeat. Even though I had on headphones, with the volume jacked up, the music failed to obliterate the voice that was getting stronger inside me every minute. *You thought you were so clever when you took that extra class. So smug.* I clenched my jaw. *You thought you were so special. That you deserved to get in. That professor saw right through you—just like Mom always did.*

John was as distant as the stars in the Jamaica night sky. Perhaps he was frightened by how profoundly out of character I had become. Perhaps he was confused about how he should respond to my sadness and depression. Instead, he offered only silence.

I bowed my head and cried. Nothing soothed, even the fine golden sand that rubbed rough against my feet. I worried that if I just waded into the water, I would be pulled out to sea. At a certain point, I would be no longer be visible. I would just disappear.

When I drove down to see Mom the day after I returned home from Jamaica, she picked up on my mood, though she didn't interpret it correctly.

"Terry. You look really tired, even with that tan."

"I'm fine, Mom." I wanted to change the subject, so I handed her a bag with a brightly colored necklace inside—a souvenir I'd picked up in the resort's lobby before leaving for home. She opened it, made appreciative noises over my gift, and then shook her head.

"You're working too hard," she chided, her fingers tracing the design on the beads. "I'm afraid you're gonna kill yourself if you don't start taking it easy."

"Mom. Really. It was just a long layover."

Her words filled me with even more loneliness, as I realized that her concern about my fatigue came most likely from her worry that if I fell apart, I wouldn't be able to take care of her.

"You need more time off before you go back," she insisted, getting up from her chair and moving toward the refrigerator. Standing up to help her, I pulled a large bowl from the shelf above her head. "You know, Terry," she went on, as she took the dish from my hands, "if you don't have your health, you don't have anything."

I slumped into a seat at the table.

"Here." Spooning the contents of the bowl into a sundae glass, she pushed it toward me. "I made some nice Jell-O." A familiar word, "nice." Nice Jell-O. A nice pot roast. A nice piece of coffee cake. Nice was her way of saying she'd taken the trouble to do something . . . well, *nice*. Though I had no appetite, I ate it, pretending enthusiasm. "I can't take any more time. Things just don't work that way." I was frustrated by her lack of empathy. In her mind, my job was so unimportant that I could take off as many days as I wanted and it wouldn't matter. I didn't say that I might need to continue at my job for a period of time while pursuing a further degree. In fact, I hadn't even confided in Mom that I'd hoped to return to school again; it would only spur on her worries that I was "doing too much."

Now, sitting across from her and spooning the soft and sweet bites into my mouth, I couldn't bear to initiate talk about what had happened with my application. I wanted simply to focus on her Jell-O and how she was worrying about my fatigue. Afterward, as I scooped up my purse and got ready to leave, I planted a kiss on her cheek.

This conversation with my mother was the first one of substance that I'd had with anyone in twelve days—the first time since I'd ripped open the rejection letter that I wasn't torn apart. I hadn't been forthcoming with her about why I was so exhausted, but I hadn't felt the urge to put on a show for her, either. No going out to lunch, no shopping trip. I'd come to the house emotionally spent and bearing a fresh wound. I'd brought her a memento, hoping—without even realizing it—that she would give me something in return. Something to take home with me. She'd offered me gelatin mixed with fruit and the usual dire predictions. Souvenirs of a different kind, but valuable nonetheless: the sort of caring she could safely provide.

A day or two after I had stopped in at Mom's, a slim envelope from Northwestern University arrived in the mail. *Bad news*, said the voice inside me. *Acceptance letters always come in a fat package of materials. But what did you really expect?* I stalled, afraid to open it. In the aftermath of my "safety school's" response, I had been so overloaded with emotion that I'd blocked out the likelihood that I'd have another rejection. After a minute, I forced myself to slip my fingernail under the flap. The first word jumped off the page.

"Congratulations."

I let the paper float to the floor.

A new door had opened in front of me.

An Unsafe Neighborhood

The unconscious insists, repeats, and practically breaks down the door, to be heard.

—Annie G. Rogers, Ph.D.
The Unsayable: The Hidden Language of Trauma

IN THE SUMMER OF 1982, several weeks after receiving my acceptance letter, I began my first class at Northwestern. Mostly as a joke, I referred to the university as "The Big School" when I told family and friends of my new venture, but in truth, I really *did* imagine myself as a half-pint heading off to kindergarten. Wishing for someone to hold my hand.

I'd enrolled in a seminar in late June on the assessment of severe psychiatric disorders, hoping that beginning coursework immediately would make acclimating to the program easier, before I had to manage a full load of classes come fall. Apprehensive, I really believed I wasn't ready. The clinical training facing me over the next six years would emphasize how the unconscious mind worked—with both the therapist and the patient mining the internal, mostly unseen world within us all—and then observing how it influences our behaviors.

Now I would need a different, deeper level of insight—one of which I had only a hint. I would be required to touch down on emotions running far beneath the surface, understanding for the first time not only what motivated the behavior of others, but what motivated *me*. The woman who would become my first training supervisor emphasized that we would all need "ruthless honesty." My success depended on being able to carry that honesty like a beam into the unknown.

By the end of the third week in that summer seminar, my fear had spiked skyward, and worry trumped perspective. Stuck in a quagmire of doubt, I imagined what would happen if my academic instructors and clinical training supervisors knew of my anxiety. I was as poorly put together as a sweater with a dangling thread. One wrong tug and I might unravel. At the time, even greater anxiety came from how I would react if they recommended I leave the program. In my mind, such dismissal would not simply be a commentary on my classwork, but would be the old refrain once again: "We don't want you. You don't belong."

Given all this angst, what a relief to settle in on campus in September knowing that I'd completed my summer class without raising my professors' suspicions about my stability, academically or otherwise. I'd hidden my nerves and my fear. Just as I had as a young girl in grammar school, and especially when I began work on my master's, I'd put all my efforts into my studies and kept my mouth shut. By following the rules, I hadn't had to concoct even one lie about myself. As the semester began, a little bit of comfort came over me like a warm blanket.

October arrived. On the steps outside the library, sitting in a patch of sunlight and taking a break from studying, a shadow fell across me. Jerry Welch, another first-year "doc student," carried a book in one hand and massaged the back of his neck with the other.

"Unreal, isn't it?" he commented.

"No kidding!" I was sure that Jerry was referring to our course syllabus, which lay open in my lap.

"I saw Gayle in the lounge a few times." He sat down next to me. "But I didn't really know her. Did you?"

I turned to look at him. Confused. Gayle Byrne was the first person I'd met when I'd taken the summer Clinical Assessment class.

"Sorry—I thought you'd already been over to the department," he said, as he scratched at his beard. "She killed herself. Last night."

Stunned, I thought I must have heard him incorrectly, but then he apologized again for having been so abrupt with bad news. My questions tumbled fast. Did he know what had happened? Or why? Had anyone in the department known that she was struggling and tried to intervene? All questions for which Jerry had no answers. The only other bit of information he could tell me was that an emergency department meeting for students was scheduled for later that day. I turned down his offer to head to the student union for coffee, lying about having something I had to do. I wanted to be alone.

Under an awning of maples that hadn't yet shed their leaves, I walked fast, trying to escape the image of my classmate on that first day of our class back in June and the way she'd stood with such confidence in the doorway. As the term had moved onward, I had watched her from a distance, intrigued—and intimidated—by the strange aura of both intensity and detachment she projected. She often dominated others with questions that were smart and opinions that were cogent. But she had another side as well: sometimes she retreated to a corner of the room, quiet and aloof. Now, as hard as I tried to repress this picture, I failed. I didn't want to think about her. I didn't want to think about suicide.

The news of this young woman's death skewed my world. *If she couldn't make it here—how will you?* Looking out over the rocks that butted up against Lake Michigan, I tried to breathe evenly. *What are you doing here, anyway? How can you be sure you won't be next?* The questions, unanswerable, elevated my agitation.

That evening at the emergency meeting, I huddled among other grad students, but did not reveal my vulnerable state. Were they, too, frightened? Did they wonder, as did I, whether suicide could somehow be contagious? And then my mother's voice chimed in: "You're doing too much, Terry." She always said something like this when worried that I was pulling back from her. Soon, another voice resonated with a different message. *Maybe she knows that you really can't handle stress as well as you think you can. That you're too ambitious for your own good.* I shifted my weight in the chair: *Maybe she's worried that you're headed for a breakdown—just like Jeanie.*

My sister had been twenty-eight.

You're twenty-nine. And alone.

No one in my family could provide the reassurance I needed. Instead, I'd come to the meeting hoping to discover that I wasn't on my own, that someone else was "in charge." That there were answers for a peer's suicide. I was hoping to find someone who would guarantee our safety. It suddenly seemed to me that we were only children, looking for more support than our instructors were offering. I needed someone to assure me that nothing else tragic would happen to any of us.

When the gathering came to a close, another first-year student commented that we were like a family. I recoiled. *Nice wish. Even if you were a family, how would that help? Your family never protected you.*

I left the building still very unsettled. When I reached the parking lot, the questions I should have asked now plagued me, playing with intensity in my mind: did her family know she was in trouble?

I steered my Honda toward home, down the twists and turns of the road. But the voice kept recurring in my head. *Mom would have warned you, in that prickly tone of hers. She'd want to know who you're getting mixed up with in that school of yours.* I imagined my mother waving her hands in exasperation as she delivered the blows. "Surrounding yourself with people who think they're so smart, telling everybody else how to live." And how she'd shake her head, impatient. Not only with the situation—but with me. "If they're so good at all that, how does someone wind up killing herself?"

I drove with both hands tight on the wheel. *What if this prestigious program is as dangerous as Mom says? What if you've really joined a club that causes people like you to self-destruct?*

The forty-five-minute drive had wiped clean all the confidence I'd developed during the summer semester. While some part of me recognized how irrational my anxiety was, another part of me wasn't so sure. As I pulled into the driveway, I turned off the engine and just sat there. Dad's voice came to me, repeating as usual the words he always used to reconcile disappointment, worry, or misfortune. His mantra.

"What are you gonna do, Terry?" He'd have shrugged his shoulders and leaned in, as if he were revealing a secret. "It's part of life."

I sighed. Dropped my head down against the steering wheel. Remembering Dad's common sense philosophy didn't quash all the emotions this woman's suicide had brought—but no one ever got as hysterical as Mom. Remembering his common-sense reaction reassured me, relegating Mom's paranoia to a corner of my mind.

I was going to do the only thing I could. Exactly what my father had taught me. I would just keep on going.

Over the course of the next year, Dad's recommendation just to keep moving worked. I battled anxiety by spending a lot of time in the library and structured my days so that I had little to do beyond researching and writing papers. Slowly, the fear that had me by the throat at the beginning of the year abated. By the start of my second year, I was enjoying the support of my professors, had made friends with classmates, and was settling into my first clinical rotation at Northwestern's Institute of Psychiatry.

At last I felt safe enough to explore all I'd avoided, and that included beginning my own psychotherapy—which proved to be intense. No graduate training program could mandate that their students enter treatment, but nearly every student in the department did so. It was considered critical to learn about oneself and experience the "other side of the couch."

The first time in the waiting room of my new therapist, in October of 1983, I was struck by the predictable art reproductions and the requisite copies of *The New Yorker* fanned out on the glass coffee table. Dr. Jensen always opened the door of his office precisely at the appointed hour, and he was courteous—but stiff as an undertaker. Still, I knew that he adhered to many of the tenets of classical Freudian psychoanalysis, and so was not taken aback by his formal demeanor—just a little spooked.

Once inside his office, I was surprised at first by what was missing:

candy-filled dishes, butt-filled ashtrays, Styrofoam coffee cups—not even a box of Kleenex. He offered no small talk, either. Many clinicians who worked from a "psychodynamic" model saw such small comforts as being "against the rules." They could be construed as incorrect messages about the therapist's role—as an acquiescence to a patient's desire, however unconscious, to be treated as a dependent child rather than as a conflicted adult. This would not be the soft, fluffy kind of therapy that offered comfort but not growth.

In this strict environment, my therapy progressed predictably because it relied on clear emotional, physical and social boundaries. These boundaries inhibited the therapist from expressing emotions, or even personal reactions. He or she was meant to be a blank wall against which the patient could bounce his inner experiences; protected in this way from personal interactions with the therapist, the patient's fears, fantasies, and wishes could be explored safely. This was the heart of the treatment: the patient would learn to live a more comfortable life enlightened by insight into both his conscious and unconscious selves.

My reaction to this whole enterprise, despite all I had learned in class? Terror.

Each week when I got off the elevator, two different Terrys tiptoed down the hall into the waiting room: Compliant Terry, who wanted to be the best patient ever; and Controlling Terry, who could not imagine unlocking the mental vault inside her. Controlling Terry was committed to keep hidden everything that would be too difficult, or too shameful, to voice aloud. Compliant Terry became the "good patient," just as she had tried to be the good daughter. And the good wife. As the weeks progressed—October into November and throughout December—I kept many things secret from Dr. Jensen. And myself.

Still, just as I wanted to impress my professors and clinical supervisors with my abilities and potential, I hoped to demonstrate to Dr. Jensen that I could succeed at the deep therapy he offered. I wanted to be better at it than any other patient he might have had. In those early months, I did nearly all the talking, just as he expected—but remained wary about what I revealed. Outside our sessions, I worked feverishly to ascertain the deeper meanings of what I'd shown him. Sitting opposite him during a session, Controlling Terry strove to make the story of her life fascinating. She liked to entertain him: carefully constructed and colorful sketches of her family—although I left out many details that might make Mom and Dad and my siblings seem unattractive. I also gave him the "we weren't people of means" speech, but never said that we were flat-out poor.

Compliant Terry offered up her earliest memories, without Dr. Jensen having to inquire, chatted about her "feisty" Mom, and even attempted some snappy interpretations about snippets of her mother's behavior over the years. Throughout, his reactions could be measured in large doses of silence, carefully doled out nods, and a pinch of commentary.

But Controlling Terry wasn't going to risk admitting she needed him for anything, just as she had never admitted that she'd ever needed her mom. Even in Dr. Jensen's office, to be "needy" seemed to be an open invitation to criticism and the inevitable subsequent disappointment. My goal was to keep him awake and fascinated by my stories. By doing my own private therapy outside the consultation room, and deciding exactly what I would reveal in my next appointment, I sought to avoid exposure. I spent time culling my memory for the nuggets of revelation that I could offer him. Carefully. Gifts for the wise and competent.

The twin Terrys made every appointment on time, each committed to pursuing her own personal end game as hard as she could. However, Controlling Terry wasn't above using deception and obfuscation to avoid making herself vulnerable—in fact, her careful release of information wasn't the true work of therapy at all. Was Dr. Jensen aware that Compliant Terry was approaching the issues while Controlling Terry was simultaneously ignoring them? I had no clue. Dr. Jensen wasn't much for talking.

As for me, I did have some sense of how keeping up this charade was affecting me. While I didn't yet know the twins well enough to call them by name, just being in the same room with them left me nervous and exhausted. And more often than not, feeling like a fraud.

New Year's Eve arrived and when I woke that morning, the first thing I noticed was a sense of being unsettled, with a knot forming under my ribcage. Why? I had completed thirteen classes successfully, was holding my own in a primo training rotation, and my relationships with both John and Mom had become steady.

Yet, as the day progressed, panic began to flow inside me. For no reason. My heart jumped and my palms were sweaty. I paced, hoping that what had obviously become anxiety would dissipate. By midafternoon, it did. I took a shower, pulled on clothes and did my makeup. A next round of classes would soon begin and I had looked forward to this holiday. John's and my plan had been to eat, unwind, watch a movie and welcome in the New Year together. But before my hair had dried, a new surge of fear hit.

"I don't think I can cook dinner like I planned," I told him.

We'd been married for more than nine years by now and I no longer had any expectation that my husband would offer support, though I had hoped that letting him know what was happening inside me—by putting it into words—would diminish its impact. Like driving alone on a deserted road at night, all I could see was a red light flashing across the dashboard: *Check engine.* I just kept on driving with no idea how to solve the problem, and my anxiety kept on humming.

At no time throughout the day did I ever think to call Dr. Jensen. And even if it had occurred to me to reach out to him, I'm not sure I could have brought myself to dial his number.

To ask for help. How dare I bother him on a major holiday? What if he told me to check myself into a hospital? Worse: what if he thought my call was insignificant and decided not to return it at all?

By ten o'clock, the churning mix of dread had escalated until I couldn't think. I crawled under the duvet on my bed, certain I was losing touch with reality, totally. When John finally slid in beside me, I stayed mute and reached for him, believing that if he would only take my hand, I might once again find some peace. Sex was out of the question, having lacked any robust quality since I'd gone back to school. Eventually, John did pat my hand, but a short time later he turned on his side and fell asleep.

Through what I had learned about myself in therapy, I did understand the despondency that sometimes overwhelmed me as a consequence of rejection: first by my mother and then later by others in positions of authority. But on this New Year's Eve, both depression and anxiety had caught me completely off-guard, and my panic did not appear to be connected to anything recognizable. Squeezing my eyes tight, I was as overwhelmed as a child without a nightlight when the dark presses in. Nausea then, and my heart pounding in my chest. Just before the hall clock chimed twelve, I imagined I heard a rumble, like the sound of a wall collapsing under the force of a powerful push. I tried to ignore it. Only one way out existed. Sleep.

Compliant Terry couldn't even close her eyes, and Controlling Terry was making a strong bid to take over. Resorting to what I did only in times of desperation, I prayed. "Please, God. Don't let me go crazy." I rolled over, curling my body into a fetal position, clutching my stomach. "Please don't let me die." Over and over again, for what seemed like hours, I repeated my prayer. Mercifully, fear and exhaustion finally pushed me over the edge into sleep.

On New Year's Day, I woke as fragile as a cracked egg. Still, I was somehow back on the right side of reality. Nevertheless, even though I had regained some measure of control, I hadn't regrouped. I remained afraid. What if yesterday's emotions returned? I knew only that I was being pulled between the future and the past simultaneously, without any sense of the present. I dragged myself down to the kitchen, wrapped in a shroud of trepidation.

That day—and for many that followed—I moved as if trying to ward off a migraine. Winter term classes had not yet begun. While I was relieved to have time before facing the pressures of studies and training commitments, I still felt rattled. I imagined looking into the mirror, certain that I would see the reflection of someone I didn't recognize. Or, worse maybe, I would see no reflection at all.

To distract myself, I took a drive to the campus library one afternoon to search for articles to be assigned in an upcoming class. But looking out toward Lake Michigan, I shivered my way across the snow-covered campus and was seized again by that now familiar swell of anxiety. White caps crashed against the rocks lining the shore in tune to the erratic beat of my heart. I hurried past the waves that seemed to mimic my churning emotions. Inside, surrounded by books, my fear reverberated in the safety of the overheated room. I didn't want to die, but could falling into the violent lake be any worse than the dread that kept climbing up my throat? The dread that made me short of breath? The dread that seemed as if it might kill me?

A week later, I worried what I should tell Dr. Jensen about New Year's Eve and the fear that remained inside of me. Would admitting to everything that overwhelmed me lead him to diagnose some kind of breakdown? If he did, every dream I'd had for my future would vanish. Equally disturbing: what if I took the risk of plunging into my story and he just sat there? Silent. Disinterested. What if he judged that I was overreacting—and demanding attention.

By the time he opened the door to greet me, the familiar wall that Controlling Terry always used for protection had risen brick by brick. Smiling, I brushed past him and eased myself into my seat on the sofa. My pulse quickened as he took his usual place in the dark leather chair—the power chair—and angled it in my direction.

But it was Compliant Terry who began to speak. "It's been a pretty rough couple of weeks." Looking down at the carpet, I did not meet his gaze or check to see if he was interested. This side of me had apparently become strong enough to squelch the evasiveness of the much more controlled twin. "Worst I've ever felt, actually." I hugged myself tight. "Things got bad over the holiday—and haven't let up."

"Bad in what way?" He smoothed his tie and then brushed at the sleeve of his herringbone jacket.

"At first it was anxiety. Now I'm depressed, I guess." I steeled myself. "Numb." He waited, a measured pause, and shaking my head, I continued. "I don't get it. Classes went well. My cases are hard, but I'm getting great supervision." My eyes began to sting and my voice dropped near to a whisper. "Everything just crashed for no reason— that's what made it so scary."

He remained quiet, one leg neatly crossed over the other, hands folded in his lap. A few minutes went by and it seemed an imaginary clock ticked into the silence. I was supposed to say more, but I couldn't find the words to tell him how unnerved I was about what he might say. How much I hated my inability to relate my anxiety to anything happening in my life at this time and then interpret it—as Compliant Terry so ached to do in her quest to be the perfect "experienced" patient.

As I sat there in the silence between us, I had never felt so alone. Or so abandoned. "Maybe this therapy has been too much," I finally offered, still avoiding his gaze. "Too much, too fast." This idea had disturbed me all week long: was my therapy perhaps actually the gateway for my distress? Since we'd begun our sessions, I'd been obsessed with every one of my hours with Dr. Jensen. Unpacking each word from the suitcase of my memory, ruminating over all the emotions which had surfaced, I unfolded my confessions like dirty laundry, kept trying to squeeze out interpretations to illuminate my past. I wanted to show him that I knew what I was supposed to be doing: living a more peaceful life enriched by understanding my turbulent history.

"Maybe I need to slow down," I said, looking at him directly for the first time that hour. He looked back at me without speaking. I couldn't read from his expression whether he agreed with my answer.

Finally, he spoke. "Too fast?" He regarded me steadily. "How so?"

"I'm not sure." I lowered my head again. And then explained the sensation I'd had the night the anxiety had come crashing in on me. The rumbling noise I'd surely imagined. The wall cracking. And then the void. "I mean, it was like *nothingness.*" My voice dropped. "Like I was disappearing. Like I didn't exist." He uncrossed his legs, his eyes at last registering concern. "I'm thinking that maybe in talking so much about the past, I overreached. Stirred up more than I realized."

His eyes flickered for a moment, maybe with concern. Maybe there was hope for me. Maybe he could actually help.

He suggested then that the swell of anxiety might have taken on a life of its own and everything around me had become distorted along with it. "Including your sense of yourself." He tapped his fingers on the armrest, as if he were choosing his words carefully. "I don't yet have a clear sense of what that wall was protecting you from, but perhaps as we sift through the rubble and take a look at all the emotions it unleashed in you, we'll better understand why you had such an extreme reaction."

Relief and confusion intertwined as I tried to absorb the insight he had offered. He hadn't reacted with alarm to the story of my disintegration and had implied that I probably wouldn't always feel as incapacitated as I did now. Perhaps my future wasn't ruined, after all. Still, I couldn't relinquish my upset so easily. It had been a frightening experience and one I'd had to weather alone.

Were such pain and turmoil necessary to help me better understand myself right now? Was this sort of therapy *supposed* to feel as if the scab over a fresh wound was always being ripped off?

As I tried to unwind these tangled questions, he shifted in his chair.

"It's time for us to stop for today." He smiled and once again smoothed his tie against his crisp white button-down.

He always signaled the end of an hour with this sentence—which was in reality just another way for a therapist to maintain his boundaries. For me, however, his announcement always came as a rebuff—even though I knew its purpose from a professional viewpoint. On the one hand, he was supposed to guard my vulnerability, and yet on the other hand he was indicating that he had no more time for me. His manner of terminating the hour always transformed me into the little girl I'd once been—one who had been caught wanting more than she was entitled to have.

I chastised myself for not having tracked the time on my watch. I could have anticipated the end of the hour and avoided hearing the phrase I so hated. I stood and scurried toward the door.

"Right," I said. "I'll see you next week."

I stepped into the elevator, awash in embarrassment. Once outside on the sidewalk, my stomach twisted harder. I was bereft. Perhaps even more confused. I'd found no answers in his office today.

After many more months of work in Dr. Jensen's consultation room, I eventually came to accept that my anxiety—which was always lurking beneath the surface—had simply spiraled into orbit and, overwhelmed, my mind had shut down. I'd been unable to reconcile the two warring Terrys inside of me. The two who, prior to therapy, I'd been able to suppress. I had never before tried to merge Controlling Terry with Compliant Terry. Therapy had opened the door between the two and a collision had followed—but I still didn't understand why I hadn't been able to rally from the sweep of terror and helplessness that encircled me. Just as I had never believed that I could reach out to anyone for help—not John or my mother—it now seemed as though I couldn't trust this man, who was the most important person in my psychological sphere at that point.

Despite all this, however, I was also discovering that the vulnerable side of me was much stronger than I had ever recognized. Compliant Terry had backbone, after all. As I wrestled with all this, I couldn't decide if my ambivalence toward Dr. Jensen was warranted. Was he truly removed from me and my feelings, or did his type of therapy simply prevent him from giving me comfort and the feeling of being nurtured?

Perhaps Dr. Jensen already was aware of what I was only just beginning to appreciate—that Compliant Terry and Controlling Terry now showed up hand in hand at every therapy session. Perhaps he believed our work was moving along well. I could imagine him thinking, "What a good sign!" I could imagine a lot of possibilities, but I didn't know if any of them were true. No surprise then that I never brought up such questions in any of our sessions. I was inexperienced at this game. In the end, I had a lot to figure out.

However, a year later, my attitude shifted. Doing well in my classes and clinical training, I was beginning to take the supervisory tenet about being "ruthlessly honest" seriously. In my thrice-weekly supervision hours, I was discovering that the more open and attentive I became to my own reactions and behaviors as a therapist—as well as to my own unresolved problems and issues—the better my work with patients became. I was turning into a good clinician.

In my own therapy, I now tried to talk about whatever came to mind rather than censoring my thoughts, no longer planning out what I would offer Dr. Jensen. No more golden nuggets. I scrambled right there during the therapy hour to make my own interpretations about memories I had, dreams I remembered, and spontaneous thoughts. This, I told myself, was progress, as I was moving beyond the desire to impress or please him with my developing skills. And it was progress—though of a limited sort.

In some critical ways, I continued to struggle with the process in my therapy sessions, skirting emotions like humiliation and shame. I never spoke of the robbery, or what I was at last able to recognize was a rape. I never described the pain of my wedding day. I never talked about how, when I was a young girl, my mother's behavior had cut so deeply, with her sharp-edged words. I hoped not to awaken those memories. My ability to be "ruthlessly honest" had parameters. Without even realizing it, I was still guarding the door, not trusting how much pain I could afford to shepherd in. The room was crowded enough already.

Nevertheless, I was discovering how to express anger for the first time, rather than driving it down deep. One evening, about two years into my therapy, I walked into Dr. Jensen's office and took my usual seat. This time, however, I was the one who sat in silence. As stone-faced as my mother had ever been.

At last I spoke. "For the last three sessions, you've been nearly ten minutes late for my hour." I glared at him and crossed my arms over my chest.

He said nothing, but nodded, inviting me to continue.

"I shouldn't have to be kept waiting every week," I challenged. Then I just stopped talking.

He took a long time to respond, finally asking if I thought he was cheating me on time. I shook my head, confused. And then irritated— although his question had hit on the truth. What I'd really wanted was an acknowledgement that he hadn't adhered to the rules. I wanted an apology from him. What I got was his telling me that he had adjusted the time, accordingly. That I had gotten my full hour.

"I don't give a shit," I shot back. "I shouldn't have to wait! You're supposed to be watching the clock!" The look I gave him matched the tone of my voice. The one he returned, however, was impassive. "When things aren't *predictable,* I don't feel *safe.*" I spat the words out. "I *told* you after I went into that spiral on New Year's. The therapy was going too deep, too fast. And you said *nothing* to reassure me!" I no longer cared whether he had anything to say. "If this crap continues, I'm leaving."

My wrath dominated the hour. The spouting of my mistrust and resentments, coupled with long periods when I stonewalled his questions, left little time for any exploration about what I was experiencing or saying. No connections were offered by either of us. Not even the most obvious—and correct—psychological interpretation: my rancor with my therapist mirrored my rage with my mother.

During that entire hour, with my anger boiling over onto many subjects, Dr. Jensen said almost nothing. But the following week, his consultation room door opened at precisely the appointed time. He'd listened to me, and my fury hadn't destroyed him. It wasn't the same as it had been with Mom, when her rage inevitably and always cut away chunks of my self-esteem and my emotional safety. And so another door—a crucial one—opened wide. A door behind which sat all my long-closeted wrath.

Now, it became easier to resurrect old childhood memories: I had been twelve when, in a fit of pique and with one vicious sweep of my hand, I destroyed a treasured model car for which my younger brother had saved his allowance in order to build it one precious bit at a time. And it became less difficult to uncover and examine all the nights John and I had spent arguing: how easily my anger had transformed into malice and my words morphed into screams laced with invective and profanity. Even then, as an adult, my rage had been savage and uncontrollable; I'd needed hours to talk myself down after those midnight tirades that ended with me alone in my car, sobbing and wishing I were dead. How impetuous and mean I could be when I wasn't watching myself; I certainly possessed the muscle to hurt others. Including myself.

To figure out whether I was really any different than my mother was hardest of all: she was the master of the cut-and-run, and her shrieks and accusations always seemed to culminate in proclamations about wanting to die. *Wasn't it worse that she had wished all her children were dead?* I asked myself. How desperately did I not want to admit that, some of the time, I was, indeed, my mother's daughter.

Despite the pain of these sessions with Dr. Jensen, what kept me working hard in his office was that I could perceive my continuing growth. Without a doubt, therapy was an art that had to be learned a little at a time. Using metaphor and dreamwork, and searching out new ways to tell my story, I was beginning to gain the insights into myself I had so craved only two years before. At last I had begun to understand the cost of burying my emotions—as well as the price of living in my own mind's unsafe neighborhood.

In 1987—my fifth year in the doctoral program and my fourth year in therapy and clinical work, I finally managed to drop my "good girl" persona and learned to advocate for myself outside of therapy—neither resorting to, nor fearing, the rage I associated with my mother. A new supervising psychoanalyst, for example, began to criticize me constantly in our evaluation sessions, in ways that seemed to be centered more around his need for power than any desire to teach. Distressed, I requested a meeting with my training site's director, a man who knew me well. My speaking up paid off, as shortly thereafter a new analyst began to evaluate my progress with my patients. In the interns' study room afterward, I leaned toward the mirror in my locker and nodded to my reflection, as if welcoming, at last, the reflection I saw.

That mirror reflected something else new in it, as well: motherhood. Perhaps this was not an unexpected goal for the woman I had become. As did several of the close women friends I'd made at Northwestern, I, too, had begun to believe that my generation *could* have it all: a fulfilling career, a marriage built on love, and the tenderness and responsibility of motherhood. Nor was the timing of my desire for a child unexpected—especially considering the position of a medical establishment that deemed the biological clock for a woman in her midthirties to be drawing close to midnight.

Around the time I was completing my research for my dissertation, I confided to John my desire for a different kind of future, one that he and I might create together. Hoping that he might be persuaded to consider having a family of our own, I pressed him with reasons why he might want to reset the button on parenthood: he couldn't erase the mistakes he believed he'd made with his sons, but his thirteen years in recovery—the longest period of sobriety in his adult life—boded well for making a fresh start. In that conversation, the first of what would become many, he leaned back in his chair and tamped tobacco into the bowl of his pipe. "Well, that's some news," he said, with a smile.

After that discussion, I closed my eyes and tried to imagine how my mother would react if I told her what I had just confessed to John. "All that money to get another diploma that you thought was so important and now you want to throw it away?" she'd probably say. Or would she advise me that motherhood would be a drag, an anchor that would keep me, as it had kept her, mired in the mundane? I took a deep breath and let my mind wander into places more pleasant to visit. Places that were safe.

A year later, two days before Mother's Day, I completed the oral defense of my dissertation—the last requirement before being awarded my Ph.D. My nearly six-year tenure at Northwestern had culminated in the delivery of my "dissertation baby," the baby who wouldn't be enough.

After receiving congratulations from professors and peers, I walked out into the warmth of spring. A soft breeze touched my cheek as I headed alone toward the Shakespeare Garden, a partially secluded place on campus that featured a tiny stone chapel. Slightly disoriented—tipsy, even—I sat quietly, my mind unfamiliar with this brand of *happy*. I inhaled the smell of freshly turned soil and the fragrance of a blossoming tree, my senses heightened by the fullness of the day.

I was ready to think in earnest about the dream that had formed so intensely inside me. The dream that I'd shared with John. The dream I had yet to share with my mother—largely because I'd wanted to protect it from a reaction that might be painful. For now, the dream was still in the making, like the peonies and day lilies that had yet to push forth from the earth near my feet. I wanted to become a mother. The kind that could touch with tenderness. The kind that could enfold. The kind that could sing lullabies of love.

Acts of Balance

The world was suddenly still;
nothing was being required of me;
I could stand in the quiet of my own skin.

—Maggie O'Farrell
I Am, I Am, I Am

I'D INVESTED IN KEEPING secrets for my entire life. But now, eight months after graduation—and eighteen months into the intensive outpatient staff position I'd held since I finished my training—I harbored the biggest secret of all. I was two months pregnant. And could think about nothing else. At the time, not sharing this news so exciting to me—just as I'd resisted letting anyone else know I even had plans to have a baby—seemed totally rational. It had taken a full nine months to conceive, and many women lost their babies in the first trimester. Insecure, I wasn't about to jinx it all now. Surely I could reduce that risk by waiting until it was no longer feasible to keep the truth hidden.

I worried, too—more logically, perhaps—about how others would react. For one, John, despite his expressed pleasure, seemed concerned about becoming a new dad. This, despite months of discussion before I'd graduated, reiterating that having another child could be his second chance at being a better father.

"You don't see many men in their midfifties steering a stroller," he'd said. "Unless they're grandfathers."

And he was right. In 1989, I knew only one other couple with an age difference mirroring ours who had undertaken what we were about to do. Despite his lingering reservations, however, we were already making guesses about the baby's sex. Because John already had sons, and I'd had to care for two younger brothers, I found myself wishing hard for a girl—unable to think of anything beyond pink bows, frilly dresses, and lace-trimmed socks. Even the list of potential baby names I'd compiled was gender specific.

As I considered others' reactions, how my bosses would respond was of particular concern. Would they regret having hired me when they heard the news? Support my request for a reduced schedule after the baby arrived? Write me off for advancement if I had a baby at home? Though women were making strides in the workplace in the late eighties, we still couldn't be honest about wanting to have children—or to raise them—while working simultaneously. The negative repercussions for the career of every woman of child-bearing age was all too real.

I vowed to find a balance: I would keep working, albeit part-time, with the hope that the university would grant John a year-long sabbatical. Although his time away from teaching would require independent research instead of his flexible work schedule, it would make possible sharing the responsibility of childcare. Still, all these uncertainties increased my wariness about revealing my pregnancy until I began to show and could avoid it no longer.

And, in the same way I'd refrained from any celebration with Mom, Dad, or my siblings upon the completion of my doctorate, I wanted to savor this event quietly, as well. I was neither looking forward to the unsolicited opinions and advice of my brothers and sisters, nor to hearing what would be, I imagined, a lukewarm reaction from my mother. Better to stave off the possibility of that disappointment until I couldn't step around it any longer. So, as was my custom when it came to family, I opted to revel in my test results the same way I always had: in the safety of my own company.

One Friday evening, ten weeks into my pregnancy, I was looking forward to basking in the excitement I'd repressed all day long at work. I put behind me the thought of jinxes and other people's demands for

attention, eager to get into my nightgown and head off to bed. Since
the positive pregnancy test and our first doctor's appointment, both
John and I had at last given in to a giddy anticipation; we spent more
and more of our free time together planning. And so I wanted to be
ready for all Saturday would hold.

In the bathroom, I dropped my dress to the floor, peeled off my
stockings and panties. A rust-colored stain bloomed up against the
white cotton crotch. I held it up in front of me for a closer look as
the moment dragged onward. Filled with disbelief, I just stood there
staring at the stain. My heart pounding like an animal in my chest.
I yanked a fistful of toilet paper from its roll. Rubbing it across my
vagina, I took a deep breath, and looked at the tissue. A pinkish blot
was smeared across the middle, a Rorschach image I knew all too well
how to interpret. I didn't need any time to know what it meant.

Pressing the tissue between my legs a second time, and then a
third, I willed the paper to come back clean. "Don't get freaked," I
told myself. "Spotting isn't unusual." However, my efforts to reassure
myself that everything would be okay did not succeed, and once again
anxiety welled up inside me. Overwhelmed and wanting to cry, I
could hear an echo in my mind: *What should I do? What should I do?*
The same panicky refrain I'd repeated to myself when I was scared as
a child.

The only way I knew to shut down the noise in my head was to
retreat physically. And, just as was true during childhood, the idea
of reaching out for my mother—a perfectly natural solution for any
daughter fearful of a miscarriage—never even registered as an option.

Shaking, I crumpled the tissue and flushed it down the toilet.
Then, lowering myself to the edge of the tub, I sat without moving.
Danger was threatening my dream, overtaking me as quickly as the
minute hand ticks over onto the new hour. Despite all the emotional
strength I had gained through my therapy, despite all my efforts to
change and to grow, I could find no way to cushion myself from this
shock.

After a long time, I rose, stepped over my pile of clothes on the floor, and turned out the light. In our bed, I lay flat on my back and tried not to jostle what I hoped was still safe inside me. Frozen by worry, I waited for John to turn in for the night. Then I told him what was happening.

"I wondered why you hadn't come back downstairs." He slid in beside me and held me in the dark. "Are you okay?"

"No. I'm not."

John ran his hand up and down my arm and fell silent. Minutes passed. My body stayed tense and rigid. My answer had obviously worried him and he had no clue what to say. He was all I had—and we were trying hard to be a couple—so I pushed away the idea that the silence he was offering me wasn't nearly enough. Taking a deep breath, I dismissed the significance of the bleeding, trying to reassure both of us that sometimes spotting could be a natural occurrence.

Saturday passed saturated with fear. I kept returning to the bathroom to study what was on the toilet paper. How much? How red? By Sunday afternoon, with more of the tinged tissues now making it impossible to calm myself, I reached for the phone at last.

A short while later, my call was returned and I described with care my symptoms to my doctor.

He got to the point without any preamble. "Rather obvious that you're suffering a miscarriage." No alternative explanation. No softening of what I now must face as reality. Rattled by his pronouncement—delivered in such a matter-of-fact tone—I stumbled for the right words.

"But isn't it possible . . ." I asked, my eyes on John, who'd stepped into the room. "Doesn't bleeding begin sometimes and then just stop? Couldn't it be something other than a miscarriage?"

"I wish I could tell you that's likely." He paused. "Best if you call when the office is open and make an appointment. We'll need to confirm with an ultrasound and decide whether you need a D&C. To make sure nothing of the fetus remains. We don't want an infection."

To wait even one more day more seemed an eternity. And the words "D&C" increased my sense of desperation. I did not want my baby scraped from my body—not while there was a chance that there still might be a heartbeat, a chance for arms and legs bicycling away, life.

"First trimester miscarriage is a common occurrence, as I'm sure you know." Before I could tell him that knowing this helped me not at all, before I had even thought of asking him what to expect as our situation moved forward, he continued. "It's just nature's way of weeding out the fetuses that will have chromosomal abnormalities. Sometimes it happens early enough that a woman doesn't even know she's pregnant. It's really for the best."

I closed my eyes at the thought of my baby being "weeded out," somehow "abnormal." In the background, I heard his pager beep. As he ended the call, I looked at the bedside clock. The first round of discussing the possible loss of my baby had lasted less than three minutes.

"Is there anything I can do for you?" John asked, looking sad and confused as he sat down beside me. Too upset to speak, I curled on my side. And lay that way for the rest of the day.

But on Monday, the obstetrician's supercilious pronouncements proved wrong. The ultrasound showed a heartbeat. Slowly, the spotting stopped. After another day of calling in sick and fielding guilt for lying about why I was out, I forced myself up out of bed and back into my clothes. Nonetheless, going to the bathroom was traumatic, and for the next few weeks I checked my underwear several times a day. I couldn't relax. Not even for a moment. And especially not before an amniocentesis procedure recommended by my obstetrician proved uneventful. Given the constant nausea that, in my case, didn't abate until almost the twentieth week, I convinced myself that the only way to harness control was to stay silent about the pregnancy as long as I could. *Just in case.*

And, naturally, withholding the news also applied to Mom. While I did not let myself think—at least not consciously—about why this was so, maybe the reason was simple: saying nothing about the pregnancy protected me from conversations that would be distressing. I couldn't bear to hear her anxiety as well as my own. Confiding in my mother—seeing her as an oasis for comfort—required too much distortion of reality. Mom was as comforting as a mirage was real. And so, not only did I not share what was happening in my life, I didn't think much about her at all. At least not during this vulnerable stage. Adding more worry and confusion to an emotional mix that was already conflicted made no sense.

Finally, five months into a pregnancy now proceeding normally— and when I could no longer hide the full globe of my abdomen—I made the move to open up to my parents, but decided to leave John at home when I made my announcement. Would he know how to support me? Maybe. Maybe not. But in case Mom did have a negative reaction, or opined that he was too old to have another child, I wouldn't have to risk both of us feeling mortified.

It was a sticky, early June day when I arrived without notice and found them sitting together on their patio, a table with a pitcher of iced tea and a sleeve of plastic cups placed between them. Next door, the giggles and shouts of kids dodging water balloons echoed loudly. From another yard, the charcoal smell of barbecue wafted our way. Not yet noticed by either Mom or Dad, I paused for a moment to absorb these proofs of summer, hoping to offset my worry with the lightness I associated with the season. Then, I walked over, pulled up a chair, and without any lead-in, told them the news.

My mother responded first. Waving a pair of scissors she'd been using to cut coupons from the Sunday *Tribune*, she said, "Oh, Terry! Thank God! You've looked like hell for so long! I thought for sure you had cancer." My father, less effusive than Mom but clearly as pleased, announced that he hoped I'd have twins.

An animated conversation followed: Mom asking what John thought; my sharing with her his excitement and our plans for a short getaway before summer's end; she thought it was "swell" when I revealed that I'd been tested and the baby was a girl. Only when she peered over her glasses to get a better peek at my tummy and asked me when I was due, did her expression change. A look of confusion crossed her face when I told her early October. "You're that far along?"

Stymied for an acceptable answer, I found myself—at least for an instant—second-guessing my decision to keep quiet about the pregnancy. *Why didn't you tell her sooner? You should have known that she would've picked up on your physical discomfort and then worried that you were sick. You could have calmed her instead of shutting her out.*

I explained about the bleeding at the beginning, aware only of my desire to redirect the conversation and to keep the positive vibes between us alive. Pulling for something that would make *her* feel special, I told her that I hadn't wanted to worry her until I knew everything was okay. A straight-up lie. But she responded to it with a smile, then added how good it would be for me to be staying home with the baby after she was born.

My anxiety reignited. "I'm going to see patients privately, but only twenty-hours a week," I said quickly, hoping that she would simply accept my plan. My father just shrugged his shoulders, both of us knowing that Mom would have more to say.

And she did. "Why would you want to kill yourself?" she said bitterly. "You know what I had to do! All those rotten jobs I had, sorting clothes and punching a cash register! Hour after shitty hour. And that was after taking care of you kids all day." Mom leaned in close to me then, backing me against an invisible wall. "I'd come back so exhausted I couldn't pour myself a cup of tea."

"You had it rough, Mom."

It was a story that had been repeated a million times, although she and I still treated it like a call and response song: Mom sang the blues and I chorused the affirmation. Each of us knew that failure to acknowledge her hardships would resonate as me acting dismissive. Tension in any conversation to follow would be sparked. I pitched my reasons for wanting to work, but my mother simply continued. "Think of your health!" she persisted. "Why would you want to take care of other people's problems when you'll have enough of your own?" She pushed herself back in her chair at that point, away from me.

I just sat there, silent now. This argument was exactly what I had feared would happen. How could I get her to look beyond her own history, I wondered. How hard I wanted her to see that I had crafted a different kind of life for myself. To realize that we weren't twins. My emotions see-sawed. A part of me could hear her concern, however unconscious, that what had happened to her shouldn't happen to me. That she cared about everything I was going to face, even if she didn't understand that her past need not be my future. But I was made uneasy, too, by the "You know what I had to do." Did she envy me for my lighter load? Was this, too, part of her resentment?

And then, suddenly, how to move past it all seemed simple. "Are you surprised I'm pregnant?" I asked, with a smile. Circling back to talking about the baby would bring her around to my side again, I knew.

The wrinkles in her face grew deeper as she spoke. "I prayed hard to the Blessed Mother—prayed that someday you would have somebody to take care of you. And now that prayer has been answered."

I smiled. Hadn't mine been, as well? Wasn't my baby turning somersaults in my belly even now?

Closing my eyes, I turned the words in my mind, over and over again, hearing them like a magical refrain I could twist, as pliable as wire warmed by the soldering iron my father once used for electrical repairs. These were words I could imbue with whatever meaning I wished them to have. *See! Look how much she thought of you—her prayers were special and that makes you special, too!* How I hoped this fantasy might stay with me, indelible as the engraving on a wedding band.

But it lived for only an instant, when reality returned with a vengeance. My wish—surely created by the little Terry who lived on in my woman's body—vanished as I opened my eyes. I saw then that while both our prayers had been answered, they were radically different. I took one deep breath and cleared my mind, facing her meaning at last. The revelation rendered me speechless: how could she actually imagine that I would want a devoted girl child to take care of *me* the way I'd felt compelled to take care of my mother? What an angry and unfulfilled mother I would have to be to have such an expectation of my child! And if I became the kind of mother who viewed caregiving as some kind of transactional deal, what would then follow inevitably? A girl whose devotion to me would, in the long run, render her a rage-filled mother herself, worn down and out by her own stint at child care.

As much as I wanted to claim certainty about how different my mother and I were, I had to consider the family history—and what had happened so far. I wondered: could I be the one to break the terrible hold of an inadequate mother's grip? Resentment settled like a stone behind my ribcage as I tried to ignore a sudden blooming rancor toward Mom. And my fear about the kind of mother I might actually become.

"Take it easy," I told myself. "Patterns can change. They don't have to be passed down."

But the truth pushed at me like a sermon. *Who are you kidding? When you've got a mother who's starving, she just passes that hunger along and it goes down from generation to generation, one daughter to the next! A virus. That kind of girl doesn't get to be a child. Unless she rises up and rebels, she'll just model herself on Mom's good-old example. Stop hiding from what you already know, Terry.*

I blinked then, and looked over at my mother. Her smile was still wide. She didn't even begin to understand the import of what she'd just said to me. Wishing the sharpness under my breast would dissolve, or even just shift, I pushed myself up out of my chair, struck once more by the power of my emotion. Pregnancy held turbulent and evocative experiences for mothers and daughters alike, I reminded myself. It was inevitable that such intense sentiments would come to the fore. That old fears would look for a new home.

As I adjusted the elastic on the waistband of my jeans, I was rewarded with a brief poke from the baby. Pressing the spot where her foot or elbow had landed, I telegraphed back to my little one that I had gotten the message and knew what was in order: breathing room for us both.

"That's really sweet, Mom. All your prayers."

I stood over her, then bent in close, inhaling the smell of her shampoo. Just as a loving mother might. Just as I might one day with my own daughter. And then I straightened my back. Realizing I was readying to leave, she protested.

"Come inside. I've got some nice lunch meat. I can make you a sandwich."

"What's your rush?" Dad interrupted. "Why don't you stay?"

"I can't eat right now, Mom. Too hot." I patted her arm. Told her I was happy that she was excited about the baby. Reaching over, I pressed my hand to my father's shoulder. "Errands, Daddy," I added. "I've got errands to run."

In my confusion, my old coping strategies had taken over once again. They'd ignited the urge to get away, to be separate and emotionally insulated. I was alone again, just as I had been through so much of my life. On my own, I could sift and sort through all the resentment and angst that stirred inside. Walking back to my car, I wondered, for the first time in my pregnancy, whether it had been so wise to wish for a girl. How was it possible that I had not appreciated that—for me— raising a daughter would be infinitely more complicated, and more daunting, than raising a son?

For weeks afterward, I wrestled with all the conflicting emotions that had been aroused during my conversation with Mom. Her criticism of my decision to keep working now climbed to a prominent position. And so I became very careful about what news I shared with her about my job and our plans for what would come following the baby's birth. Outwardly, I remained pleasant, but inside I chafed, and nursed my irritation over her strong opinions and her unsolicited advice. Like an old injury that flares up unexpectedly, I'd heard her words as I'd heard them most of my life—as a repudiation of my accomplishments. And as disapproval of *me* for choosing a different path.

I was frustrated with myself, too, annoyed that after nearly six years of therapy, I was harboring the same resentments toward my mother and could still feel myself withdrawing when she said something that hurt. But I tried to douse this with self-righteousness, telling myself that her prayers were outrageous, as they wished for me an awful fate. I couldn't then see the simpler, sadder truth: Mom was simply oblivious—blind to the terrible message she was transmitting.

Not surprisingly then, when the phone rang one afternoon late that summer and I heard her voice—knowing that my mother only *initiated* calls when she hoped to be bailed out of a jam—I was well primed to feel aggrieved. I was like a trap ready to spring.

Mom wanted me to come for coffee and cake when Jeanie arrived in town the next week. Having avoided traveling to Chicago for almost two decades, my sister was returning home from California for a family wedding. Sixteen years had passed since I had visited her in Los Angeles while on a college spring break. Mom and Jeanie's contacts consisted in the main of correspondence and occasional phone conversations. Considering the careful distance between them, I didn't doubt that Mom was apprehensive about how this upcoming visit would go. But I didn't care.

I told her that I had to work. That she should ask Patty or Flo. She insisted that Jeanie wanted to see me. *What manipulation!* But I wanted to see my sister, too. Especially now that I was pregnant. The news was out among family members, but this would be a rare opportunity for my sister and me to celebrate. I caved, but not before insisting that I would not leave work early.

On the appointed day, I purposely dawdled, arriving at my mother's house later than expected. Dropping my keys into my purse, I walked in. There, across the room, aproned and with her hair freshly styled, stood my mother, beaming. Next to her were my three sisters. "Surprise!" they called.

Tears filled my eyes. Behind Mom, pink and white streamers hung from the dining room light fixture, each length of crepe paper carefully twisted and anchored to the table. Like a little girl's birthday party. In that moment, I was transported back in time to my childhood and to the few neighborhood parties I'd attended. Like my sisters and brothers, I'd never had a party of my own, but now, looking at the banner that proclaimed "showers of happiness," I felt I was claiming a prize I had never expected to win.

Later—after we'd finished the meal my mother had prepared— Mom, sitting beside me, handed me a carefully wrapped box adorned with a large bow. "I hope I didn't make it too big," she said.

Swaddled in thick folds of glittery tissue lay a crocheted baby shawl. Stunned, since I had never known my mother to do handwork of any kind, I stared at her gift. That she had crafted such a lovely wrap, one that was certain to become an heirloom, moved me beyond words.

I knew I would think of my mother each time I looked at this shawl, each time I held its delicate threads against my cheek. As I sat there beside her, I imagined her fingers twisting the yarn and how they must have ached from her arthritis. And the patience it must have taken—all the more impressive in that Mom had no patience at all. I found myself daring to think that the time she'd spent creating each stitch was time she'd spent thinking about me. Intuitively, especially in light of how I'd first responded to her "answered prayer," I realized this was a wonderful—yet potentially dangerous—hope to have. But I also recognized something else. A different response inside me. My palms swept gently across the fabric. I fondled the edges between my fingertips, needing to savor the moment. I held in my hands the most meaningful gift my mother had ever given me.

"Oh, Mom, it's beautiful," I whispered, pressing myself closer to her. Then, resting my head on her shoulder, I added. "And the size is perfect. Just perfect."

"It can get nippy fast in the fall," she responded, as she patted my cheek. "She'll be bundled up nice without getting too hot."

As I absorbed my mother's gesture, her words, I wiped at my eyes, suddenly aware that her generosity was resonating as too much. So accustomed to chasing a mother beyond reach and so unaccustomed to experiencing her warmth, I felt disoriented. Like I'd run out of a dark room I'd been holed up in, and had, without pausing, stared into the sun. Here was my mother, celebrating my pregnancy—celebrating *me*. Overwhelmed by her thoughtfulness, I was a bit frightened. too. Could I tolerate this unfamiliar feeling—this unadulterated pleasure? And what if it disappeared as fast as it had come? I let out a long breath and reached for my mother's hand. Then laced my fingers through hers.

One September afternoon following the shower, I sat in my office and reflected on the journey my pregnancy had become. It had begun as a secret, one which I'd sprinkled with magical thinking to protect myself, the same kind of secret I'd always used to soothe myself through emotional turmoil and uncharted terrain. But now, in these last weeks of childbearing, with my belly big and my mind overflowing with emotion, I felt incredibly exposed. Nothing was a secret anymore.

Preparing to cross the threshold into motherhood, I found myself curiously free of any desire to keep further secrets. I wanted to come fully forward, into plain sight, arms stretched out in exhilaration. I would hold this daughter of mine closely—this daughter who, even in the womb seemed to be demonstrating her ability to throw her own weight and to push against me.

Looking out my consultation room window, a contraction gripped my middle; my belly hardened and, after a minute, softened. My uterus, practicing. Getting ready. In my ninth month now, that long muscle inside my abdomen had found a new pattern: hold and release. Hold and release. Each interval of tightening and then letting go was a metaphor, perhaps, for the paradox of mothering. I vowed I would learn to give my daughter a lot of breathing room, along with the abundant love I carried deep inside. My mother had never been able to manage this act of balance. But I would.

Missing in Action

Absence is a house so vast that inside you
will pass through its walls and hang pictures
on the air.

— Pablo Neruda
"Sonnet XCIV"

THE HOUSE WAS QUIET and I relaxed, rocking in my chair. Replaying the moment I first held the bundle now asleep in my arms. I remembered how my daughter had met my gaze with eyes dark as midnight, eyes that seemed not to blink at all. And how that introduction to joy altered everything. The world as I knew it had changed its tilt.

I'd been home from the hospital for nearly two weeks, and happiness shaped my mood as I rocked and waited for my parents, who'd just returned from a trip to the east coast to celebrate their fiftieth wedding anniversary. Their first order of business had been to call and set up a time to hug their new granddaughter, who'd arrived three weeks prematurely, while they were still away.

Mom burst through the door ahead of my father, arms raised and hands flapping like a fundamentalist preacher's. "There she is!" She raced toward me and my dark-haired beauty, and Dad hurried in behind her with a wide, lopsided grin.

"Ha! Those were John's exact words when she finally popped out." I laughed. "And all I could think was, 'She's too early! Is she okay?'"

"Let me see this little dolly." Mom leaned in and gave me a small kiss. "I need to have a look at my girl." She smiled down on her twenty-third grandchild, appearing as enchanted as if my baby had been the very first in a long line. "And that little rosebud mouth."

"She looks good, Terry," Dad commented. "Good color. Solid."

"Geez, Dad," I protested, "you sound like you're talking about a table you just varnished."

"I'm saying she looks great! Very healthy!" He bent in closer. "Grace, huh? Are you gonna call her Gracie?" He poked a finger inside the delicate shawl that Mom had made, to tickle the baby's cheek.

"Grace Elizabeth Marie," Mom said brightly. "I agree with you, Terry. You should call her Grace." Mom pushed Dad's hand away and peered closer. "She most certainly doesn't look like a Gracie."

"I'm gonna call her Grace-a-lina. Or maybe Gracie Allen, like the old-time radio star," Dad teased.

I turned my head to look up at him and rolled my eyes.

"It's probably not what you expected, Mom," I said, feigning an apology. "But it is a saint's name, so she's covered, right?" From inside the blanket came a hiccup and a brief bit of fuss. "And you both have the same middle name—I thought you might like that." Suddenly, a bit of shyness crossed over me.

"And Elizabeth was Grandma's name, too," Mom observed, treating me to a full-on smile.

"Grandma was a pain in the ass," Dad quipped. He sank down on the couch, chuckling at his own joke. "So, Terry," he said, folding his arms across his barrel chest. "Where's the guy with the pipe? Has he changed any diapers yet?"

Ah, John. John, with his excitement and physical hovering—especially through the last months of the pregnancy—had been such a constant for me.

Had been. Since Grace's arrival, he had suddenly become very hard to find.

The first time he'd gone missing—shortly after our baby's late-afternoon arrival—he had taken off without much explanation, which I attributed to his wanting to make phone calls and it having already been a very long day. Had I not been so enthralled by this new life

I cradled—and too wired to sleep—I would have wondered more the following morning and afternoon about where he was. When he finally arrived for what would be a brief visit that evening and I asked where he'd been for so long, he blithely replied that he'd been shopping for a crib; in a distant sort of way this seemed odd to me, as we'd already set up a bassinet and had no immediate need for anything bigger. But in my drowsy, post-delivery bliss, I coasted and didn't let myself see the only thing that mattered: not where my husband had been, but where he hadn't. He'd left Grace and me all alone in a strange hospital room, only hours after her birth.

Not until we'd returned home and I'd settled Grace and myself in, and when he still seemed removed—doing work in his study—did his explanation about the crib fully register as odd. Further, I now recalled that, during our two-day hospital stay, friends had dropped by to see the baby and offer congratulations, and I had had to make excuses for John's continuing absences. Inside me embarrassment and then annoyance flowered.

The end of our first week at home approached, and one afternoon I decided to go looking for him after I put Grace down for her nap. Now on sabbatical from his teaching responsibilities at the university, he was again holed up in his study, a stack of research texts piled up on the floor next to him. "You're like a damn ghost," I said, in an angry tone. "The minute she was born, you checked out."

He didn't answer immediately, using the time to make a penciled notation on an article he was reading. "Really, Terry? Just because I happen to be doing some reading in another room?"

His professorial tone rankled, but I tried to hold back. Perhaps he was right in suggesting that I was overreacting. Maybe my hormones were to blame.

But a minute later, I stormed out of the house and into the garage, pulling the lawnmower out onto the lawn. Too angry to care about my physical discomfort and pain, I tried to calm my fury by pushing the machine hard, creating rows of freshly-cut grass. When John interrupted me twenty minutes later, carrying Grace on a pillow as if she were made of glass, I flipped the switch on the motor and muttered under my breath. "What the hell is this?"

"She's crying," he announced soberly as he approached me. "She needs you."

I reached for my daughter, and dripping with sweat, breathing hard from exertion, I hurried inside. Leaving the mower in the middle of the yard and my impassive husband with the pillow. But later that day, unnerved by how angry I'd become, I pledged to let go of my resentment and make a fresh start.

Now, as I rocked, awash in my parents' joy over their new grand-daughter, I considered for an instant whether I should mention John's behavior. However, my ecstasy at showing my daughter off to her doting audience overrode my suspicion that my husband's current disappearing act had any significance. And so I dismissed it. "He may have gone over to the library to get some work done," I said, in response to Dad's question. I sneaked a glance at my watch. Maybe he really had gone to the library. It was almost twelve. "Hopefully, he'll get back while you're still here." And as I spoke, Grace began to stir.

"All these beautiful flowers, Terry," Mom gushed. "It's like a garden in here!" Then, as she headed toward the kitchen, she called over her shoulder. "Let me wash my hands so I can hold this baby."

Into the noon hour, I stayed in my rocker, content to watch my parents pass Grace back and forth. This was the second time in two months, and only the third time in my life, that it felt safe to touch and be touched by my mother. Only my first communion day and my baby shower had offered a match in the warmth and attention that settled now across my shoulders.

Grace began to fuss and I reached to take her from the cradle of my mother's arms.

"She's getting hungry." I hesitated, afraid I was about to spoil the moment. Mom had been outspoken about breastfeeding as long as I could remember. "Breastfeeding!" she'd say as she wrinkled her nose. "Only people with no class feed their babies that way." She had always spoken with vehemence. Avoiding looking at my mother directly, I wanted to avert making her uncomfortable. "I'm going to take her upstairs to nurse." I tried to sound nonchalant.

"Will you eat a grilled cheese if I make one?" She looked me up and down. "Too thin, Terry. You hardly look like you were pregnant at all."

This was not the response I'd expected. Yet, here we were: I was breaking her rules and she was making me grilled cheese.

"I made lasagna," I answered, delighted that the day was unfolding with such magic. "If you could just reheat it and pull out the salad, that'd be great. I'll be back down in a few."

Later, after the dishes had been cleared from the table—including the empty plate that had been set for John—we walked onto the front lawn. Even the sound of the leaves, now dry, and the way they crunched beneath our feet, seemed filled with serenity. With Grace tucked in the crook of my arm, I gave my mother one last hug.

"Bye-bye, peaches and cream," she called to my baby as she opened the car door and slid into the front seat. A waggle of fingers and a kiss to the air.

Peaches and cream? Here was Mom, using the same gesture Grandma Healy had. She gave us one last wave as the car rounded the corner. Grace began to stir and I placed my finger against her lips. I hoped the visit foreshadowed what was to come—that my daughter would have a deeper connection with her grandmother than I'd had with the very same woman. Maybe my mother would at last be able to nurture someone.

I had an abundance of hope that first year of motherhood: hope that my baby's future would be bright; hope for the private practice I was beginning to build; hope that I would become the mother I aspired to be. And there was ample reason to have such an emotion. Grace was thriving, meeting each benchmark outlined in the child-raising books that sat piled next to my bed. Through referrals from colleagues and former supervisors, my schedule to treat patients was beginning to fill. And I did my best to do good work. I was fortunate, too, to secure extraordinary childcare four afternoons a week, making it possible for me to weave work responsibilities with my first priority—my daughter. As both a mother and a therapist, I wanted to be as different as possible from my own mother.

And my relationship with Mom had continued to blossom throughout that first year. Motherhood had drawn us together. The only time I worried that we might hit a bump of significance was early on—the day I summoned up my courage to tell her Grace was to be baptized in a Protestant church. To soften the blow, I'd dressed my seven-week-old daughter head to toe in ruffles and pinks that day and carried her like a basket of goodies to my mother's house.

"It's important to John," I told Mom as she poured coffee into her mug. A pastor from John's hometown—a small place where his parents still lived—had relocated to our area. Shifting Grace from shoulder to shoulder, I tried to stay calm as I explained all this to Mom. "We joined the congregation before Grace was born," I confessed. "John really likes that this guy knows his parents so well."

"You're going to do what you want anyway," she replied.

I was shocked at her compliance, though the expression on her face bore a trace of bitterness. Nevertheless, I'd expected a much stronger complaint. Maybe even vitriol. A reaction against which I would have to defend our choice with rigor.

In reality, I wanted to support John's desire to be included in Grace's introduction into a church. Her first weeks had passed and as we approached the finish of her second month, he had become even more absent than at the beginning. Perhaps I could draw him into his daughter's life through her christening.

"It's all pretty different," I said then. "But the bottom line is I don't want you to be surprised or upset with the service."

At first, she shook her head and rolled her eyes. Predictably. But then she surprised me for the second time in the span of ten minutes by completely changing the subject.

"Flo's still going to be the godmother, right?"

"Yes! Of course!" I sputtered, sorry that I hadn't reinforced this fact at the start of my explanation. "She'll be her guardian if anything happens to me." I purposely chose the word "me" rather than "us." I'd already focused on John enough, and now all I wanted was to reassure Mom. To bring this sale home. "Flo knows that I want Grace to have a religious education." This part was true, even if John and I hadn't yet considered what sort of religious education it was to be. I focused on the details as a distraction. "Jeanie sent a beautiful silver cross necklace for Grace to wear." I slapped my forehead. "And the christening gown! Flo's having it professionally made." I stood up, walked around the kitchen as I rubbed the baby's back. "It's going to be gorgeous."

Mom's face lit up with pleasure and she held her arms out for her granddaughter once again.

It was a cold and bright Sunday in December when we gathered. Mom sat in a front pew, and while I knew she must be uncomfortable celebrating as part of such an unfamiliar denomination, she never once scowled. After the fiasco of my wedding, when she'd avoided speaking to me the entire day, I had expected—and dreaded—something quite different from her. Mom sat next to me, where I held my baby in my arms, pleasure coursing through me. Her fingertips trailed lightly over Grace's beautiful dress, and she leaned in to absorb with pleasure the baby's mouth, her feathery lashes, her rosy cheeks.

The next day, still marveling at Mom's aplomb, I decided to stop by and thank her. It was late afternoon when I arrived, and we sat at her kitchen table. Grace slept in my arms.

"You were really great yesterday, Mom." I gave her a smile, watching as she poured cream into her tea. "I know it couldn't have been easy. But at least it was a religious ceremony. Kind of the same."

The silence of the room echoed. I knew, in only the beat of a moment, that I should have just expressed my gratitude and then shut up.

"It is *not* the same," she snapped. "My God! No BVM for one thing." BVM was the acronym she sometimes used when describing the Blessed Virgin Mary. Her voice was elevated. Insistent. "C'mon, Terry. That was no baptism at all."

I looked away again, wishing Grace would interrupt us by crying—anything to change the charged atmosphere of the room. But rather than launching into all the ways in which I hadn't "gotten it right," she waved her hand dismissively instead. "Ah, what the hell." She sniffed. "You don't go to church anymore anyway." Taking the dish towel she had draped over her shoulder when our arrival had interrupted her cleaning routine, she began to wipe spots from the table. Invisible ones. She rubbed harder. "When I watched Grace for you here . . . A couple of weeks ago? I took care of it then."

"What do you mean?"

"You have to abide by the sacraments, that's what I believe." She raised her head, her brow creased. "So I took care of it."

"You said that already." Filled with consternation, I wondered what she meant by "took care" of it.

"Someone Catholic had to say the prayers. So I dipped her head under the faucet in the bathroom. I didn't have the special oil, but I put holy water on her afterward." She sniffed again. "I baptized her myself." She looked at me directly, a familiar expression on her face, an expression that spelled just one thing: defiance.

But instead of feeling angry—for using her secret as a weapon against me—I shrugged it off. After all, what did it really matter? Expressing anger toward Mom had always been my weak spot, and perhaps unconsciously I viewed the lack of a Catholic ceremony as victory enough. And yet, if I'd given it any thought, I would have seen that I'd allowed everyone else's needs to take control of my baby's significant day.

I'd acquiesced to John's desire to choose a church, colluding with him by trading whatever he wanted for his acceptance of our daughter. I'd allowed Flo to dictate what Grace would wear. And though, on some level, I felt Mom had a point, at least for herself, I'd tiptoed around her. I had swapped the love I wanted others to give to our daughter for resentment. Even though I couldn't see it, on this special occasion, I'd dealt with my anger just the way I'd done so often in my life. I buried it under a smile.

As I listened to my mother, I seized the only solution that seemed possible to me then, starting to laugh and turning what she had done into a joke. I couldn't really challenge her on this, not when she believed that her act—however covert and unwanted—would safeguard her granddaughter's soul from that warehouse of poor babies who had not been baptized: limbo. Or, as in this case, one who hadn't been baptized according to the rules and traditions of her church.

"I was making sure she was protected," Mom said, crossing her arms with obstinacy.

Protected. Not a word I would ever have considered part of her vocabulary. It brought me up short. I stopped laughing, tried instead to absorb what she'd said. But before I could take it all in—before I could reply—the protector of my daughter's soul had moved on to other, more mundane matters.

"Have a piece of coffee cake, Terry." She slapped the dish towel back over her shoulder and pointed at a box on the counter. "Just bought it yesterday. It's still nice and fresh."

And, as far as she was concerned, that was the end of it.

With all going so well with Grace and with Mom that first year, I found it easy to distract myself from thinking much about my marriage. John's disappearing act when he wasn't on "baby duty" had only increased and by the time Grace could scoot on all fours, he'd mastered the art of the fast retreat. Our shared childcare routine, also predictable, helped blind me to the gap widening between us. Now, as we traded off parenting responsibilities and juggled our work demands, something new began to take shape. With my little girl balanced on my hip and a private practice running smoothly, I felt as if I'd won the lottery—but John acted as if he'd been suckered into a pyramid scheme.

In public, he was animated when talking about Grace or about his time away from the university, but at home he was quiet, on edge. With the end of his twelve-month sabbatical nearing and the pressure of the approaching deadline for completing his research growing, he seemed to be developing an escalating resentment and an unarticulated antipathy over the division of his time between Grace and me and his work.

Earlier in our relationship, I would have reacted to his irritable moods just as I had Mom's when I was a child—as if I were tap-dancing on a thin sheet of glass, searching for both love and safety delicately. However, I'd worked hard to change and grow in our sixteen-year marriage, so now, when John signaled his distress with a cold silence or a sharp word, I had an entirely different response. I ignored him. To dismiss him turned out to be easy. Remarkably so, because I was so slaphappy in love with my daughter. Even on the days when Grace was fussy, or sick, or just impossible to please, even on the days when mothering was exhausting and closer to a chore, even on the days when I doubted my judgment as a parent, my heart brimmed with fulfillment.

The resentments both John and I carried certainly contributed to the way our marriage was whizzing down an ice-glazed hill. But right then, I was certain that John alone was the problem. And it only took one shriek from Grace, shortly before her first birthday, to convince me that I was right.

The evening had begun quietly enough. John and I had done the handoff when I'd arrived home from work, and after I fed Grace her dinner and gave her a bath, we'd taken turns reading to her before putting her down for the night. Bedtime had its challenges, though. Colicky as a baby, Grace had trouble with the sleep routine and still woke frequently during the night. As the one who typically got up with her, chronic fatigue plagued me. This particular evening, she'd nodded off easily enough, but two hours later, she was awake again, crying and screaming from her bedroom on the second floor near the top of the stairs. Ten minutes passed and still she cried. I began the touch and go—lay her back down, leave the room, repeat ten minutes later if necessary—an exercise in frustration that had become all too frequent in recent months.

After the third round, I looked at John with a weariness that felt bone deep.

"Your turn." I rolled over on the sofa where I'd been reading a book. He sighed and went upstairs.

Time passed. Good. He must have got her back down. But just as my body sank deeper into the couch, my eyelids closing, her cries started up again. A high-pitched wail this time. Seconds later came the sound of feet pounding from our bedroom into the nursery across the uncarpeted hardwood floor. This was followed by silence, a momentary one. And then, there was a muffled thud. As if something had been dropped, hard, onto something soft. As if onto the mattress of a crib.

Operating on instinct, I struggled to get up as fast as I could.

I took the stairs two at a time, ready to burst into Grace's room, when I was blocked by John, who stood in the open doorway. I pushed past him, the spill of light from the hall making it just possible to see her. She lay sprawled on her back. Without a word from him, I knew exactly what had happened, exactly what that overhead thud had meant. He'd thrown her down onto the mattress. Raised her up and then let her fall. Eyes wide, my daughter stared me as I arrived at her side. Stunned now, it seemed, into silence.

"Are you okay, sweet thing?" I could hear the note of agitation in my voice. "Does anything hurt?"

Lowering the crib's side rail, I reached down and lifted her gently. But her lip quivered. When she moved her arms and legs, I whispered a thank you to God. Pulling her close, I stroked her damp hair and her sweaty body melded into mine.

"You're okay, huggie, you're okay," I repeated, trying to comfort both of us. "Hush little baby." Now she began to cry, loudly, desperately, gulping for air. "Shhh, shhh." I rocked her in my arms.

Behind me, John moved from the doorway into the room.

"I think there's something wrong with me." He sounded panicked. "I think I need help."

I took a step back. In that instant, I could not have cared less about how he felt or what he needed. I was too angry to look at him. And so I didn't answer. Not a single word of comfort or understanding. But then I thought about what could have happened: a picture of him out of control—smashing kitchen drawers onto the floor—washed through my mind on a tide of fear.

Only long after he'd gone back downstairs—after I'd finally gotten Grace's gulps to turn to sniffles and she'd at last bowed out to sleep— did I go back to where I'd been sitting on the living room couch. Only then did I look at him directly.

"Listen to me." My voice was hard as steel. "It's one thing to be so tired and frustrated that you want to throw your kid out a window. Nobody'd argue with that kind of feeling." I stared at him, so that he had no choice but to look back at me. "To actually throw our baby down! You make me want to vomit!" I barreled on, fueled by fury. "Tomorrow." I spat out the word. "Get the name of someone to talk to. And you'd better have an appointment set up by the end of the day." I didn't let myself dwell on the idea that he might simply ignore my ultimatum. Unconsciously, I knew what I would do if he didn't respond to my demand, but I wasn't able to parse that through in the pitch of the moment.

As it turned out, I didn't have to deal with that possibility. John found a therapist and had had his appointment before the end of the week.

"How did it go?" I asked, when he arrived home afterward.

"Fine."

"Did you talk about what happened?" I tried to keep my voice calm, somewhat conversational, even though I wanted to scream "What did he say?" Ordinarily, I would never have pried into his session with his therapist, knowing as a practitioner that privacy was paramount. But now I felt he owed me an answer.

"Terry, I don't need two therapists," he answered in a careful, even tone.

"That's it? That's all you're going to say?"

"I'm taking care of it." He sighed. "What more do you want?"

"For it never to happen again," I rebuked.

"Be fair. It's my business—whatever goes on during my therapy hour. You know that."

"When my daughter is involved, it's my goddamned business, too."

As the months passed, and John continued in therapy, I often wondered: what had he told his therapist about his appalling behavior? Had he even brought it up? Day to day and hour to hour, I was pleasant on the surface, but inside I remained as detached as I had been enraged on that terrible night, unable to believe that I could ever trust my husband again. He displayed no further signs of violence toward our daughter, and in fact, spent time with her in constructive ways—especially time spent reading her stories—but I could see that underneath his calm, professorial manner lay a volatile nature.

Nothing changed for the better during the year John spent in therapy, which shouldn't have been surprising, since I continued to ignore him most of the time. My world overflowed with the delight of my daughter and I told myself that she was more than enough for me. And although I couldn't articulate it then, any physical attraction I still had for my husband had died the night he'd thrown Grace down in her crib. I convinced myself easily that doing a solid job as a parent was far more important than being happy as a couple. Who needed companionship, anyway? Intimacy? Sex? The answers were simple: Not me. Not me. Not me.

I avoided confronting just how unhappy I was. Avoided realizing, on a conscious level, that I no longer loved my husband. Avoided acknowledging how ashamed I was that my loveless marriage set me apart from the neighborhood stay-at-home moms with partnerships I perceived to be solid. I'd already felt that I didn't fit in, and under this new burden I now knew that I truly wasn't one of them.

Staring down any of these emotions meant acknowledging that I was failing at one of the central aspects of my life: my womanhood.

Not yet ready to face the situation, I looked off to the side instead of straight into the mirror.

❧

But just as John had long been "missing in action," so had I. Neither of us were committed to making the marriage work, no matter how strenuously we deluded ourselves. I had built a set of rationalizations—excuses, really—about why it had deteriorated. And also about what we should do about it.

One afternoon, when Grace was three, after an all too familiar episode of bickering in front of her, I pulled John into the kitchen, where she couldn't hear us.

"We're terrible role models, you know," I said, sounding smug even to myself. The therapist in me took over, easily settling on a one-dimensional way of explaining the roadblock we faced. "We never present ourselves as a united front." I was on a roll now.

"What do you mean, exactly?" *Typical John*, I thought. Sounding defensive rather than interested in the counsel I had to offer. "What are you suggesting?"

"Why can't you see it? It's so damned obvious!" I sighed, as loudly as if I were talking to a child. "We're just leading parallel lives. Grace doesn't have parents who love each other, talk to each other, give her the security she needs. The love she needs."

"Terry, I think you're overreacting. Of course she knows she's loved." His tone matched the patronizing look on his face.

"We don't love her *together*. We don't share her—we're always separate. Why don't you see that?" I asked, irritated by his obtuseness.

He just sent me a puzzled look.

I charged on. "It's not like I ever had a role model for any of this, you know. My own mother never cared enough to worry this way about her kids." I lowered my voice. "Or maybe she just didn't *know* enough. But we do—for Grace's sake we've got to pull this together." I waited. Unsure if John would even respond. In his slow-motion way, he finally did and nodded.

I went plunging on to my next idea, encouraged by his small acknowledgement. "I think it would be good for us to see somebody." Reaching over the sink, I opened a window. "In the long run, it will be good for Grace. We need to do it for her."

"*Another* therapist?" John sputtered. I turned to look at him. He looked testy.

"A different kind," I corrected. "For couples." I crossed my arms, annoyed again. "We owe it to her to begin acting like a normal family. There's no choice here."

And so, two years after the incident in the crib, we began a long run of Monday nights, sitting on a comfortable sofa, on the other side of a coffee table that separated us from an experienced marriage and family specialist who had been recommended by a colleague. Each week he'd greet us with an affable smile and we'd fill the hour practicing new ways to talk with and understand one another, while also devising practical strategies for spending quality time together. The next Monday we'd return to his cozy office and begin the process again—making little, if any, progress.

For more than a year, we slogged along, with no end in sight, avoiding the true issues in our marriage by pushing the reason for our therapy behind a very effective screen: how to be better parents to Grace. If I had been honest with myself, perhaps I would not have pushed for, or stuck with the marriage counseling for as long as I'd insisted we do. After the first year, maybe I would have gone back into my own individual therapy instead. Maybe I would have focused on lifting my half of the weight—my contribution for the split in the marriage—instead of putting Grace right in its middle, choosing to believe that motherhood was reason enough to do so. However, I didn't then have the ability, or the courage, to dip into that well.

I was determined not to let John stand in my way: I would be a different and better mother than mine had been. My rationale that he and I should simply keep working at the marriage to provide better role models for our daughter was exactly that: a rationale. Much of what I believed about John and me *was* the truth—we were leading parallel lives—but not the essential one I needed to face.

So, in lieu of truth, I opted for show—just as I had in the early years of our marriage. I was playing a different role this time, now the earnest and savvy and put-upon wife. Yet, once again, John and I were cast in the same type of drama. One that guaranteed a dissatisfying ending. The only question, it seemed, was how long this current production would run.

The Prayer Broker

That's the way prayer do. It's like
electricity, it keeps things going.

—Kathryn Stockett,
The Help

SHORTLY AFTER GRACE TURNED four a new issue arose, one
that not only distracted us from the problems in our marriage, but
also weighed it down even further and smothered what remained. She
began to suffer from a severe and unrelenting gastrointestinal upset.
It began with a single episode of violent vomiting every twenty minutes—finally abating after twenty-four hours—but soon morphed into
a clockwork cycle. Roughly every twenty-eight days, with the pattern
always the same, each attack started without warning.

Cheerful at this stage of her life, Grace played happily by herself
and with others. But now, periodically, a taut look would come over
her face like a cloud blocking the sun. Turning to me, she'd announce,
with tears, that her tummy hurt. Then she'd race to the bathroom. A
day later, after the vomiting had ceased and she'd been rehydrated, my
girly girl would bounce out of her sick bed as if nothing untoward had
occurred. Once again, she would look perfectly healthy.

Still, I worried. As time went on, that worry grew into fear. In
our couples' therapy—which would continue for another weary and
unproductive year—I held back from talking about our issues with
each other, not wanting to add to the tension between John and me.
I pretended that we were using our sessions to collaborate on solving

our daughter's mysterious health issue. In reality, however, I was on a solo mission. The mistrust I still felt about the night he'd dropped Grace more than three years earlier—mistrust I had never dealt with openly and honestly—festered. The anger I carried internally provoked my insistence that I handle everything on my own.

This unexamined resentment made it easy to undermine and vilify my husband, and thereby rationalize my behavior as "efficient." I never encouraged him to accompany me to the pediatrician's office, and whenever Grace endured another bout of the illness, I dropped everything. Canceling my appointments with patients, I took care of her alone, stayed at her bedside, held her head over the toilet, cleaned up the mess. Reassured her. Although considerably anxious, I never coordinated these times of our daughter's physical crisis with John so that he was the one to stay home. And once the immediate problem had passed, for the first time I found myself reaching out to my mother—not my husband.

Although I told her nothing about the demise of my marriage, I often asked her to babysit and to keep a watchful eye after Grace had an attack, so that I could go back to work. Mom never turned me down, and, in fact, encouraged me to ask her for help. She never once commented on my return to my practice—a lack of reaction that amazed me, in light of her opposition on the day I'd told her I was pregnant.

Her willingness to pitch in did not surprise me, however, given her fondness for Grace. Perhaps I was witnessing a tenderness and care my mother was capable of providing when no longer burdened and overwhelmed by the responsibilities of mothering. Whatever the reasons for such availability, and in response to her generosity, I relied on her help more and more. How much had changed between us. For the first time, we related as a mother and daughter should. I could see that she felt the same way I did.

But time passed and Grace's problems continued. No one had ever suggested that perhaps my daughter's attacks were a way of eliciting more opportunity for mothering from me—nor did I imagine this to be true. I had the flexibility to schedule my appointments around Grace's needs and I believed I'd calibrated our separations well. One evening during this difficult period, however, my mother made an astute remark, one I quickly rejected.

Having arranged for her to babysit while I attended a work-related dinner, I dropped Grace off at her house. Into the living room my little girl marched, hunched over because her two over-stuffed grocery bags were so heavy. In her flannel pajamas, robe, and fuzzy slippers, she resembled a tiny old woman as she unpacked her "supplies." Out came a small mat, her blanket, stuffed animals, and several books, all of which she arranged carefully in the middle of the living room rug. Surveying her handiwork with her eyes as big and round as buttons, she put her hands on her hips. Then nodded, causing her shoulder-length chestnut curls to bounce. Finally, as if saving the best for last, she pulled a framed picture from the bottom of the sack. A photo of me that she'd taken from a table back home. Holding the picture as if she were offering it up to the gods, she gave it a big kiss, patted it lightly, and then tucked it under the pillow on her makeshift bed.

"Oh, Terry," Mom observed, as she watched her granddaughter. "I'm telling you now—she's never going to be able to let you go."

"It's okay," I replied. Leaning in toward my daughter, I tickled her chin. "You know Mommy's coming back soon, right?"

"I don't mean 'let go' *tonight*," Mom corrected. "She's so attached," she went on solemnly. "I mean, she's never going to be able to let you go. *Ever*."

But I didn't want to hear that my relationship with my child was less than optimal. Or that if such dependence on me deepened, it could spell trouble. Not even as a professional did I see the situation with clarity. And so I didn't really take in what my mother had said and process it. I wanted to believe—just as I had vowed during my pregnancy—that I was orchestrating the delicate dance of attachment and separation with my daughter perfectly. That I was breathing in. And breathing out.

∾

Throughout Grace's fourth year and into the early part of her fifth—with her doctors still searching for an answer to her illness—my distress mounted. Exhausted and scared, unable to find comfort in John, I reached out to the neighborhood moms and to some close friends from grad school. However, unaccustomed to relying on others for emotional support, I often became flustered about how much to share, and feared being overwhelmed. More often than not, I would leave the meet-ups with the people who cared about me feeling jittery. Anxiety always trailed me home.

As the months spun by, only one thing remained absolute and clear: my resolve to help my child was not curing my sense that I was failing her. I'd consulted with a variety of doctors of all persuasions, as well as having researched vomiting syndromes and their possible causes on my own. Eventually, however, I had to face the growing skepticism in the pediatrician's eyes as time passed and no obvious physical cause could be determined.

"Well, we've explored the allergies angle, food issues, checked for possible migraines." He ran down the dozen possibilities we'd considered, any of which would have given us a definitive diagnosis. "You know . . . sometimes emotions can be a factor." His voice held a note of consternation. "I see a bubbly little girl when Grace is here in the office, but . . ."

I didn't have to wait for him to add, "Is it possible she's responding to stress?" My pulse shot up and a familiar voice jumped into the conversation, as harsh as always. *Of course she's stressed! How could she not be? She picks up on everything you feel, Terry!* That voice, which had berated me since childhood, continued to list all the reasons why my nearly five-year-old daughter was suffering. But one charge from the voice hit me hardest: *You pushed her into kindergarten this fall knowing she would always be the youngest kid in the class. By nearly a year! You did to her just what Mom did with you. Push, push, push. No wonder the kid's a wreck.*

I'd looked over at the pediatrician, overwhelmed by guilt, feeling defensive. Wanting to justify my decision by explaining that Grace had been tested and placed early into kindergarten by the school district—and not at my insistence. Wanting him to understand that I'd pursued the option only because there were so many neighborhood girls starting school that year: I'd decided that my daughter, as an only child, needed to build on those friendships. Fostering her social skills had seemed important.

But I said none of these things, and only took a deep breath. "I know we shouldn't rule anything out." I projected calm into my voice, but I certainly didn't feel calm. "On the other hand, what I see at home is the kid you see here in your office. A highly verbal, tell-you-what-she-thinks-and-feels little girl. What I see—except when these episodes hit—is a healthy, happy camper."

And so, what he did next startled me. I sat up in my chair.

He pulled out his prescription pad. "The next time she has an episode, I don't want you to wait to see me. I want you to call and let me know what's going on. Then you run her over to the emergency room with this order, and we'll have them work her up." He handed me the slip of paper on which he'd scrawled "abdominal ultrasound." "Let's do this, and we'll go from there."

I walked out of his office holding Grace's hand and fighting back tears as all the frustration and anger of the past year surfaced. Finally, something that spelled "action." This, after all the appointments with various physicians and even a bogus nontraditional healer. This, after all the anxious hours huddled with my sick little girl. As we got into the car, I strapped Grace into her seat and tried to sound lighthearted.

"You were such a good girl at the doctor's," I said, with a smile. I kissed her cheek. "How about if we stop at Mimi's on the way home?"

Mimi. The moniker Mom had chosen when her first grandchild was born thirty years before. The name all her grandchildren used.

"She'll probably have a 'little something' for me, I think," Grace said eagerly, giving me a kiss back. And she would be right about that hunch, I knew. Mom liked to pass out trinkets from the dollar store.

"She's a little Shirley Temple," she often said. And that was a high form of flattery: my mother remained as starstruck over movie idols as she'd been when I was a child.

Arriving at my parents, I ushered Grace into the house and smelled onions roasting in a pan.

"Please don't tell me you're frying liver to go with those onions, Mom," I groaned. I hugged her and then stepped back. Was my mind tricking me or was she losing muscle? She looked more bony and frail.

After I settled Grace in, Mom and I sat at the dining room table and I told her about the pediatrician's plan.

"You spend more time with Grace than anybody else except me." I clasped and unclasped my hands.

"She's fine here, Terry. I can watch her as much as you want. Or need."

"No, Mom, that's not what I mean. The doctor asked me if I thought she could be stressed." My voice began to break. "Do *you* think she's a nervous kid? Stressed out?"

Even after all this time, I'd still said nothing to Mom about the trouble between John and me. I'd said nothing about the two years we'd spent so far in our useless marriage counseling. So conditioned to keeping secrets—in spite of my vow before Grace was born that I would no longer do this—I found myself unable to bring any of it up. And yet, here I was, asking my mother's opinion, the same mother who, before Grace's birth, I'd never have sought out for support— much less counsel.

"Terry! She's got the life of Riley." She brushed her hand, large knuckled from years of manual work, over the table's lace cloth and smiled. "You take such good care of her. I've never seen her act any way but happy."

"I'm so tired." I closed my eyes and then rubbed them hard with my palms. "Just tell me she's going to be okay."

"I went from doctor to doctor with Tommy when he was little, and all they wanted to do was put him on drugs because he was nervous."

"You just said you didn't think she was nervous!" I fought tears.

"Look, she's nothing like your brother was." She sounded impatient now. "What I'm saying is just that these goddamned doctors don't know what they're doing a hell of a lot of the time."

I stood up and went to the door to check on Grace, who was playing with the stuffed animals that she'd lined up against a wall. I looked back at Mom.

"When I gave Tommy those rotten pills, he started hallucinating. Damn near put him out of his mind." She shook her head as if trying to banish the memory. "Terry, if you let yourself worry about everything they tell you, you'll just make yourself sick."

We sat without saying anything for what seemed a long time. Mom waiting, me trying to regroup. The only sound was Grace, instructing Mouse and Pat the Bunny to quiet down, that it was time for their naps.

Then, finally, hands resting on the table, Mom spoke in a much more serious tone. "I've prayed the rosary for her, you know. I pray every night that she'll be protected." She leaned closer. Lowered her voice. "And you know, Terry, no matter what anybody says, prayers *are* protection." Slowly, she unlocked her fingers and placed one hand over her heart. "That's the God's truth, and it's what I believe."

Driving home at the end of that afternoon—with the object of my mother's prayers nodding off against her seat belt—my tears began at last. Soon, I was sobbing, though I tried to repress my crying because I didn't want to upset Grace. I failed and released a year's worth of worry, despite my continuing fear that something terrible was happening to my daughter. Could it cost her her life? Unlike Mom, I felt helpless to protect her. And bereft, too, because I so wanted my mother to protect *me* from whatever was going on.

I pulled on to a side street, shifted the engine to neutral and just sat there, occasionally wiping my nose with the back of my sleeve. After a while, spent, I forced myself to take several deep breaths. My tears dried up. I tried to settle my thoughts and they circled back to Mom's words: *Prayers are protection.* The phrase played over and over in my mind until I heard it as a steady chant. Perhaps she was trying, once again, to instill in me her beliefs about the purpose of prayer. As I gathered myself toward calm, I heard her voice—the voice of the rogue baptizer: "I did it to make sure she was protected." The voice of the prayer broker: "I pray every night that she'll be protected." How far apart were we, really? Mom was certainly a fervent defender of the faith, but now I saw her in a new way. As a devout mother who—though compromised in her ability to provide security in the expectable ways—nonetheless tried to offer it in the only way she knew how, through spiritual intercession.

I peered at my sleeping daughter in the rear-view mirror. *Don't worry, baby girl. Your Grandma's got you covered.* And knew, to the extent that it could be, I'd told her the truth.

❧

A month later, on a late December afternoon in 1994, I stood bent over the bathroom sink, squeezing the contents of a bottle of Miss Clairol onto the top of my head. A do-it-yourselfer since my late twenties when I'd opted for a more dramatic, less mousy shade of brown, I'd just massaged the last glop of hair dye into my scalp when I felt a tug at my jeans.

"Mommy." I looked down to see my five-year-old girl, her eyes filled with tears. "The medicine isn't working."

"Oh, baby girl, let's go over here." I coaxed her toward the toilet and a moment later saw the tiny undigested letters of alphabet soup floating lazily in regurgitated broth.

The nightmare had begun once again.

As we turned to go out to the family room, I bumped into John, bundled in his winter coat and ready to make a grocery run. He grasped the situation after taking one look at Grace's pale face as I steered her to the couch. He kissed the top of her head, while I ticked off my plan: get her settled, notify the doctor, and wash the dye out of my hair while I waited for him to respond.

"Don't bother with buying a lot of stuff. Ginger ale and crackers," I said. "And maybe just enough for a meal or two."

Twenty-five minutes later, as I held a cool cloth against my daughter's forehead, the phone finally rang. The doctor. "Right, right." I replied and then repeated his directive. "The emergency room. And you'll call me as soon as they've done the ultrasound."

A surge of adrenaline raced through my body. Hearing myself say "emergency room," even though we'd discussed this step previously, made the crisis all the more real. "Emergency" meant that now I had to move fast. Tucking my still wet hair inside a hat, I sat down on the couch next to Grace, drawing her in close.

"The doctor wants us to have his friend put special cream on your tummy to figure out why you keep getting sick," I told her in a gentle voice. "Do you think it will tickle?"

She gave me a tired smile. Maybe, after all she'd been through, she didn't care anymore.

Trying to appear calm as I slid her rubber boots onto her feet, I tucked her arms into her parka and pulled on my own. "We'll stop real quick at the Jewel," I told her, "and pick up Daddy." Without waiting for the engine to warm up, I headed out of the driveway and down the three blocks to the big parking lot, then past rows of cars until I spotted the Toyota. Why had he parked so far from the Jewel? I wondered. I slid the car into a space next to his. It occurred to me then: he had forgotten something and decided to pick it up here—at Walgreens—where it might be quicker.

"Mommy will be back in a jiff," I reassured Grace as I got out. Locking her in, I double checked each handle to be sure the doors were secure.

Inside, I sped down the center aisle, my eyes shifting left and then right as I jogged past aisle after aisle of merchandise. *There!*

John was scanning the shelves along a rear wall and then stretching up high with one arm. He gripped something tightly, as if he were holding a trophy, then pivoted in my direction. I started to call his name, but the word caught in my throat when, like a thief trying to hide what he'd pilfered, he shifted his arm until a fifth of scotch disappeared behind his back.

Dumbfounded and speechless, I just looked at him. Couldn't think of a word to say.

He blinked. Dropped his head as if he'd been caught in a police searchlight. No explanation. But then, what explanation could possibly make sense?

"*Really?*" I hissed. "*Now?*" I held up both hands as if I were warding him off, an unnecessary gesture, since he hadn't moved. "Now— when Grace . . ."

"I know. I shouldn't have come here."

"I'm taking our daughter to the hospital." I began to feel the magnitude of his betrayal and I froze in in my voice now. "And don't bother coming with us." As much as I wanted to punish my husband, the prospect of sitting in a hospital emergency room with a drunken spouse was simply more than I could tolerate. "Wait at the house. I'll call you when I have some news."

My body shook all the way to the hospital. While waiting for Grace to be admitted to the ER, I dialed the first call I would make that evening from the pay phone. I sketched out the events of the day for my mother, omitting any mention of John.

"Oh, Terry, you must be a wreck. How are you and Grace holding up?" The worry in her voice echoed down the line. "Is John there with you?"

Part of me wished I could tell my mother that I was *not* holding up—that my husband was an alcoholic and had slipped back into the booze. Somehow I couldn't. Couldn't take the risk of being uncertain as to how Mom would respond. Memories of her addicted brother might get in her way. A decade ago, Uncle Buddy had been found dead in the stall of the men's room in a neighborhood tavern. While Mom had been afraid of him most of her life, after he died he became, in her eyes, a tragic figure. The misunderstood underdog who'd been discarded by his family. I couldn't take the chance that she might waffle in her support for my circumstances—and see John in a sympathetic light—when I needed her so badly. I told myself that the timing was "off" for spilling a twenty-year-old secret about his alcoholism.

"We're OK," I lied. "He went to the store to pick up groceries for when I get Grace home. I'll just call him as soon as I know anything."

"You should have someone there with you." She paused, as if mulling over an idea. "Do you need me to come?"

My mother's offer shocked me. Was this the woman who had raised me? The mother who, when our lives got tough, ran as far and as fast as she could? Though touched, I declined. Outside, it was cold and dark and the last thing I needed was for my seventy-seven-year-old mother to slip on the ice. In addition to which, I wanted no distractions while taking care of Grace.

Promising to keep Mom apprised of our girl's progress, I hung up, but imagined her, still sitting in her kitchen chair, a hand resting in her lap as she murmured "In the name of the Father," and touched her forehead with her fingertips. Then, "the Son," as they brushed the space over her heart, and finally, "the Holy Spirit," as she tapped each shoulder and bowed her head, ready to get down to the serious business of negotiating prayer.

The hours crawled by as machines beeped and the patients in nearby beds groaned in pain. Between Grace's bouts of vomiting, I talked to her in a low voice and stroked her hair. Told her silly jokes and tales of adventurous girls. All the while, I listened for a voice— not that of the doctor, but of John—fearful that he still might come stumbling into the room where our little one lay, her face so wan on the pillow.

And of course my mind was overflowing with other "what ifs" as well. *What if they find something? What if they don't? Which is worse?*

Finally, sometime later in the night, after the ultrasound was finished but before the IVs for dehydration and nausea had been disconnected, I was summoned to the nurse's station. The pediatrician was waiting on the phone.

"Well, we do have some results." He sounded almost excited. "The radiologist could see that one of Grace's kidneys isn't working."

"Her kidneys?" Fear spread like fire ants under my skin. "How can that be?"

"No, no—just the left kidney." Sensing my alarm and confusion, he slowed down his words. "The right one looks okay." I braced my back against the counter and tried to absorb what he was telling me, grateful that I was not getting this news from a stranger who knew neither of us. "I have to say, I'm really surprised," he continued, sounding almost apologetic as he gave me the name of a specialist he'd like us to consult.

I could hold onto little of what he had said: "congenital," "atrophy," "ischemia" and "nephrologist" were the only words—the scary words—that stuck in my mind, though I didn't really understand them. Nevertheless, the gratitude that he had listened to me that day in his office rang loud and clear. He had given me what I'd sought for so long and what I'd needed for both my daughter and me: to be heard.

With a sheaf of papers and a medicated child in tow, I settled Grace on a waiting room bench and placed the follow-up call to Mom, gave her the news.

"Oh, Terry, the poor little thing." In the background, I heard my father's hacking cough. "Are they keeping her there? Do you think you should get another opinion?"

"I can't think, Mom. I'm taking her home. I just want to get in to see the specialist as quick as I can."

What I meant, more precisely, was that I couldn't think *straight*. The "what ifs" that had bombarded me earlier were attacking again. The what ifs that I'd forgotten to raise with the pediatrician. What if she gets slammed on the playground? Or hurt in a car accident? What if something happens and the good kidney fails? And this: What if you're wrong and the other kidney really *isn't* okay?

"Would it be easier, Terry, if you came here instead of going home?" Mom offered. "My house is closer to the hospital than yours."

"I'm just so worried, Mom." My throat tight, I fought back tears. Named the fear that had been hiding just below the surface of my thoughts, ready to be named. "I'm not going to lose her, am I?" I whispered. "Do you promise me that she's not going to die?"

"Oh, no, Terry," she answered, her voice firm. And then, as if she actually did have the power of prediction, she said exactly what I needed to hear. "There's no way she would ever die."

I lingered at the pay phone, the coins for my call to John growing warm in my palm. What would I say to him when he answered—assuming that he would be conscious enough to answer at all? I waited, my mind going over it again and again, but my heart, my whole being, couldn't think of a single solution. I would never forgive him this desertion, or the insult to both our joint parenthood and our marriage. He didn't deserve to know about our daughter. Or about her diagnosis.

I dropped the change into my purse. Picking up my jacket from the bench, I smiled at my daughter. Worn out, she'd drifted off in spite of the din in the waiting room, her body tilted to one side as she sat hugging her candy pink coat like a pillow. For a minute, I sat down next to her and watched her sleep, love washing over me in a strong and warm wave. Mom's words came to me once again. "I don't care what people say. Prayers are protection." I let out the long, deep breath I hadn't even realized I was holding.

Slowly, I pulled my daughter toward me and wrapped my jacket around her like a blanket. Her head nestled into my shoulder. When I stood up to carry her to the hospital exit, her breath puffed like a soft kiss on my neck. Stepping out into the cold, I shivered and pulled her body even tighter, searching for something I couldn't name at first, something that would comfort me. This time, I realized, I had begun to look for just the right prayer. The one that would keep my daughter safe, at last.

Part Three

Homeward Bound

Home is one's birthplace, ratified by memory.

—Henry Anatole Grunwald

CHRISTMAS MORNING, 1996. SO much and so little had changed in the nearly two years since Grace's operation. Now seven years old, she'd experienced no further bouts of cyclical vomiting and was in excellent health. In keeping with what her first full sentence as a toddler portended—"Me do it!"—she remained a strong-willed little girl. Stubborn. The biggest difference now was her wider vocabulary and improved diction when she had a point to be made.

John and I had continued with our couples' therapist for a few months longer after the surgery. We'd talked about his relapse into drinking and his vow that he would do everything possible to avoid "another slip"—but except for his return to abstinence, we came away with no more insight or success than we'd had in the two and a half years spent pretending to work on our marriage. Finally motivated to do what I should have done at the start, I'd decided to end our couple's work and begun seeing a therapist of my own. John showed no reaction—he simply shut down. The couples' therapist offered to work with him in individual therapy, and for a few more months, he did—but the subsequent year and a half of our marriage passed in stagnant silence, while my own therapy made good progress.

What I hadn't expected in this season of the Epiphany was to have an epiphany of my own. I'd grown accustomed to the family routine—sitting in a room across from John, with few, if any words being exchanged between us. This Christmas, John and I were simply making up the holiday as we went along, with no connection at all—just the way we had faked our way through so many others. We diverted all our attention onto our daughter. If I thought about him one little bit, it was only to wonder if he was still drinking. Or, if as he insisted, he'd actually stopped.

But on this day I stepped out of the marital fog in which I'd enveloped myself since Grace's surgery. I'd walked through that fog—saying nothing about the precarious state of my marriage except to my therapist and two close friends—believing that such a thick cloud had its benefits as a protective place where no one else could see me. A place where no one could probe or prod the vulnerable person I was and always had been. On this particular Christmas morning, however, I finally saw that my haze had offered no real protection at all. I needed to open my eyes. To take the lid off the box of my emotions.

I'd picked up several pairs of slacks, two sweaters, and a new winter coat for John from JCPenney's—practical items purchased so that Christmas would look normal to Grace because her father would have something to open. As he always did, John seemed flummoxed by the packages that bore his name. I looked down at a wrapped gift that lay at my feet, and wished, so very hard, that we could skip this part of the charade.

"Open it, Mama! Open it!" Grace prodded.

And so I placed my mug on the coffee table and picked it up.

Inside was a cheaply made flannel nightgown, the price tag still dangling from one sleeve. A ten-dollar purchase from a cheesy, local discount store. I was stunned. John had never been generous with gifts, but how well he knew my aversion to wearing inferior quality items that reminded me of being poor as a child. He'd heard all about the incident with the Bishop's Relief Fund and the way Sister had instructed me to paw through other parishioners' discards. My loathing of bargain basement and secondhand stores was hardly a secret. Walking through such places, I responded as if a heavy veil were being sewn around my body. Short of breath, I'd race to the exit and push hard against the revolving door.

Gathering up the box and the wrapping, I tried to smile at Grace as I crushed the paper into a tight ball. Then, I looked over at John and stared at him, emptiness replacing my shock. I was unable to come up with even one single word. All that I saw staring back was a blank gaze that mirrored my own. Whatever had once been between us had finally evaporated. I knew then that the time had arrived. That I could no longer live this way. Telling myself that how we were existing was no way to raise a child, I decided I was ready to file for divorce.

One week later, I told John of my intention to consult an attorney. We sat together for a long time, but didn't speak much. After I left the room and its silence, I drew a hot bath and sat there until the water grew cold, sobbing. Pouring out all the grief I had for the death of my marriage. In the weeks and months to come, as I began to create a new life for myself, I wrestled with fear and anxiety, but that day in the bathtub would be the first and last time I would cry by myself for all I had lost. After that, relief always trumped sadness.

The day after I declared the marriage officially finished, I drove to my parents' house to break the news. I gripped the steering wheel, worried about the reaction I might now face. At one point, as I sat waiting at a traffic light with the sun glaring off the windshield, my anxiety mushroomed and I hesitated. Would I be able to handle Mom if she got all worked up? Or if she took John's side? I dreaded the possibility that my news might be met with anger and judgment. When I pulled up at the house, I tried to compose myself. *They're going to be shocked, you know. You never once said anything about all that was wrong. If they get angry it'll be your own fault.*

Beyond that: no one in our family, or even extended family, had ever divorced. It just wasn't done, no matter how unhappy the marriage, and so my imagination ran untamed: "It goes against the sacraments!" Mom would probably exclaim, throwing her hands up in the air. But surely they had suspected that my marriage was not good. Hadn't they wondered why I never talked about John? Hadn't they been curious about why I treated him like the Invisible Man at family gatherings? And now, wouldn't they feel shut out by my failure to have taken them into my confidence? I'd dipped under the radar on this one, the same way I had so many other times in my life. My temples throbbed as I got out of the car.

Minutes later, after some perfunctory hellos, I moved to the living room and sat stiffly on the floral-patterned couch.

"Can you two come in here?" I asked. They looked puzzled—the kitchen, after all, was the usual place where conversations occurred—but somehow, like delivering news about a death and then discussing funeral plans, the formal setting of the living room seemed a more suitable location.

"I have to tell you something," I said when they'd settled into their chairs, my voice dropping to a near whisper. As my story gradually unfolded, I started to cry again. Sobbing in public for the first and final time, I realized that this conversation was not unfolding the way I'd anticipated. It seemed I had no control after all, as I detailed all the years of unhappiness and stress. I recounted John's long history of alcoholism, and my mistrust of anything and everything he said or did. "It's been a living hell." I took a deep breath and swiped my palms across my cheeks. "I have to get out. I have the name of an attorney and I'm getting a divorce."

I waited, my head pounding from all the tears, but the room remained quiet. I looked at Dad, then at Mom—confused until I saw the expressions on their faces.

"Terry, I feel so bad for you," Mom finally said. "This is such a damn shame." Her fingers, stiff with arthritis, touched the gold crucifix on her neck. "John's so quiet, I never would have imagined that he'd give you such grief! My God, how will you be able to manage?" She pulled the cross on her necklace back and forth along its chain. "That big house? All the bills? I don't know. I worry you could end up on the street."

This was the fear that my mother had harbored for herself her entire life. The terror of being homeless. She looked at me wide eyed.

"It's not right, Terry." Dad shifted his weight slowly. "What the hell is wrong with him?" He drew his mouth tight. "You don't drink like a son of a bitch when you've got a wife and a kid."

I wiped my eyes again and studied them both. It was my turn to be shocked. Both Mom and Dad were supporting me. Offering me their sympathy. I sat without speaking, listening to my parents try to comfort me. Together. Somehow they had become parents who were expressing their indignation and sorrow for me, parents speaking in one voice.

I couldn't remember a single other time they'd responded this way.

But somehow, in that moment, it didn't matter. It seemed that right now, right here—when they'd said all the right things—might just be enough.

"Let me bring you a nice cup of tea, Terry." Mom stood, steadied herself, and moved slowly toward the kitchen.

"Not necessary, Mom."

She just raised her arm.

"Watch your step, there. It's easy to fall." Without even realizing it, I had slipped into the role of the worried mother, just as I did with Grace some of the time. As my daughter had grown older, so too had my mother. She needed me in new ways and that need forged a different sort of bond between us. Even in this time of my own trouble, I was concerned for her. And that felt good.

I turned to my father, and saw the worry on his face.

"Believe me, Dad, I feel just like you do. Terrified." But I don't want this kind of life for her. It's never going to change. It will only get worse." After all, wasn't this the same card I had used on myself: the reason, ostensibly, that I was getting divorced?

"You've gotta find a lawyer who's going to look out for you, Terry. Someone who will get John's paycheck yanked if he doesn't pay." He leaned forward and winced, the sign that an old leg injury was causing him pain. "After all, you're entitled to support. You've got Grace to take care of."

"Why don't you take a rest in my bed, Terry," Mom coaxed, coming back into the room with the saucer wobbling in her hand. "You've got so much on your plate. Take a nap if you can."

I said yes to her offer, surely surprising her by taking her advice. "But I want you to make a list. I can run some errands for you afterward. You look beat, too."

Minutes later, I crawled into her bed, and pulled the double set of blankets up to my chin. Breathed in the scent of extra-strength Bengay. I imagined Mom sitting on the edge of the bed each night, squeezing the ointment onto her wrinkled, papery skin. It was that image and this scent that I last remembered before drifting into a sleep that was deep and anxiety free.

One unseasonably warm day in early March, two months after my announcement to my parents, John and I settled into what had become our "faceoff" chairs in the family room. Grace was today's topic. She was heading toward completion of second grade and I had let her know that her dad and I were having problems—but she had yet to be told about the divorce. Surely after two months of no meals together as a family, and silence when her father and I passed one another from room to room, she had figured out that something was wrong—her sensitivity to the adult world once again clueing her in.

"I don't see why we have to do it now," John repeated. The same words he'd used at least a dozen times before. "Isn't it enough that you're pushing me to move out?" Irritated, he began shuffling the neatly organized tabbed folders that lay in his lap, folders which held his copy of the draft of the divorce papers he'd been served the month before. "Isn't it enough that I have no money and I have to find a place to live?"

"We agreed you'd move out after she's out of school for summer. That's only two and a half months away."

"That's your timeline, Terry. Not mine."

"I want to be able to talk with Grace's teacher after we tell her!" I snapped. "We need *time* before the end of the school year to get her feedback. *Time,* so she can give Grace support." A memory of my first parent–teacher conference sprung up in my mind and I heard her kindergarten teacher's voice: "I was a little concerned at the beginning of the year," she'd said. "At circle time, Grace would crawl under my desk and just sit there, cross-legged, watching the group." I'd been alarmed, wondering how, after two years in preschool, my daughter had regressed into a withdrawn child. But the teacher had quickly reassured me that the difficulty had passed. "She's quite the happy dreamer, really," the woman laughed. "Academically, she's ahead of the curve. I think she just needed time to acclimate to so much change."

The plan I'd outlined for telling Grace was the best route to take for her sake, I believed, but I also couldn't stand the waiting game anymore. The game of pretend. Of silence and isolation. Of something approaching hate. But like everything else we tried to discuss, we could come to no agreement about when to talk with the school, or when to sit down with Grace.

"And timeline! You have no timeline at all!" I said, throwing up my hands. "You haven't even started to look for an attorney, for God's sake! You won't provide me with numbers so that I know where I stand financially!" Then, in a tone meant to sound threatening, I added: "You think you can keep your head in the sand, but that's not going to work. At all."

"You always do what you want, anyway, Terry," John shot back. "I'm sick of fighting with you." He waved me off. "Go ahead and tell Grace. You're the one who wants this divorce anyway. So you can be the one who upsets her life more than it is already."

"Fine! You don't want to be a part of this. I can help her better than you anyway." John's words were what I'd expected—and unconsciously wanted—to hear. I marched out of the room, angry, but victorious, too.

❧

Several days later, I sat with Grace in the parking lot of our neighborhood McDonalds. Positioned sideways behind the wheel, I looked over at her, felt sad for her. I didn't know how she would adapt to the new home situation I would soon be creating. Still, another part of me also felt devious, and therefore uncomfortable: I knew that I'd chosen this particular time to tell her because I wanted to move the divorce along. We sat there for a while as I wrestled with my conscience. One minute I was sure I was doing the right thing. And the next, I felt like the witch in Hansel and Gretel. As if I'd substituted Chicken McNuggets for breadcrumbs and was enticing her into my cottage where only bad news was to be discovered.

"So, are you excited about Family Violin Camp this summer?" I asked, as we sipped our milkshakes.

"Yes, yes, yes!" Grace said, a wide smile on her face. "Annie's going too, isn't she?"

"I don't know yet, honey. Her mom is still trying to decide."

Grace took a long draw on her shake, and laughed as she patted her belly.

"I want to tell you about something, but I need to ask you something first." Anxiety pressed against my chest. *No, no! Why don't you just stop?* "Have you ever wondered why Dad didn't come with us last summer? Or why we never do things together?"

"No," she replied, elongating the sound of the *o*. The way she said it made it clear that I'd asked a very dumb question that she had no intention of answering.

"Hmmm." I could feel myself trying too hard now. Sounding like a therapist, but unable to stop. "Well, sometimes kids think it's weird if their family doesn't do things the way other families do."

Silence.

"And I think that a lot of times, they're right. It is kind of weird." I tried to keep my voice calm and relaxed. "And that can be sad."

"I don't think it's sad," she said evenly. "Why is that sad?" She lowered her chin and took another slurp of her drink.

And here the memory train stops. For a long time after that day,

I tried to invent what I'd said to my daughter to ease my guilt. Tried to convince myself that I *had* found all the "right" things with which to reassure her, like "Daddy and I tried our hardest." Or "We gave it our best." And, "Some things will change but other things won't. Like how much you're loved." In my inventions, I substituted fantasy for fact when "recalling" how I'd helped Grace understand the concept of divorce: "Remember when you and Julia used to be best friends, Grace? But then you were getting into too many fights and decided that it just wasn't going to work to play together anymore?"

In this story of my imagination, Grace always smiled at me. Nodded her head to demonstrate that she "got it."

But nothing that neat or tidy happened that day in the car. "Oh, Mommy, no," she whimpered, a plaintive, wounded cry impossible to forget.

Sadness and guilt swept over me as I fumbled with my seatbelt— and then hers—to move closer and gather her in. Her limbs went limp, as if my words had sucked all the air from her body. Why was I doing this to her? Putting her through so much stress and pain? A chorus of self-recrimination grew loud in my mind: *What kind of mother snatches away her child's innocence and trust? Sacrifices her child's needs to satisfy her own?*

Not yet able to grasp the irony of these thoughts—that I was judging myself as harshly as I had once judged my mother—I did the only thing I knew how to do just then. I held my daughter closer and murmured "I'm sorry," again and again. And then I waited. Waited until I could muster the words that I *wanted* to be true.

"You won't always feel this sad, sweetheart," I promised. "We'll all be okay."

She lifted her head and pulled herself away. Then, cast her eyes downward. Toward the milkshake still in her hands.

"Please stop talking, Mommy," she said, in a voice that was suddenly as resolute as it was forlorn. "I want to go home."

∾

Fortunately, by the spring of the following year—nine months after John moved out of the house—Grace seemed to be adjusting to the new life that was still unfolding for us. Just as she had after her kidney surgery, she was showing herself to be a girl with plenty of sparkle and pluck. As her annual violin concert approached that year, the fourth such event in her eight-year-old world, she was excited. Eager to be one of a hundred other young performers from the area schools who were set to demonstrate how much progress they'd made since last year.

The morning of the concert, I pulled from Grace's closet the white blouse, ironed crisply, and her floor-length navy skirt. This was the dressy attire that all the little girls wore. As I spread the fancy outfit across her bed, the memory of my Communion Day came rushing back. I was lingering, fingering the material—remembering how my mother had helped me into my beautiful dress with such gentleness—when Grace appeared in the doorway.

"Will Mimi be coming to hear me play today?" she asked, hope in her voice. That Grace had inquired about Mom—testimony to the deepening of their relationship—filled me with pleasure.

"You know how it is with Mimi," I responded. "She loves to see you perform, but she never knows until the last minute if she'll be able to come."

I phoned Mom at least once every day—short interactions intended to reassure her that I was keeping watch. She still loved having someplace to go. It seemed that, as it had with Grandma Healy, almost any outing would suffice. But it was also true that she enjoyed seeing her Grace perform. Now, she no longer referred to her granddaughter as a "little Shirley Temple," but instead said, "I love how she plays that violin. She's got a real talent there, Terry." Which made it easy for me to want to include her every time Grace performed in front of an audience. Harder to predict, however, was the activity level her eighty-year-old brittle bones could tolerate, especially when she had to navigate through crowds. Or to predict what sort of attitude she'd have on any given day. Now riddled with near constant pain and still adamant in her assessment that life had cheated her, Mom was as susceptible to the same barometric drops in her mood as she had been during my childhood, fueled as ever by the struggles that had plagued her all her life: her fear of being abandoned and her fear of loss of control over her world. But now, rather than seeing her as a mother afflicted by demons, I saw her simply as *emotionally* afflicted. Much the same way that she was afflicted by *bodily* pain.

"And what about Dad?" Grace had a puzzled look on her face. "Will he be there?"

"What's with that father of yours? Doesn't he ever tell you his plans?" I snapped, too late to catch myself. Being angry and perturbed with John in front of her had become a reflex that I regretted but still seemed unable to rein in. And the divorce was nowhere near final. My interactions with her father had devolved into quibbles over nickels and dimes. "I'm sure he'll be there," I said, trying, not very convincingly, to sound less annoyed.

A short while later, I put in the call to Mom.

"I hate to miss hearing Grace play, Terry. But I had a hell of a time falling asleep last night. One damn leg cramp after another. And this morning, I woke up even before the birds."

Undeterred, given that this sort of dialogue now characterized the design of all of our plans, I suggested something else—something that would tell me just how much to push.

"Why don't you see if you can get dressed, Mom, and then try to take a little nap on the couch." I paused, allowing her time to protest.

"I don't know, Terry. I never know how my stomach will be."

This was a good sign in the transaction. She needed me to understand that nothing was easy, but that she hadn't given me a final no.

"How about if I call you when we're leaving? I'll pick you up at 12:30. If you change your mind, you can let me know when I phone."

At 12:35, I held the pretty lavender raincoat I'd bought her the year before and watched her slowly and carefully guide her arms into its sleeves, as if even she knew how fragile she'd become. The purchase had been a gift—but also was a move to save face. I would encourage her to put it on if I arrived and discovered that she was wearing one of her old, stained blouses over an even older pair of pilled, polyester slacks. On this day, however, Mom—like Grandma Healy when she'd been invited out for an afternoon—had upgraded. She was wearing the lightweight pantsuit that she reserved for visits to the doctor.

We arrived extra early at the high school auditorium—as we did each year—to avoid the rush and to nab seats that provided the best view of the stage. Once situated, Mom scanned the aisles, and then the doors, her neck strained like a tortoise's as she peered around the hall. Reverting quickly to her usual impatience, she soon began fidgeting, not unlike the little kids around us who had been shepherded into their seats. Childlike, she sat perched at the edge of her chair, her hands clutching the seatback in front of her. Looking from left to right, and then right to left.

"Relax, why don't you?" I suggested after a minute. "There's still twenty minutes before the concert begins."

She sunk into her seat with a sigh. "You know, our Mary played the violin," she said. As if this were news. As if I hadn't heard the stories about Aunt Mary—Mom's long-dead, oldest sister—and her love for the violin at least a thousand times.

I recognized my cue. "Now *there's* somebody who had an awful life."

"Mary played like a dream. She knew all the songs by heart." Mom looked up toward the ceiling as if trying to catch a memory. Then, waving her crooked index finger like a baton, she began to hum. "I always liked that one."

"'Humoresque', by Dvorak."

"Oh, I can't remember the names anymore."

"Grace's group will actually be playing that today!" I smiled, but Mom, preoccupied, rolled onward with her memory and didn't acknowledge that she'd heard me.

"Poor Mary. Twenty one. What happened to her was a crime." She paused, fumbling with a roll of Lifesavers she pulled from her purse. "Open these for me, will you, Terry?" she said. I took the candies from her hand. "She had an abscess this big on her back." Her fingers formed a circle the size of a baseball.

"Mary should have never died like that. Alone in a sanitarium." Mom massaged the skin on her neck, loose with age. "Beautiful girl, she was." Then nodded her head slowly. "Had a real talent, for sure."

"How come there aren't more pictures . . ."

Mom interrupted me with a long sigh. An exhale of air that signaled she was done talking about Mary. As if the memories she'd resurrected were now too heavy through which to sift.

"All these people here," she said, after a minute or two. Her tone had shifted: less lament; more of an edge. "I tell you, these kids today. They've got everything under the sun."

Now it was my turn to take a long breath. I knew just where this conversation was going.

"A lot more than you ever had, Mom," I said, patting her knee. I glanced at her out of the corner of my eye and then looked at her directly, convinced that in the span of ten minutes, she'd grown smaller.

"Are you comfortable enough?" I asked. "Why don't I roll up my sweater so that you can use it like a pillow behind your neck?"

She brushed me off. Sitting next to me in the flash of an instant was the petulant little girl my mother became when she needed to trade her sadness for fight. Undisturbed by this—or at least, unlike how I would have been in the past—I didn't worry that Mom would create a scene that I would find too hard to handle. Nonetheless, I hoped I could soothe her sufficiently—distract her enough to keep her in line. I reached into my pocket. "Here, Mom. Have some Peppermint Patty instead."

"Do you hear that one behind me?" she announced, leaning toward me as she took the chocolate. Her voice loud enough for "that one" to hear. "What a joke."

"Mom, stop."

"But, Terry. It's so ridiculous. All the 'my Johnny this, my Johnny that.'"

"Are you going to make me wish I had tape to put over your mouth?" I said with a laugh.

Here we were just like in the days of old. Mom ready with the wind-up pitch before she whipped her opinion across home plate. Ready with the insult she threw when her irritation with mothers who bragged on their children got loose.

"I'm sorry, Terry," she insisted. "But—"

"Don't," I said, embarrassed now.

"I have to say it."

"No, you do not."

God, Almighty. Don't let whoever she's talking about be someone you know.

"But it's true! The way she's going on, you'd think her kid could shit gold."

Just then, the house lights went down, the curtain went up, and my relief was palpable. Now excitement rose within me. From the wings of the stage, the youngest, most inexperienced violinists began to enter. Kindergarten-age boys wearing shirts and ties and tiny girls in flowing skirts, their matching sashes cinched at the waist. Each child held a small polished violin under his or her arm. They marched like tin soldiers, all quite serious as they found their marker on the stage floor. Behind them, the second group assembled, and then the third, until the most experienced players—usually the fourteen-year-olds—stood behind all the others.

"There, Mom. On the left midway toward the back." I whispered. "Do you see her?"

"Which one, Terry? Which one is she?" Mom asked, her eyes squinted as they explored the stage. "Oh, I see her! With the white bow in her hair!"

I smiled. Then placed my hand on Mom's hand and got a catch in my throat. Here was my mother happily exclaiming that she could see her granddaughter—could pick her out in a sea of other children—even though her vision was poor. The same mother who had always seemed to me like someone who'd been blinded by our births. Blinded in her ability to recognize me as a person in my own right, a woman separate from her.

And now here was Grace. I sat at the edge of my seat, straining to get a good look at my daughter. She stood tall on a riser that made her more visible. How confident she looked with her half-sized instrument tucked under her chin, her curved bow held above the violin's strings with care. I smiled. My girl was ready to play. And in that moment, I felt as much pride as I would have had she been center stage at Carnegie Hall. My daughter was cherished and therefore privileged. Safe. A child recognized for who she was and who she had yet to become.

I sat back in my seat as quiet settled over the audience. Could Mom really see Grace? I wondered. *Why are you always looking for more? Isn't it enough that she wants to be able to see her? That she's forged a bond with her granddaughter? A bond that you've gotten the benefits from, too—even though it's a bond that, during your childhood, the two of you never shared?*

As the music began, I drifted back and reflected on the last several years of my life—and the bond Mom and I *had* developed, one based largely on her increasing dependency and her heightened anxiety, as her world continued to shrink. She had a greater capacity for gratitude now. Penned in her spidery cursive, notes would arrive after those times I'd visited. "Terry," she'd write, "I don't like you spending your hard-earned money on me. Put some gas in the tank. Love Mom." And, invariably, there'd be an underlined "PS" at the bottom: "Be sure you cash this check or I'll be mad!" I always took each five- or ten-dollar check and stored it in the drawer in which I kept my small treasures.

As I sat next to Mom that day at Grace's concert, an important piece of the puzzle that had always been our relationship snapped into place: what mattered the most to me was to be able to see both my daughter and my mother with clarity. That I be able to mother them both in ways appropriate to their different needs and their different life stages. I had no idea what the future would bring—how much longer Mom would live, what the roller coaster of adolescence would mean for Grace. I could not have imagined that a new man would come into my life. What mattered most—at least for now—was the sense that I was on the right course. That I knew in which direction to go. Finally, I was bringing us all home.

Tone Deaf

And so it became a household of silence. As if in the aftermath of a violent detonation.

—Joyce Carol Oates,
We Were the Mulvaneys

"TERRY! GOOD TO MEET you. I want to hear all about your divorce!"

It was a joke delivered with the enthusiasm of a teenage boy's cannon ball from a high dive. And a loud one. From the surprised looks on the faces of the restaurant's other patrons, my blind date had succeeded in making a splash. I blinked as this taller, somewhat corporately dressed version of the rocker Phil Collins rounded the table and held out my chair.

Despite the inauspicious beginning of the first date since my divorce—and my first blind date ever—the dinner with *this* Phil did not turn out to be disastrous. We laughed. Traded quips. Riffed on a host of topics. I left the restaurant afterward in good spirits, pleased that our lighthearted conversation had touched all the right notes.

Fifty-two years old to my forty-nine, Phil was a successful businessman who had divorced the prior year after twenty-years of marriage. He had three daughters—a twelve-year-old, like Grace, who lived full-time with her mother, and two older girls who were off on their own.

"You're kind of a newbie to the divorce world," I commented that first evening. And while I hadn't asked, I did wonder how well he and his children were adjusting.

"Newbie shnewbie. I like to think I'm a fast learner," he shot back with a wink.

"Right." I said. And then we both laughed.

Only much later would I wish I'd asked more.

Six months into our relationship, we began calling it love. Phil was a generous and kind man, and we were well suited, despite our quite different personalities. As much of an extrovert as I was an introvert, like me he enjoyed his own company and wasn't afraid of being alone. A long-distance motorcyclist for decades, Phil had described doing his "best thinking about life" while riding solo across Canada, or up through Alaska toward the Arctic Circle.

Also like me, he nurtured his friendships, but whereas my circle was small, he gravitated toward others more easily. And because he traveled frequently on international business, he had friends around the globe. We differed in how we greeted the world: more often than not, I met it with trepidation, while Phil epitomized optimism—a quality I admired. He was someone who seemed to have been born with a happy gene. "Do you always wake up smiling?" I sometimes teased.

Perhaps what had attracted me most, however, was his devotion to his children. A hands-on kind of dad, Phil addressed his girls as "sweetheart," or "honey-girl" or "big one," and his eyes shone when he talked about them. His daughters knew they could count on him, and perhaps that helped them to respond pleasantly to Grace and me. And Phil was good to Grace, too. But just as I kept a respectful boundary with his kids, he didn't push himself into her life.

Occasionally during that first year, Grace and Sarah, Phil's youngest, would join us for a dinner out, or a movie on TV—usually at his home. Though both Grace and Sarah were young adolescents, they were more dissimilar than alike. Physically, Grace was tall and slender, artsy, with long, brown wavy hair; Sarah was petite, preppy, a blue-eyed blond. My girl could be flippant; Sarah was staid. Days apart in age, they were in the same grade and did well at their respective schools. Both were quick-witted. Fun to be around.

"Phil's a great guy," Grace would say. "But don't get married until I'm away at college." When she saw our relationship turning more serious, she soon began cautioning me about our home, where she had lived as long as she could remember: "And don't ever sell our house, Mom. I want to keep it forever." I'd dismissed these proscriptions, telling myself that she was simply nervous about how this new change in my life would impact hers. Over time, when she continued the same chant, I reasoned that she was just being an only-child-budding-teen-ager-trying-to-make-the-rules. A kid hoping to wield a power that was not hers to have.

In any case, at that time Phil and I were not considering marriage. Agreeing that we had hold of something special, we had both adopted a "Let's see how this thing unfolds" attitude. And with high school looming for Grace, I knew I needed to stay focused on her. Phil and I could take our relationship slowly. Grace would be fine. After all, hadn't I long ago vowed to be the kind of mother who would know what her child needed as she guided her toward independence? A mother who knew how to balance? Who understood when to grasp tight and when to let go?

Adolescence. Grace started high school in the fall of 2003 the way she'd entered kindergarten: aloof with her peers. A week or two after freshman classes began, I received a personal note from one of her teachers who informed me that Grace had yet to open her mouth in class and had to be coaxed out from sitting behind a divider in the classroom. "We look forward to getting to know her!" the message continued. I responded to the words with the same reflexive cringe that I'd had upon learning that my daughter preferred to mark part of her kindergarten days under the teacher's desk. What, I wondered, was this one *really* saying? Did she think Grace was weird? Incorrigible? Did she wonder about what sort of mother I was?

I didn't press the issue with my daughter. In new settings, I knew she became shy, but Grace also wasn't beyond carrying out small subversive acts that were borne of her stubbornness. "It's okay to be nervous," I'd told her, "but you can't make your own rules. And you can't make yourself invisible." Over the next few weeks I grew relieved: no further updates arrived in the mail and Grace had begun participating in extracurricular activities. I reassured myself that she was just a quirky kid who'd needed time to adjust.

By sophomore year, Grace demonstrated all the attributes I'd hoped she would as a high school student. She was an independent thinker, a good friend to her peers, motivated in her studies and committed to her artistic pursuits. And not only did she have a good ear for music, she could claim equal proficiency for understanding what people were really saying, for picking up the meaning behind words that could be superficial. But on the home front, a new Grace appeared: I now had a just-turned-fifteen-year-old antagonist living under my roof. A daughter who challenged my understanding of her at what seemed like every turn: her belligerence seemed misplaced, given how much I prided myself on my abilities to listen to her, to interpret and respond in ways that enriched conversations. Wishfully, I'd thought we would escape so much of this contentious behavior because I believed I understood her so well.

In my friendships and with Phil, I was a masterful listener. And in my role as a therapist, and as caregiver to my eighty-eight-year-old mother, my brand of "good ear" continued to be an asset. With Mom, my empathy and compassion had become so finely tuned that I rarely felt rattled when she became angry or demanding. I'd accepted her shortcomings as a mother and we'd achieved an intimacy I'd never before thought possible. All those years spent in therapy had helped me to declare a truce with her and to find calm—as did my vocation, which had taught me so much about myself and our relationship. But perhaps becoming a mother had helped the most of all, providing me with a deeper appreciation for how difficult child-raising could be, how overwhelmed Mom must have been.

Despite my nascent strengths in dealing with Mom, however, Grace—still the spirited girl she'd always been—appeared quite pleased to inform me about how tone deaf I actually was. Roxanne, my business partner and friend who had become like a sister to me after my divorce, and who was one of the best child and adolescent therapists with whom I'd ever worked, knew Grace well. "What did you expect?" she'd tell me. "Grace is off-the-charts smart." Then she'd lean back and laugh. "Besides which, she's a teenager, Terry! You should want her to push back in ways that are safe." I knew, of course, that she was correct—but such knowledge didn't make it any easier to emotionally deal with my daughter.

Even with my friend's counsel, I wrestled with my frustration. As she challenged me, Grace focused on my "listening" skills with a gaze like a tractor beam: surely, on some level she sensed my need to be recognized as a different kind of mother than the one I had had as an adolescent. A mother who paid attention. And thus, her dismissal of my abilities to understand her was artful: the just judgment of a canny teenager.

During that year when she'd turned fifteen, I didn't see Grace's ability to tune in to people—especially me—as a gift. I wanted a daughter who did not give me a tough time. Unconsciously, I'd been pulling for a girl who would demonstrate some of the personality traits—the better ones—that I had possessed at her age. A teenager who worked hard; who was generous and kind.

So, when she got sassy or threatened to explode—neither of which she ever did in public—I chose to believe, despite all my experience in working with adolescents, that the problem was not with my ears, but with her mouth. I hated having to parent an insubordinate teenager. Especially one who could be so emotionally intense. I didn't want an unhappy, edgy daughter who might slide off the rails, or one who opposed me at every turn. A daughter whose temper might escalate into rage as had Mom's, or like her father's. Or my own.

On one particular night, in the early months of her sophomore year, I had stopped after a long day's work for groceries. I'd greeted Grace pleasantly enough when I came in the door. But, as I began unloading food from paper bags onto the counter, she just stood there and watched me. With boredom. Or maybe even annoyance. Despite the fact that I was suddenly ticked off that she wasn't offering to help me, I nevertheless wanted to avoid a confrontation—especially considering that this was our first opportunity to check in with each other that day. And so, repressing my irritation, I tried to chat her up instead.

While the conversation began benignly enough, something unnameable suddenly shifted, and whatever we'd been talking about swelled into an angry exchange. Grace said one thing, I said another— and all I heard was her insolent, demanding tone. Back and forth we argued, the routine far too familiar: I took offense at how Grace was talking to me, and she responded by digging in deeper. "There you go again, Mom," she said, her voice heavy with sarcasm. "You never like my tone. With you, everything's a *tone*." We went at each other, over and over again, until—fueled by exhaustion, frustration, and fury with her disrespect—I saw only an irredeemable brat standing on the other side of the room. *What a prima donna,* the voice inside me sneered. *She needs to be brought down to size.*

As if some internal switch had suddenly flipped, I grabbed a card-board box of saltines and a package of cold cuts and whipped both across the kitchen dead at her. I missed and hit the wall, but it took only a second for Grace's shock to bloom into outrage. "What kind of mother are you?" she shrieked. "My God, I was just trying to talk to you!"

As she stormed off to her room and slammed her bedroom door, I stood rooted in place, speechless. I was trying hard to justify my behavior—reassuring myself that I'd never before done anything so out of control—but I couldn't. It had been foolish to lose my temper that way, and I was alarmed by how quickly I had descended into the same kind of behavior, powered by rage that my mother had so often exhibited. The entire exchange made me feel small. Mortified by the way I'd sometimes acted with my younger siblings—being the child instead of the adult—throwing something at my daughter the same way I had once thrown and smashed Robby's model car when he hadn't helped me with the housework. Leftover emotions repeated, and made for embarrassment and shame.

My hands shook as I tried to brush it all aside and attribute it to a long day spent apart. I waited, hoping Grace might reappear so that I could apologize. But I was not yet ready to go to her room in surrender, or to do my part to clean up the mess I'd created—though Grace and I did eventually talk out our emotions very late that same night. I expressed my remorse for my role in the debacle, and then headed off to bed, my spirits in the gutter.

As Grace continued to move through her sophomore year, I also found myself debating, then second-guessing, and then triple-guessing a host of decisions, many of which centered around her. The previous August, with the culmination of dedication to practice and a successful violin audition, she had been invited to participate in the coming summer's five-week international tour with a Michigan-based youth orchestra. This honor was giving me the most trouble of all. For the past six months, we had traveled to Michigan one weekend a month for day-long rehearsals bookended by a five-hour trek to and then from Twin Lake. I sat in the back of a dark, drafty concert hall for hours. So, when she returned home each time beside herself with anxiety and indecision about whether she would participate in the tour, I began to doubt the wisdom of our efforts.

It was not the practical considerations that maddened me, but rather that I was trying to help Grace manage her fear. And not doing a particularly good job at it. Conversations meant to reassure her inevitably ended in silence. She could hold on to her courage for only so long before it evaporated as she tried to make an informed choice

about whether she was ready to be so far away from home, and me—
though naturally this went unsaid—for such a long time.

During the final months of tour preparation, Phil and I began
talking about joining our own lives together permanently, even enter-
taining the possibility of marriage before Grace finished high school.
Excited by taking the first step, a formal engagement before the end
of the calendar year, I was also nervous, remembering Grace's dictates
about waiting to marry until she was in college, and about never sell-
ing the house. Yet, waiting another two and a half years until college
happened began to feel counterintuitive. Didn't she need a real sense
of family before she was launched? Phil agreed with my assessment.
After my daughter left the nest, a new but familiar home would have
been established—even if it wasn't exactly the same house.

Nevertheless, I refrained from telling Grace of our conversations,
reasoning that the summer trip overseas had her in enough of a spin.
Why risk overwhelming her with so much "new" simultaneously,
when big changes could be tackled incrementally? Logically, waiting
to talk with her until after the trip made sense. Just as, *logically*, I knew
that wanting to marry again represented a normal desire and a decision that I had a right to make. But making decisions that were guided
by simple observations of situations and facts—giving myself over to
"common sense"—also offered what I saw as my one hope against the
diatribe that played in my mind, its presence exhausting, its through-
line clear: *You know damn well that Grace won't adapt well to a change
in your tightly knit twosome. You're thinking only of yourself. Who are
you trying to fool?*

Unfortunately, at the same time I was "refraining" from saying
anything to Grace, I was avoiding sharing any of my struggle with
Phil. I wanted to revel in the excitement that circled us, not dampen
it. Nor did I want to spoil Phil's idealized image of me as the wise and
steady mother who had everything under control. Remaining silent,
at least for the time being, seemed the easiest way to achieve what I
wanted most: to shove my worries aside.

Grace and I continued our monthly treks to Michigan that spring,

where an amiable, mature way of handling herself in social situations—including her rehearsals—belied how wired with anxiety she
was beneath her calm facade. Her qualms about the tour persisted and
she was still conflicted when I dropped her at the Michigan departure
site in late June. Only when I explained to her that her reluctance to
get out of the car meant we should return home did she reach for her
violin case and push open the door. I helped her with her luggage and
gave her a quick hug goodbye. Then, primed by adrenaline and jangled nerves, I scrapped my plan to spend the night in a nearby hotel
and drove the long distance home instead.

I didn't consider that perhaps Grace's reluctance and indecision
about this trip was being caused by a more serious issue with anxiety.
Or allow myself to think that perhaps she, with her highly developed
emotional radar, was intuiting that Phil and I were discussing marriage.
Maybe the anxiety was a protest: her way of saying, "Don't do that!" And
perhaps she was worried that if she left home, beyond her reach, I might
make a decision with which she didn't want to live. Or couldn't live. A
peek down into her anxiety might have helped to explain the reasons she
felt so torn about leaving on her trip. But, once again, unfortunately, I
didn't see how these things might be related. I hadn't heard the message
behind the message. I wasn't listening to her very well.

Grace returned from the tour in early August, her mood ebul-
lient. She'd made new friends, had loved traveling from city to city,
living with host families and playing long concerts before appreciative
audiences. Days after her arrival back home, I sat in the park with my
mother and described my relief.

"Thank God it all turned out okay," I said, as I handed Mom a
Chicago-style beef sandwich, her favorite, from a brown paper bag. "I
can't imagine going through anything like that ever again. Trying to
figure out if she should go almost killed me!"

"She's a funny kid," Mom said, her voice raspy. "Most of the time,
Grace's so determined. I've always thought of her as knowing exactly
what she wants. With a mind of her own."

Reflecting on what a cyclone of emotion the year had been, I slipped off my sandals and felt the grass warm against my feet. "I don't know how you did it, Mom. Trying to raise eight kids."

"Oh, Terry." She shook her head as she pulled a bit of gravy-soaked bread from her sandwich. "I remember nights on Campbell when I'd come home from Walgreens with such a backache. And I'd sit on the couch looking at the big heap of shoes piled up in the hallway. All I could think of was how I'd ever be able to keep buying them."

"Did you ever wish you'd had only one kid? Or maybe just two?"

"I wished for a lot of things, Terry," she replied, dabbing her lip with a paper napkin. "But what choice did I have?"

"Daddy was good to you, though, don't you think?" This was a question I'd asked many times before. Always hoping my mother would give a simple "yes." "He stood up to Grandma. Got you out of her house."

"Yeah, and I traded one prison for another," came the familiar reply. "And I'm still in it, taking care of that man."

"C'mon Mom. You're still in your own home—which is what you always wanted. And, God help us all, you're going on ninety and still driving."

"I only go to the store, the library, church. That's my whole life."

"Your own little Bermuda Triangle. You could disappear, you know."

"I've never gotten lost."

"Well, you could end up on somebody's lawn." I stopped. I was about to add "or kill someone," but realized I wanted to avoid a contentious conversation. Not again. Not now. I reached over and touched her arm. "Okay, so what did you wish for?"

"I wished I'd had a man who gave a damn about me," she said, evenly. "Your father never wanted to go anywhere—it was always about the kids. Other women, they had husbands who took them places, had men who wanted to travel." She gazed off into the distance. "He sure sold me a bill of goods."

I looked at my mother and allowed the sadness to seep in as I thought about these, her last years, still so littered with disappointment and regret.

We moved from one slow topic to another, mostly remembering the past—visits made easier because, working for myself, I could create my own schedule. The same as arranging my availability for Grace's activities, I could now free up blocks of time in the day, or plan our get-togethers around a patient's need to move an appointment. These were visits where we'd sit together quietly, me sharing news about Grace as Mom sifted through her boneyard of memories. The times spent together usually ended the same way: "Do you want me to stop at the store for you, Mom?" "Should we go someplace for coffee?" "Do you want to take in a play next time?" Simple queries that were meant to convey that I could give her the gift of my undistracted presence. Demonstrate that I could anticipate her needs.

My daughter deserved to hear a message like this, but it was one I was still failing to provide. Instead, I clung to my script: that dating Phil for as long as I had was plenty of time enough for Grace to adjust. And, after all, they got along well. Most importantly, I was her *mother!* Who better than I to draw the line between what my daughter might *want* from what she might *need*? Wasn't it, in the end, up to me?

Several days after the outing with Mom, I finally reached out to Grace to tell her about my plan to marry Phil, but each time I introduced the subject, the conversation took a nosedive. Grace said little, but nevertheless made it clear that what she wanted was to keep things status quo. "We'll see," I'd mutter before walking away. Nervous and afraid of disappointing her, I'd leave her each time with the impression that the wedding was still just an idea. Feeling terrible for misleading her, but frozen, too.

Had I been more willing to go inward, to dig deep for answers that would explain my behavior, perhaps I would have been able to see the ghosts in the room. Maybe then I would have understood that I was reenacting my time as the adolescent Terry, the girl whose mom resented all her decisions to move forward—to leave home, to find a job, to go to college. Acting as the insecure Terry who had had to wait a long time to make her move. The Terry who kept silent and steered away from confrontation. Maybe then I would have realized that I had lost sight of my daughter. On an unconscious level, I was reacting to Grace as if she were the mother I'd once had.

Mixing the two of them up in my mind, I was holding Grace in reserve, the same way I'd held my mother at arm's distance so many decades before: trying to tiptoe around her acrimony, hoping to drown out the accusatory voice that told me that, with remarriage, I was abandoning my daughter. Sadly, I was too distracted to listen to my daughter's fears about separations and transitions. There were still too many voices speaking from my past to haunt me.

September came and with it, my decision to remarry the next June. Finally. By then, Grace would have completed her third year of high school and be a rising senior. I still wasn't listening to her in the way that she needed me to—but now, I wasn't even hearing myself.

Just as I'd done with the divorce eight years before when I hadn't admitted to myself how desperately I'd wanted out of the marriage, I framed my decision to remarry all in the name of Grace. I perpetuated the myth I'd created for myself when I'd left John: that I was doing what was best for my daughter. Reprising the same rationalization that I'd pitched to Phil before Grace had gone overseas with the orchestra, I told myself that my primary motivation for marrying in the near future was to ensure that she felt a part of this new family Phil and I were trying to create, that she feel secure in our new life before she ventured off on her own.

Grace had just settled in to her junior year classes when Phil and I began looking at engagement rings, and she continued to excel. Heartened that she seemed to be on a good trajectory—that she was, despite my fears, a girl who had goals and who followed the rules—I reassured myself that these good signs would ease the news that Phil and I planned to wed early the next summer. The timing, I rationalized, would allow her some months to adjust to the changes my marriage would bring for us all, before revving up her search for a college. Phil and I would each give up our homes to buy a place together—exactly what Grace had asked me not to do. All of it, however, was one way to create a fresh start and I tried to convince myself it would work.

Several weeks later, on a cool, dry, October Saturday afternoon, Phil and I drove to the jeweler's and picked up the diamond band I had chosen instead of a traditional ring. Then, as we sat together on the front steps of my house—the home where I'd lived for the past fourteen years—my excitement waned. I was finally prepared to tell Grace we'd become engaged—or so I wanted to believe.

I glanced at my watch and tried to catch my breath. She would be home soon. "I think your girls will take the news better than Grace," I said slowly.

"What do I know?" Phil asked, with a shrug. "It'll be an adjustment for her—after all, you two have always had an us-against-the-world kind of attitude. But I have faith." He grinned.

"You know, I had to make it as a single parent," I said, my tone defensive. "Even when I was married, it seemed like it was just Grace and me. And now? It still makes me angry that John never made a space for her at his place—filled what should have been her bedroom with storage boxes. So, yes, I'm really all she's ever had." Folding my arms over my chest, I sighed, as if my calling out my ex-husband's behavior covered everything about adjustments that needed explanation.

And then I moved from good sense to cowardice. "What do you think—could you tell her about the engagement by yourself? It shifts the dynamic." I was speaking faster now. Liking this new idea. "Brings you into the picture in a special way."

Desperate to avoid any unpleasantness, I didn't want to face the fact that I was afraid Grace might say something cruel that would spoil the moment for me. Or even worse, create a big scene that might surprise and dismay Phil. Just the way my mother had always had a tendency to do. His childhood had been spent in a *Leave It To Beaver* kind of home. One where everyone is cheerful and the kids know their

place. Once again, as I had weeks earlier, I worried that any imper-
tinence on my child's part would make him question what kind of
mother I'd been. A pushover? Would he, in that moment, see me as
the person I really believed myself to be? Somebody who was both
selfish as well as afraid of caving into her kid?

With these worries shaping my thoughts, I latched on to what Phil
had acknowledged many times before: that Grace was never anything
but delightful when he was around. So, why not aim for a reaction of
delight? Especially if it could be so easily had?

Without being conscious of all my motivations, I was also trying
to manipulate the method in which we conveyed the news of our
engagement, because telling Grace about it was too much like telling her about the divorce—something I had done alone. Once again
I would cause her pain. I didn't want to hear what I knew what would
be another version of "Oh, Mommy, no." Or to confront the fact that,
once again, I was the one to flip her world upside down.

Grace arrived home while Phil and I were still sitting on the porch.

"Grace!" Typical Phil. He was always able to make you feel as if
you were the most important person in the place. "Take a walk with
me, sweetheart." He steered her toward the backyard.

I walked into the house and peered out at the two of them through
the patio's glass. My heart beating fast. Hoping, hoping, that all would
go well.

With his hands in his pockets, Phil ambled alongside Grace
toward the hammock that hung beneath a towering evergreen. They
stopped. Phil faced Grace now, his lips moving, his body relaxed. But
my eyes were fixed on my daughter. Still hoping. However, in the time
it took me to inhale only once, her body went stiff. Then recoiled, as
if she'd been shot.

What the hell were you thinking? You set her up! My hand instinc-
tively fumbled for the latch on the patio door, but Grace had spun
away from Phil and bolted across the lawn. *Too late.*

Wait? Please wait! The yard was silent. Like a frightened deer, my daughter fled through one unfenced yard and then another. Running and running and running. Until she was gone.

When she returned home later that day, having poured out her heart to a best friend, nothing I said helped. My excuses and apologies for catching her off guard, my explanation that while I knew it would be difficult for her initially, I was sure that if she trusted me she would see how it could all work out—to all of this, she gave me only a cold stare. Over the ensuing weeks, the distance between us widened.

Grace's new refrain became "there's nothing to talk about, Mom." She busied herself with her schoolwork, her music, her friends, taking control of her life in all the ways that she could. Relieved that she was functioning well despite having shut me out, I tried to be patient. Compassionate. I held my temper when she punished me with rejection: she refused to help me pack up the house for the move. "You're the one who wants this, Mom," she'd said, spitting out her words. Sometimes, when patience failed, I found myself acting offended. But in reality I was scared. Scared that she would never come around. Scared that the fury she harbored might become even worse.

I sought consolation from friends who reassured me that Grace would adjust. "She's just going to put you through the paces until she does," they would tell me. I heard the same from Phil—the guy for whom the glass always brimmed over—who believed that shortly it would all improve.

In April, just months before the June wedding, I put the house on the market. The day the realtor staked the FOR SALE sign on the lawn, I stopped by my parents' home and shared my worries about Grace with Mom.

"But Terry, why shouldn't you want to get married? Phil's such a terrific guy." She shrugged. "So happy-go-lucky, not like that guy over there." Smirking, she tilted her head toward my father. "And you can tell that Phil's just crazy about you."

"But Grace's furious about the move." I stopped short of recounting my daughter's refusal to help me pack boxes and her outbursts of ire. I knew this would make Mom angry, despite her special bond with Grace. Daughters were not meant to be defiant. Daughters were supposed to do their mother's bidding.

"Ah, she'll come around." Sitting in her favorite chair, Mom sorted through a box of papers. "I'm glad you're moving. That house is too much for you. I don't know how the hell you've done it all these years."

What I hadn't admitted to anyone at all was how sad I was about putting the place up for sale. Because it was Grace's childhood home, leaving it was hard enough; but I also had a strong emotional attachment to the house. One that had sprung, in part, from having come into my own during those early years there, when Grace was still small. And that emotional attachment had deepened further during the years I'd made renovations following the divorce. With the house now ready to be sold, I harbored a wild, desperate, and persistent fantasy that I would one day reclaim it by buying it back, a fantasy that grew out of my desire to avoid my own sadness about letting it go, as well as my guilt over causing Grace distress. Nevertheless, these emotions remained submerged and elusive—as did an even more significant truth—until Grace left a letter to me on the kitchen table.

"Mom," she'd begun. "I'm not trying to make you mad. I just want you to consider what I'm telling you. I think deep down you know that getting rid of the house is a big mistake. You love it, too." In her typical fashion, she had seen to the heart of my feelings. I read every word of that letter printed so neatly on several pages. How visible her pain was. I swallowed hard. Then buried the letter in a moving box.

Afterward, I told myself that all had been said and dealt with; that Grace's distress was a case of "teenage angst," and that I had no need to look at the letter again. Wasn't it just that she was caught up in a maelstrom of emotion—wishing with vehemence that she could change my mind? Wasn't this all just more of the same intensity she played out over and over again? Worst of all, wasn't it proof that she knew all too well how to manipulate me to get what she wanted?

I rationalized: surely a house is just a house and it is the relationships within it that truly matter—unable to see that the house was a metaphor for our relationship. That for Grace, the house symbolized *me*; that its sale would *of course* evoke for her the loss of the person she counted on most. Hadn't she always had me as the main person—the "one" in her life? Always had me first? Her bond to me was deep. And wasn't that true *vice versa*?

But rather than having the insight to understand how complicated and tangled our attachment *to one another* was—insight that would have made it possible for me to speak to our mutual grief and then guide her forward, I foundered. I forced our pain to remain unshared. And so it became solitary. Like the white noise in between two radio stations, the static between us masked any possibility of listening and understanding. As surely as if I had been my own mother raising me as a teenager, I had allowed Grace and me to fall into a space where clear signals of communication were obliterated.

Not long after that visit with my parents and the entombing of Grace's letter in the bottom of a box, Phil's youngest daughter called him: unhappy living with her mother, she wanted to move in with us. After hearing the details, I agreed with Phil that we needed to make a home for Sarah, too. That same evening, I went upstairs to tell Grace, on my tiptoes mentally, as I prepared myself for what might be another difficult exchange. Moving in a guarded manner was something I did routinely around my daughter these days, and now I was trying to convince myself that this new twist in plans might turn out to be a good thing. Maybe they would bond? Maybe misery would love company? But her reaction caught me totally flat-footed.

"I know all that," she said, cutting me off.

"You *do?*"

"Of course." She rolled her eyes. "Sarah already told me."

"Oh!" Should I explain our decision? Or apologize? Or try to find something that would make all this okay with her? "So, were you as surprised as I was?" I asked, in a lame attempt to keep the conversation moving forward.

"Nothing you do surprises me anymore, Mom." Grace sighed, then brushed past me and headed toward the shower.

∾

In late June, on the morning of the wedding, I woke early and did several loads of wash. Then I then stepped into my strapless white gown. After a simple ceremony, my new husband and I hosted a garden party at an outdoor venue for our families and friends.

"Oh, Terry, I'm overdressed," Mom whispered as I greeted her. "We should have picked out something simpler." She looked lovely in her fancy, wide-legged pantsuit. Very Hollywood.

"You're the mother of the bride!" I protested. "The only one here who gets to look better than I do!"

Sarah and Grace hung together, smiling, laughing, even co-delivering a speech that was a toast to the happy couple, and a roast of the bride. I smiled brightly, giving our guests permission to laugh—even though, for those awkward minutes, I didn't feel much like laughing myself.

A few weeks later, in a grand and deluded attempt to bring Sarah and Grace—both of whom were studying French—into the fold of our new marriage, Phil and I took them on a vacation to Paris. But, it didn't take long for any excitement they'd felt about the excursion to disappear and for discord to develop between the two of them. Once home, tension bubbled even harder. Sarah became territorial, claiming her space in small, sometimes subtle ways: rearranging kitchen drawers; labeling her food; shifting the angle of lamps. Grace withdrew from us all. School resumed, not a moment too soon.

As the autumn days grew shorter, the weather turned cold, the house colder still. Guilt plagued me: how alone I was with my desire, so desperate, to reclaim some connection with my daughter. I waited, and watched, and then worked to engage her. Seeing how intensely unhappy she was, I now believed that if I just tried hard enough, she'd let me back into her life and her heart. That I'd finally find the perfect pitch that had eluded me for the last two years and made me tone deaf to her needs.

Of course, wishing and trying did not make it so. I had no perfect pitch; in fact, I was a mother unable to hear anything at all. A mother who felt drowned out by her daughter's silence, even as I struggled to speak, to listen, and to be heard. A mother who did not recognize that the emotional tremors beneath our new home were actually the rumblings that precede an earthquake—one that would crack the ground beneath us and threaten to swallow Grace whole.

Tightrope Walk

When suffering knocks at your door and you say there is no seat for him, he tells you not to worry because he has brought his own stool.

—Chinua Achebe
The Arrow of God

BECAUSE NOVEMBER SKIES NEVER promise anything but cold rain, I'd never liked this time of year. Everything became less in November: sunlight, color, energy. I was a summer girl, someone for whom heat was like oxygen. Even the anticipation of Thanksgiving, for all its assurance of bounty and good cheer, couldn't offset the gloom. And on this particular afternoon, five months after my remarriage, I was about to discover just how much bleaker November could become: darker and more desolate than any I'd ever known.

The wind was blowing hard when I pulled into our driveway after a full day of patient appointments, and my anxiety was high. This sense of foreboding had become a new norm for me, rooted as it was in the tension between Grace and Sarah and their mutual antipathy toward me. Steeling myself as I walked into the kitchen, I dropped a bag of groceries on the counter and then began making my rounds. My job was to see who, and what, was afoot.

Was my stepdaughter downstairs? Yes. A brief hello: "How was your day? Lot of homework? Okay." Press on. I knew Phil would not be around just yet. I glanced at the clock on the mantel: he should be home soon. Grace? Likely not here. Not with so many after school activities that kept her out until dinnertime. Double back to check with Sarah. "Sarah? Has Grace been home?" The answer came slowly: "I thought I heard her earlier. She might be upstairs."

I headed there, planning to change clothes along the way, but stopped short when muffled cries became audible, coming from the master bedroom. I took the stairs fast. There, propped against the wall, sat Grace. Sobbing. Scattered around her were booklets and brochures. On her laptop, an e-form—only one of the applications and essays for the nine colleges to which she planned to apply.

"Grace?" I asked, startled. "What's going on?"

"Go away! I don't want you near me!" She pulled her knees to her chest and then lowered her head. Her whimpers sounded like a trapped animal.

"Grace. Calm down." I crouched next to her. "Tell me what's wrong."

"Leave me alone!" she screamed.

"My God, Grace! Sarah's right downstairs—you're going to terrify her!"

Not as much as she's scaring the hell out of you right now.

Her head snapped up and she glared at me. "Sarah! She's all you give a fuck about!" In one quick swoop, she kicked the pile of college catalogs across the room. "Don't want to upset Sarah now, do we?" she jeered.

She drew herself into a ball, wailing even harder now.

I sat beside my angry and bereft child in my fancy bedroom with fear hammering in my chest—in a house that, despite all our efforts, seemed nothing like a home.

"Grace, stop. This is about *us*." I struggled to keep my voice pitched low. "I love you. Please let me help!"

"Why don't you save your therapist bullshit for somebody who gives a damn!"

I stood up and moved to close the bedroom door, hoping that Grace's howls and whatever else she might scream about her stepsister, wouldn't be heard downstairs. Then I warned myself to ignore the further barrage of insults my daughter was hurling at me. I sat down on the floor again, but this time a bit further away.

"Look, Grace. I'm trying here. I never meant for you to suffer like this."

"News flash—not everything is about you!"

I managed a deep breath. "What's it about then?"

"I don't know!" She cried out, as if I'd tossed a match in her lap and set her on fire.

I believed her: she didn't know. She was too overwhelmed to parse her anguish in any way that made sense.

"Okay, okay," I whispered. "Let's just sit then."

And so we did, even after the gray afternoon sky turned dark and the walls of the room receded and grew indistinct. Not a word passed between us, but my mind spun onward, trying to guess what had happened to provoke this level of distress in my daughter. Then, thinking that maybe she'd fallen asleep, I edged closer. She opened her eyes. Blinked several times. I reached over and took the chance of stroking her hair, unsure of whether she would flinch away.

"Honey, you're stressed to the max," I said, my voice quiet now. "We've got to find a way to get you some relief."

"My stomach hurts," she mumbled. "I think I have an ulcer."

"You're running from morning to night. You've got to be so tired." More stroking. She didn't move away. "First semester senior year is the very worst. And there's so much tension here at home. You must be wishing you could just escape." I understood how she felt. With all the strife between the girls and me, I wanted to escape, too.

"There's something wrong with my body," she whimpered. "I feel sick all the time. And my periods are off."

"Would you go back to see that lady doc you saw last time? I'll make an appointment for you."

"Yes."

It would be the last time, for nearly a year, that she willingly agreed to anything I proposed.

∽

"Grace, you're down a few pounds since I saw you last year," the pediatrician said. "You're only one hundred eleven. And almost 5'8'." She scanned through the chart, thick from all the years of routine follow-ups and labs after her kidney surgery. "Looking at colleges *might* explain why your weight's off and your periods irregular. But you've got to take it easy. No more losing weight. Okay?"

"Sure." Grace nodded, looking as if she shared the doctor's concern.

"You'll have to start having more regular meals," I said, watching my daughter as I folded my arms over my chest. "No more of this eat-on-the-go."

A month later, we were back in the pediatrician's office. She weighed one hundred and seven.

Returning home from that appointment in a state of agitation, I dropped my coat on a chair and punched in the phone number of a colleague. A board-certified clinical social worker specializing in children and teens, she had decades of experience and her reputation preceded her.

"Would you be willing to see her?" I pleaded, after filling her in on the situation. "I'm guessing it's the anxiety and depression that's driving the weight loss."

Weight loss. So less terrifying a word than *anorexia*.

It was a word I couldn't say out loud now—not even in my mind—because I didn't want to acknowledge what was already staring at me. Earlier on in my career, a small percentage of my practice had included girls with eating disorders—taxing and discouraging work because the condition often became life-threatening rapidly. I didn't want my daughter to be one of *those* girls, who faked carefree smiles all the while becoming scarecrows who wore oversized clothing that hid their bodies.

And I didn't want to be one of *those* mothers, women who cycled between begging and bargaining with their teen who had become a skeleton. Women who raged when nothing helped. Women who twisted and turned under the weight of their impotence.

I didn't want to be afraid that others judged me to be responsible. In the end, I knew, the blame would rest on my shoulders. Wouldn't it be justified? Hadn't I restricted my own eating when I was her age? Bought into an unhealthy pursuit of thinness? My insides knotted as I pushed back the thoughts that curled through my mind. What did Grace see when looking at old photos of me? What messages had I conveyed to her about body image, albeit unconsciously?

I did not call John. He had retreated further and further from Grace by then and it never occurred to me to turn to him to stem the rising tide of my fear.

"I'd be happy to meet her, if she's willing to come," the therapist offered then, and with that she'd said what I'd prayed I would hear.

When I hung up the phone, my hands still shook. The guilt that I had not paid closer attention to Grace's changing appearance swept over me again. Sick that I hadn't sought professional help for her when the unmistakable rumblings of turmoil between us arose, long before the engagement. Light years ago.

How had I not understood that in all her anger and distancing, Grace was signaling her need for my help? Telling me—no, shouting at me—that she hadn't been ready for the changes I pushed on her? Waves of remorse and worry pounded against the wall of my denial. Truth leaked through its cracks.

My daughter had been walking a tight rope for quite some time, trying to do things to perfection. And, as it had for me—also beginning in my high school years and then continuing into college—didn't her "weight loss" stem, at least in part, from her desperate desire to control her situation? Wasn't she, also, trying to stop the emotions that ensued when she failed? Despite these signs, I hadn't been able to admit that her drive for top grades, her involvement in so many extracurriculars, and her determination to "do it all" constituted only a relentless spin on the hamster wheel. A spin that both fueled her anxiety but also became her method of managing it. All this was the very hallmark of anorexia, wherein young girls sought control over their feelings of helplessness and emotional hunger and denied their needs, sometimes until they literally starved themselves to death. But surely, I reassured myself with a panic I repressed quickly, Grace was not in that much trouble.

And so, on that gray afternoon, I worked hard to deny that my daughter was in crisis, her feet slipping out from under her in the earthquake of repression over all she was feeling.

After Grace's meeting with my colleague, the recommendation was for outpatient appointments twice a week, a consultation with a psychiatrist for medication, and an internist to assess my daughter's physical state. "We'll see what we've got here," she said to me in private after the appointment, "but as far as the anorexia, I'm worried that Grace's in deep."

The therapist had named her illness. And I knew she was right. Nevertheless, her diagnosis was still too frightening for me to say the word out loud.

"One hundred four," the internist announced at Grace's first appointment with her in January. Two months since the initial visit to the pediatrician. Seven pounds down. Nausea rolled over me. I turned to Grace, who just stared at me with a blank expression. Did she even begin to understand the train she had boarded?

"I want you to see a gynecologist for birth control to reestablish your periods," the physician continued. "And we need a complete panel of blood tests." She pushed her notes aside and sighed. "I can't begin to count how many times I've had this same conversation with girls like you." She leaned toward Grace across her desk. "I myself have a sister who's been anorexic for years—and all I can say is what a nightmare it's been for everyone—especially our family." And with that, she flicked her pen onto her desk in disgust and shook her head.

Confused by her personal revelation and startled by her anger, I looked first at Grace—whose head had dropped—and then at the doctor. I searched her eyes, hoping to see compassion. But only annoyance and disdain were mirrored there. As if my daughter was just another run-of-the-mill, trouble-making girl. I looked away. In that moment, I was taken back to my own girlhood. In this woman, I saw a punitive authority figure. A towering, sour-faced nun who might misuse her power, her responsibility to help, wielding shame as a weapon that would wound.

Don't complain. You might jeopardize Grace's getting good care. Play the game to get what she needs. I decided right then that we would follow through with the lab work. Obtain a copy of the report. But I would never bring my daughter to see this physician again.

"What did you think of her?" I asked Grace, as she opened the car door.

"I hated her."

We drove off in silence. I hated her, too.

Third week in February 2007: The twice weekly therapy continued. Close monitoring by a psychiatrist and medications were now in the mix. Another consultation, this time with a female gynecologist for the irregular periods. Was it my imagination, or did my daughter appear less stressed? She walked toward the exit, ready to leave.

"What does she weigh?" I asked the doctor as Grace stepped through the door.

"Oh, right. I forgot to get a weight on her," the physician said.

"You didn't *weigh* her?" The oversight horrified me. She called Grace back to step on the scale.

Ninety-seven pounds.

The doctor's smile evaporated and she hurried back to her office. Placed a call to a colleague who was an endocrinologist and arranged an appointment for the following day.

I thought I might faint. Fourteen pounds in just over three months. My daughter was in free fall. About to disappear.

As Grace's weight dropped, the acceptance letters to the highly selective, small liberal arts schools she'd applied to, continued to arrive. "Welcome! Congratulations! We are pleased to inform you . . . !" Her number one choice had accepted her, as well. I stared at each packet, sure that the universe was playing a cruel joke. Depressed—although I couldn't admit that to myself or anyone else, not even a friend—I viewed those letters like good news being delivered to someone who'd died.

Worsening the situation, the tension between Grace and Sarah had only intensified. It seemed my stepdaughter hated Grace—and me.

"They're both crazy," I'd sometimes hear Sarah whisper while chatting up a buddy on the phone. "I can't stand her," she'd add. Whether she was referring to Grace or to me, I didn't know, but it all was an affront. Any desire on my part to reach out to my stepdaughter, to understand her pain and her fears, withered fast. Sarah was not interested in anything I had to say. She'd made that clear whenever a difficult conversation was broached: I was neither her parent nor her mother. And her brand of anger—frank dismissal, cutting remarks— unconsciously evoked too many memories of the mother I'd had, who'd made me feel as helpless as my daughter must now. Didn't Sarah have all the power while I had none?

Phil was oblivious to the rapidly deteriorating situation. In the five years spanning our courtship and marriage, my husband and I had never argued. Confused by his silence now, I wondered whether I was overreacting to Sarah's judgmental behavior, or if all the responsibility for the problem between us belonged to me. Frustrated and unsure of what to do when we were all together, I became nearly as helpless as my daughter. Just as I had once done with my own mother, I swallowed my voice and repressed my emotions as Sarah began her attacks—which were nearly always subtle.

"Phil," I said, one night as we were going to bed. "Can you please talk to Sarah about the way she's acting with Grace? It's cruel." Sarah had taken Grace's hair, falling out because of her illness and draped it over the bathroom faucet. "I'm having a really hard time getting through to her that her stepsister is in danger."

"Yeah, I can talk to her, but wouldn't it be better if you did it? After all, Grace is *your* daughter."

"No, Phil. I need help with *your* daughter. I need help with them both!"

"What do you want me to say to her?"

"Look, I get it that Sarah feels rejected by her mother, and is conflicted about having to live with us. And I know she must be scared by what's happening to Grace. But you've got to find a way to talk to her—she can't go on treating her stepsister like someone who should be punished at every turn." My words were measured. Sounding, as I often did when I was confronting something painful, like a therapist instead of an injured spouse. I tried a new tack then. "When you don't say anything to her, you're essentially throwing me under the bus." I grabbed his hand and squeezed it.

Days would pass, the strain between us like a rubber band ready to snap.

"You told me you would talk to Sarah, Phil. What happened?"

"You know, I thought about it," he answered. "I really did. But I have to tell you—I think this is just the kind of stuff that goes on between sisters."

"No." My response came through gritted teeth. "It's not. Right now, Sarah is one *very* angry girl."

"Oh, you know, Grace can be mean, too."

Every time we reached this point, my chest would grow tight and my face would flush with indignation.

"For God's sake! Grace hides in her room whenever Sarah's home! And even if she *were* the kind of kid who lashed out, we both know she directs all her anger toward me." I was desperate to get him to agree. "She's too depressed—doesn't have enough emotional energy even to know *how* to fight back!"

He'd promise to talk to Sarah again, but either he couldn't—or wouldn't. I tried to rationalize that he was trying to be a good father to his daughter. I hadn't expected the merger between our two families to be easy, but I hadn't imagined it would go so poorly, either. I needed support from him regardless of his allegiance to his daughter.

And, I wanted more than simple support—I wanted to feel

protected, and it became easy to feel betrayed. Just as I had when John showed so little interest in Grace at the time of her kidney diagnosis. Just as I had when my father hadn't protected me from my mother when I was a child.

After a while, I stopped asking Phil for his help and turned all my energies to Grace, trading my trust in my new husband for quiet resentment. Once again, I was without support from my partner. Once again, I was alone in the midst of a crisis. Silently, I wondered if this wasn't just a repeat of all I had been faced with at the time of the kidney surgery. Along with the tension, I experienced a sense of urgency, a premonitory signal familiar from childhood, and it warned me to rely on my instincts. To be wary about whom to trust, and to rely on my skill to maneuver around people who misused their power. To skirt those in authority who might exact harm.

As with the first internist we'd seen, this was the reaction I had every time I sized up a doctor. We needed quality care, and that meant we needed a physician who was compassionate, as well as expert in his or her field. Someone who was superior. My job as Grace's mother had become to save her from herself. And the internal alarm was warning me that I'd better do a good job at it—better than the one I was doing at home to protect her from her stepsister's scorn.

Early spring. Another dreary, colorless day. A phone call to my parents one morning had given me the idea of inviting my mother out to lunch. According to Mom, my eighty-nine-year-old father was falling more frequently when he transported himself from his wheelchair to his bed, and I could tell that she was worn out. But still unable to acknowledge that he needed to be in a nursing home—it would take two more difficult years of failed attempts at home health care and 911 calls before that would happen—she shifted the conversation to her granddaughter.

"My God, Terry," she said, as she fiddled with a packet of sugar. "Why can't she see how she's ruining her health?"

"I don't know, Mom."

Taking my mother out for lunch had been a mistake. I wanted to flee the restaurant, dump her back home.

"Do you think all these doctors are really helping her? She still looks so thin!"

"Mom, I can't talk about this anymore. It makes me too nervous."

"You look exhausted, Terry. I'm worried you'll get sick, too. What about John? Can't he help you out?"

"He's not involved. He's never involved."

"I lit a candle for her when I was at Mass yesterday. I put a card in the mail to her, too."

"That's good." I stayed silent for a while. Then realized that I'd been pushing my food around my plate with a fork. Just like Grace. My head throbbed. "They have rice pudding here, Mom. How about some dessert?"

Unfortunately, all my visits with my mother were like this now: touch-and-run get-togethers that exhausted me. I wanted to see her and be reassured by her exaltations about prayer, but any kind of conversation about Grace's illness—with anyone—seemed too much for me to handle. Since my wedding and the deepening problems with Phil, pretending to be "normal" had become harder and harder to pull off.

After lunch that day, I did what I had done throughout my life—especially during my marriage to John. I drove my car into a parking space somewhere, leaned back into my seat and closed my eyes. In the silence, I let myself sink into helplessness. Like assuming a fetal position without physically folding into a ball.

Alone, I worried, uninterrupted. I swiped at the tears neither of the men in my life had been able to wipe away. When the kidney condition manifested, Grace had been a small child, and I'd had more control then—been able to hold her in my lap and soothe her, know she trusted me. Now everything was a battle for control with a daughter whose defiance masked how depressed she really was. A daughter who was sealing herself off from me—and inviting death. What was anorexia anyway, if not a slow form of suicide?

And I harbored a kind of guilt that hadn't been present during the time of Grace's surgery. Now, I wondered how her profound unhappiness—especially since the time of my engagement—could be anything other than my fault? Guilt made it harder for me to be the ferocious mother I'd been when her kidney condition eluded diagnosis. Then, I'd talked back when I disagreed with the opinion of a medical professional. With the anorexia, I dealt with any disapproval I felt in silence. I advocated for my daughter by shifting treatment course without confrontation, fearing that if I made waves with a given doctor, the whole system might close ranks against us. Believing that it would then be easy for them to dismiss me as a bad mother—and make it harder for my daughter to get the care she needed.

Now, while I still moved purposefully, I adopted the attitude of a younger version of myself—the girl who flew under the radar to get things done. I made decisions about the direction of Grace's care stealthily, instinctually. We changed doctors when I—or she—had a bad vibe about them. One day a few months later, Grace and I had made a visit to an intensive outpatient treatment program, a program that would provide the closer monitoring her treatment team believed she needed. A no-nonsense nurse called Grace and took her to an alcove just off the waiting room. I watched from my seat as she flipped through the forms on her clipboard and pointed my daughter toward a scale.

"Stand facing backward," she instructed. "Seeing the number isn't going to help you one bit." Silence from Grace. The nurse spoke in a sharp tone. "You realize you only have one kidney, don't you?" She ushered Grace into another room, perhaps to wait for the doctor. But not before I heard her say haughtily, "And that it could stop working at any time?"

After the recommendation to admit her to the program came, I could see the pained expression on my daughter's face. We moved to a bench just outside the building to talk. Just the two of us, under a tree. Grace looked like a rag doll. As she slumped over, her emaciated arms were folded across her knees.

"I'll go any place you want me to. But not here, Mom," she pleaded, her voice quavering. "Those people were awful. They only made me feel worse."

"You're right, Grace," I said, standing up. "We'll find the help—but not here."

In a protest that remained silent—still the only kind of protest I was able to muster—we walked slowly to the car, without checking in with anyone. After we arrived home, I called the program to inform them of our decision, then spoke with Grace's therapist.

"Okay. Let's get her to the right place," she said. "Do you know about the program downtown?"

Her understanding made me want to weep.

Afterward, I searched my mind, my heart, and my soul yet again, trying to understand *all* the reasons Grace had become ill. But coming up with an answer—identifying the root causes of the anorexia and her depression—was like trying to confirm the source of the fire when a house is still ablaze. I simply didn't know. This was when my blackest fears threatened to break through—the thoughts about Grace's one good kidney failing, or her heart suddenly stalling—and I mentally pushed back against my terror, vowing to myself that I would not succumb to my fears.

Quickly, but acting with care and a gentle attitude, I enrolled Grace in a different outpatient eating disorders program, a program that I finally felt good about and one that was endorsed by her therapist, psychiatrist, and new internist. I discussed this decision with Phil, and then John, with both of them supporting the step and surprising me by their willingness to be involved enough to express an opinion. Grace had to attend three nights a week. This, in addition to her individual therapy, and medication visits with her psychiatrist. And school. Although I believed I had found the right program this time, and Grace had accepted her treatment team's directive to participate, it didn't mean she was pleased.

"I'll keep doing this stupid program you're forcing me to go to," she announced one day in late spring, as the two of us sat at the kitchen table. She glared at me as she spoke. "But don't think you're going to keep me from going to college in the fall. I've already sent in the forms to my top pick that I'm coming."

"I'm sure you feel overwhelmed, honey. The program. Your therapy. All the doctors." My body ached, and I shifted in my chair. "But you'll be graduating soon. Try to take it one step at a time."

"You're not *listening* to what I *said*." She stared at me, contempt flashing in her eyes. "You will *not* stop me from going to college. I'm not like the girls in this program of yours—they stay forever. Or get kicked out and then just end up coming back."

In that moment, and no longer able to contain the frustration and anger and fear that I'd kept bottled up inside for months, I shoved a kitchen chair against the wall. Once again, I had regressed to expressing my anger in the way I had done when, as a girl, I was out of control with my siblings, and even with Grace that night when I'd thrown the box of saltines at her.

"*You* said! *You* said!" I screamed at my child. "Well, I'm saying *this*, Grace! I don't *have* any control over whether or not you go to college!" My hands chopped the air with emphasis. "Are you clueless? Every college requires its students to have a physical before they come!" My entire body vibrated. "Are you so far gone that you don't realize anyone you meet will take one look at you and wonder what the hell is wrong? Be shocked? It is your *doctor* who will judge you fit for admission."

Now I could hear myself sounding just like my mother, as well, but I couldn't make myself stop. I felt pummeled. Defeated. I paced the floor, then willed myself to slow down. Failing, I grabbed at my hair. Then repeated myself, still shouting. "I don't have any *control* over what happens to you! Only *you* do!" Finally, spent, I stopped. Waited until I could breathe. "You're going to have to decide if you want to stop starving yourself and gain the weight," I said, quietly now, my voice trembling. "And like I said. It's your doctor who'll decide if you're well enough to go away to school." I looked her in the eye. "It's not up to *me*. So stop blaming me."

Minutes passed. Grace stood silent, and perhaps stunned, beside the stove. I forced myself to stay in the kitchen. Not to grab my keys and race out the door as, decades ago, my mother had done to me innumerable times, as once I had done to John. I just stood there—humiliated and scared—as my daughter dragged herself from the room. It was to be the last time I lost control with her.

Throughout this terrible year, and in contrast to my anger that day, I had sought support for my daughter as we maneuvered through the morass of the healthcare system. Not with the full voice of the ferocious mother, the voice I would later regret I hadn't used, but that just hadn't been possible: the residue of my own adolescent shame and mistrust still held me too tightly in its grip. Nevertheless, I had begun to fight for Grace in other ways, staying the course in our high wire act: striving for balance at the same time I stood underneath her as her net.

As I strove to tolerate her anger and frustration with me, willing myself against becoming defensive, I found I listened to her better for the first time. My silence, hard-won and created by love, gave her the space and opportunity to regain her footing. If I could just continue to be quietly supportive, she would mature and so would our relationship. So would I. In the end, it took years but I had learned how to listen well to my mother, and now I would strive to do the same for my daughter. Because she was, after all, an irreplaceable link in the chain of women in my life.

Early September came, and with it the reality of the central question: whether she would be well enough to attend school. Over the course of the summer months, as her weight fluctuated, Grace had vacillated between treating me as if I were radioactive and turning away from me with cold rage. *That's just the depression talking*, I reassured myself without conviction when she went off on a tear—all the while working hard to corral my anxiety, which threatened relentlessly. Still, once during that time, we did briefly connect. She was standing a little bit outside the kitchen, watching me as I walked toward the pantry.

"Mom?" Her voice cracked. Her eyes were wet. "When will I ever stop feeling so depressed?"

My heart squeezed as I saw the tears rolling slowly down her cheeks and dripping onto her shirt.

"I wish it was this minute, baby girl," I whispered, not moving toward her, afraid to spook her. "But the truth is, I don't know exactly when."

We stood there, our eyes locked in mutual sorrow. A few minutes later, I walked toward her and reached for her hands. Unnerved by how cold they were, I then repeated what I'd told her ten years earlier, when she'd been so sad about the divorce. "Honey, I promise you, you *will* feel better." And then I pulled her close. Wanting desperately to say just the right thing. Something I could believe, too. "I *promise* you," I said, drawing back to look into her face . "It's just like the seasons—everything changes. You won't always feel awful like this."

By some combination of miracle and resolve, Grace *did* leave for school later that month. Her treatment team was understandably concerned—though she had put on some weight, she still was far from reclaiming her health. Nevertheless, her therapist was willing to try twice-weekly phone sessions while she was away and to see how it went. Her primary physician, a motherly figure that we had luckily happened upon after the early fiascos, agreed that she should give college a try, provided she continue the right medical monitoring near campus. She believed that Grace needed to move forward, away from what, for her, had become such a desolate and toxic home. "Go have a normal life," the doctor said. These parting words came from a healer and brought the first smile to my daughter's face in nearly two years.

I was nervous, but was also relieved that she'd been given this chance. I was finally beginning to see that, as estranged as our relationship was, we were also too closely tied. Desperate to reconnect with her, I had hovered—watching her constantly. In advocating for her with doctors, I hadn't taught her how to advocate for herself. College, I prayed, would function for us as it was intended for all kids her age, especially those who left home to go away to school—an avenue by which emotional separation could proceed.

ॐ

The marathon drive on a bright September day had been stressful, reminiscent of those long trips to and from Michigan when Grace was fifteen. She was anxious, preoccupied, but also less guarded toward me than she'd been all year. Perhaps finally doing something "normal" had mellowed us both.

"Honey, your side of the room looks fantastic!" I enthused.

"Well, I had to go for bright colors. Gray and black are depressing." Grace responded matter-of-factly.

"And so much light through these windows!" I walked over and looked out on a wooded trail. "So many trees." A lump formed in my throat, as I was grateful for this easy kind of talking, so lost to us in recent years.

I put a birthday card for her eighteenth birthday on her pillow, as it was less than two weeks away. Then I turned to say goodbye.

"Don't make me cry, Mom," she said as she held out her arms.

"I love you, honey bun," I murmured, pulling her close.

"I love you, too," she whispered back.

Chasing Down the Dark

And what if I spoke of despair—who
doesn't
feel it? Who doesn't know the way it
seizes,
leaving us limp, deafened by the slosh
of our own blood, rushing
through the narrow, personal
channels of grief.

—Ellen Bass,
"And What If I Spoke of Despair"

DECEMBER 21, 2010. THE shortest day of light, the longest night of the year. Not unexpected. It was the winter solstice, after all. But what happened to our family that day could not have been predicted: the sun suddenly wobbling in the sky and then collapsing in on itself. The explosion eclipsed everything that preceded it: every difficult life challenge I had encountered. Then, just as unexpectedly, all light disappeared. Scorched into memory, I would never forget that exact moment, the one when Grace, home for the holidays, nearly died.

That December, Grace was midway through her senior year at her university. It seemed to me as if her recent college experiences were mirroring the happier days of her early high school years—the years before the anxiety and depression, the years before the anorexia. Sometimes, I allowed myself to think she was doing so much better because I wished it to be true so desperately. From what I'd witnessed when I'd last visited her on campus at the end of October, along with what she was sharing when we talked on the phone, it had been easy to craft a portrait of success.

Knowing Grace had good friends and was respected by her professors also provided me reassurance. In college, her world had expanded through her classes, her pursuit of the arts, and two stints of study abroad. Physically, she'd achieved and maintained a healthier weight, and our relationship had improved significantly, too. I'd worked hard to listen to her, not to push, not to pile on advice. Just to let her make her way through her own problems and her own life as it unfolded—all of which had been my goals from the time she had left for college.

But behind the outward signs of a balanced life, Grace continued to struggle with her emotions and many of the problems that had haunted her previously—problems I couldn't so easily deny.

After leaving for her freshman year in the fall of 2007, she'd made it clear that she didn't plan to come back to stay at the house during her vacations. Ever. "Bad vibes, Mom," she'd said. I intuited that she was referring to Sarah and the discord between them, but swearing off contact with her stepsister wasn't the whole story. She'd always rejected my attempts to discuss that terrible time before and after my remarriage. "You can talk about whatever you want," she would say with equanimity if I broached the subject of my mistakes and my sorrow over their impact on our relationship. "But do it with somebody else. I'm not going there with you, Mom."

Anger. Resentment. Lingering pain. It saddened me to realize that my daughter's desire for escape was, unfortunately, very similar to my own experience of leaving home.

Making good on her pledge to fly far away, Grace had nearly always found another place to land when school was between sessions. Which meant that she wasn't in town very often. And when she was, she landed with friends. She visited less with her grandmother, and that connection dwindled even further over time, reduced to letter writing and an occasional surprise phone call. During the summers, she found creative ways to avoid coming back to us: a service job in

Missouri; study in Ireland; visits to my sister Flo's—to whom she was attached—at her home near Atlanta.

I never insisted that she settle in at the house. Still feeling too responsible for her masked suffering, I tried instead—not always successfully—to steer her to make wise choices about where and with whom to stay. Throughout these continuing absences, my feelings vacillated. Sometimes I felt cheated; other times, punished. Often, I tried to dismiss my emotions as unimportant, burying my grief for the loss of the closeness we'd once shared, telling myself that Grace's search to find her own way forward was all that mattered. We maintained our connection with my visits to campus, and visits when she was elsewhere, along with calls back and forth. In this way, I offered emotional support that did not threaten her.

But I missed her terribly. And I worried. I worried. Always. She was too trusting, and the decisions she made were sometimes impulsive. Or invited too much risk.

Most difficult was knowing that despite ongoing therapy and changes in medications, despite hard work rewarded and a bevy of friends, despite her efforts to find a geographical cure, Grace's anxiety and depression continued, hanging like a heavy curtain across us all.

"What's the point of doing anything?" she'd sometimes say irritably into the phone if I probed about her mood. "Why am I even here?"

"Do you mean 'here' at college, or 'here' in life?" I'd ask, wishing that she were—and aware that she wasn't—talking about school.

Just from her tone, I knew that these questions did not stem from the "quest for meaning" so typical of a young adult her age. I understood them as evidence of her easy slides into despair. When she was really down—even if she was traveling—these calls home, colored by long pauses and flat responses, became more frequent. Our conversations went something like this: "You sound awful," I'd say. "Any suicidal thoughts?"

"No, I just feel like shit," she might respond. Or, "Yes, I have a lot of thoughts," if that was the truth in the moment.

"I'm sorry you feel so bad," I'd sigh. And I *was* sorry. "Are they more than just thoughts?" Then I'd force myself to ask whether she had any kind of plan. "No. I'm too scared to do anything," she'd answer glumly. However, if she was in an especially bad way, she'd often add, "But I want this pain to be over. I wish I could just die."

"I know that's how you feel," I'd counter. "Let's talk about better ways to get some relief."

Along with holding room for hope, I strove to be empathetic. I talked with Grace as if I were ladling chicken soup long-distance. Seasoning my words with understanding and patience, I believed my job as her parent was to be a sounding board for her distress. And thus, to gently redirect her back to her therapist to figure out what it all meant—as well as to her psychopharmacologist when she had questions about her medication. Still, hearing the pain in my daughter's voice was difficult—sometimes fiercely so.

Nevertheless, I continued to have faith that sustained relief was possible. I knew Grace had grit. She'd shown resilience in her battle with her eating disorder—and had stayed engaged in the arduous work of therapy all through college. And even though she wore a mask of normalcy in her social life while inside she wrestled with despondency, I believed that she could and would gain the insight necessary for growth, as well as master the tools required to manage her dark and anxious moods better.

Even though I never knew exactly where she was going to be on the mood meter, when I'd visited campus that late fall weekend, I wanted to believe that she was finally in a good place. She had the lead role in a Tennessee Williams play, and in the theater lobby afterward, I watched from the sidelines as she accepted hugs and compliments. For the first time in a long time, my daughter beamed. How happy she looked!

"Okay, my turn!" I handed her a bouquet. "I loved it! And you were wonderful in that part," I whispered, as I pulled her in for a hug.

"Yeah? You think so?" Grace laughed. "Of course, what else would you say, you're my mother!"

Back in my hotel room that night, I called Phil. "She seems more upbeat than she has in years," I told him. Taking a sip from the glass of wine I'd brought up from the bar to celebrate, I wished he hadn't been away on business. "You would have been so impressed by her performance!"

Only later would I wonder if a price hadn't been exacted for taking on a dramatic role of a young woman lost to herself. A character whose emotional struggles Grace might have too closely identified with on an unconscious level. Perhaps she had slipped into a part she couldn't easily shake off afterward.

As winter approached, and the New Year of 2011 grew ever larger on the horizon, I was fooled once again into the belief that Grace was doing better than she was. Her school's academic schedule meant students had a six week reprieve from classes that lasted from Thanksgiving until the first of the year, and her plans developed differently this time around: she had a boyfriend who attended school locally; she'd snagged a seasonal job at a large chain music store; and her beloved Aunt Flo was planning to visit for a few days before Christmas. With her stepsister still away at school and not expected back until after the Christmas holiday, along with this bounty of other reasons to come home, Grace decided to set up camp with Phil and me. I was thrilled, as she had only rarely done so before. Maybe she was coming back to us for good after the long and painful periods apart.

But my happiness did not last long. Phil and I first became suspicious that she might be feeling rocky as soon as she arrived home.

"Hey," I said to her one afternoon, as she sat cozied up next to the boyfriend who'd been glued to her side ever since she'd dropped her suitcase. "Do you know this guy?" I handed her my laptop and waited while she read an all-community alert blasted from a parents' group. A student was missing.

She only skimmed over the screen, clearly disinterested and with empathy in short supply. "I think he graduated last spring," she said, in a dismissive tone. "I didn't really know him. I just knew *of* him."

No curiosity. No concern. I was stunned by her nonchalant response—so unlike any other she would have offered in the past.

"Well, obviously a lot of people are worried about him," I said, quietly.

She shrugged, and then turned to her boyfriend to resume the conversation I'd interrupted. Her posture said it all: "We're done here, Mom."

I did not pursue the topic. At least, not just then. But a few days later, another email arrived from one of the parents. The young man's body had been located. Suicide.

Disquieted, I approached Grace once more. Asked her what information she'd been provided by the college, by friends. Again, she appeared detached, giving answers that were vague at best. *How odd is that*, I thought. Even though I'd grown accustomed in the past three years to Grace pulling me in when she really needed me, and pushing me away when I hovered, this felt different. But then I caught myself. *Why can't you get a handle on the situation?* an inner voice sneered. *You know how hard it's got to be for her to be here at home. Can't you just give her some space?*

Days passed. Grace was busy with her job at the music store. Busy spending time with her boyfriend and childhood friends. *Busy was good*, I thought.

Wrong.

Late on the night of December 20, she stomped into the house, sped past the kitchen table where Phil and I were sitting, and went straight to her room without speaking to either of us. Instead of annoyance that she hadn't bothered to return my greeting or answer my question about why she was in such a headlong rush, instead of worrying that her noisy clomp up the stairs might wake Flo and my brother-in-law, I was confused. Earlier in the day, she'd phoned to say that she'd be working her shift and then seeing her therapist afterward. What had happened to alter her mood so drastically? I looked at Phil, saw concern in his eyes. Pulling the belt of my robe tighter around me, I headed upstairs.

I stepped into her room, without bothering to knock. She had not even turned on the light, but had simply collapsed into bed.

"Honey, what gives?"

"Nothing," came the disembodied voice from under the covers.

"Well, *something's* wrong. Are you going to be okay?"

"No."

"Well then, for God's sake. Let's talk."

"No," she growled.

I felt my pulse quicken. "Did you make it to your appointment?"

"Yes. Now shut the damn door."

"Grace! How can I just 'shut the damn door' after you tell me you're not okay?"

"Jesus Christ," she muttered.

No movement from beneath the blankets. And then an admonishment, flatly delivered.

"I need to go to sleep. Just leave me alone."

"Listen," I said in the quietest voice I could manage, hoping to lower the tension in the room. "Are you working tomorrow?"

"Yes. Now go away."

As much as I felt reluctant to do so, I left, closing the door behind me.

A while later, I peeked in on her, and was relieved to see that she'd fallen asleep—even though, because she'd thrown off the blanket, I could see that she was still dressed. Downstairs, Phil and I whispered about the way she'd stormed into the house.

"Let's just take it one step at a time," he suggested at last, in his most sensible voice. "Maybe tomorrow will be better."

I agreed, but, despite his reassurances, my anxiety worsened. I fought to convince myself that most likely Grace had had a really painful therapy session and needed to regroup. Before heading to bed, I took a quick look into her room yet again. Even as I chastised myself that I was behaving like a mother with a newborn in a crib, I could not resist the strong impulse to see her chest move up and down, to hear the slow breathing that meant she was alive.

In my own room, as I lay awake—my anxiety now twisting in my gut—I seized upon the one hopeful answer Grace had given me: she had to work the following day. This was a good sign, and so I turned on my side and pulled the comforter up around my shoulders, falling asleep with one last thought: her mood might improve tomorrow.

Grace had been asleep when I left for work the next morning, which relieved me—until her therapist called with the message that sent my world off its axis. I'd been sitting at my desk in my office, first checking emails, then looking out the window and clearing my mind before beginning my day, when the telephone rang.

"Terry, I'm calling because Grace was in really bad shape when I saw her last night." Never before in the nearly four years she'd worked with my daughter had Evelyn Bloom contacted me without Grace's permission. But now she breached doctor–patient confidentiality.

"What's going on?" I asked, responding to the urgency in her voice. The unsettling conversation I'd had with Grace the night before flashed into focus: she'd been agitated. Unapproachable. Her dark mood had rattled me.

"She's deeply depressed and I told her in our session that I was worried for her safety. I want to arrange for her to go to the hospital to be assessed." She paused and then her voice dropped. "She agreed to phone me first thing this morning. But hasn't. And she's not picking up either."

After the call, as if propelled by rocket fuel, I speed-dialed Roxanne, my business partner, to cancel patient appointments. Then ran to my car. Panic set in as Evelyn's warning echoed through my mind: Grace was deeply depressed. And now, she had broken the contract she'd made with her therapist—to contact her first thing this morning. Perhaps worse, she hadn't answered her phone despite numerous attempts on Evelyn's part. And so I, too, began to dial my daughter's cell over and over. No response. I pulled out of the office parking lot fast enough to go over the curb.

Driving over the speed limit, I called Flo. Before I'd left for work that morning, I'd shared over coffee how Grace had thundered into the house the night before and my worry about her.

"Ah, she'll be fine," Flo had insisted. Now, I questioned her with desperation about Grace's whereabouts.

"She left about an hour ago," Flo answered. "Why? What's wrong?"

"Did she say she was going to work?"

"She was up and out pretty fast. I did offer to make her breakfast."

"Breakfast doesn't matter," I said sharply. "Was she dressed like she was going to work?"

"I'm not sure!" Her tone turned defensive. "I think she had on a long coat! What's happening?"

"I'm trying to find out!" Then I hesitated, unwilling to repeat the therapist's concern that Grace might need to be hospitalized, certain that my sister would bombard me with questions for which I didn't have answers. The end result: I would become even more frightened. "All I know is that Grace's not doing well," I said, shifting into management mode. "Do you think you could stay at Mom's tonight?"

"I guess I can figure something out," she said, sounding dubious. "I mean, if I were alone, it would be easy. But with Mike, well, it's not as if she's up for guests."

My anxiety ballooning, I hit the car's turn signal. Shifted lanes. "I'm on my way to check on her at her job."

Flo must have heard the fear in my voice because she didn't press further for details.

"Don't worry about us," she reassured me, "I'll figure it out."

Twenty minutes later, I discovered Grace at work, where customers were queued up at her counter; she was moving back and forth to the cash register, looking efficient and calm. For anyone who didn't know her, nothing would have seemed amiss. Had her manager walked by just then, he likely would have smiled, glad to have hired such a capable employee. But as her mother, I saw something different: Grace was too animated and cheerful, her diction too precise. Always a consummate actress, my daughter was performing for everyone—even if only to customers in a music store. My panic slowed. Little by little, I became annoyed.

When she saw me, a scowl crossed her face and she ignored me. With the long line that she had to take care of, a lengthy wait stretched out in front of me if I wanted to speak with her. A half hour went by as I vibrated with impatience. I watched as she rang up each purchase, her tone with the shoppers courteous and upbeat. She demonstrated how to replace a string on a young boy's violin with aplomb, at the same time she answered the phone without a single misstep. But while standing there, my irritation slipped away and fear began to stir again, remembering Evelyn's insistence that Grace was "in really bad shape." And then, recalling what Grace had told me the night before brought on another swell of panic. "No," she had said from under the blankets when I'd asked her if she was going to be okay. *She told you NO! Why did you let that go?*

When I finally trapped her—alone at last—she made a dismissive gesture. "You need to leave. I'm working." I'd been so anxious when I'd tried to track her down that it hadn't occurred to me that she'd probably listened to her therapist's increasingly concerned voicemail messages—or at least knew she had called—and had chosen not to respond. Ignoring Evelyn as she was now ignoring me. She was aware, without a doubt, exactly why I stood there in front of her at the counter. And had decided to shut me out.

"Grace, Evelyn called me at work this morning. Why didn't you return her calls the way you promised to last night? She's worried about you. And I'm worried, too."

"It's none of your business," she said, looking back over her shoulder to make sure no one was listening to us.

"When is your break, sweetheart?" I asked, keeping my voice gentle. "We have to talk about what's going on. This is serious."

"I don't have a break," she said. Now anger flashed in her eyes.

"Lunch then," I countered, nearly in a whisper now. "I want to help if you're in some kind of trouble."

She turned her back on me. A minute later, another customer

approached. Grace's fake smile reappeared. For the better part of another hour, wedged in between store patrons who needed attention, my attempts to coax her out with me did not succeed. While I continued to hope that she might somehow say something, anything, to quell my fear, she offered not a single word. She didn't admit that she'd failed to call her therapist back, didn't insist that she was fine, didn't claim her therapist had overreacted, didn't mention plans with friends after work.

My anxiety grew more intense.

I tried hard to project a calm demeanor. "You know Evelyn would never have called me if she didn't think this was an emergency." I moved closer. "Just tell me the truth."

She tapped a pencil's eraser against the counter.

"How bad do you feel?" I asked, my desperation surely evident. "Enough to hurt yourself?"

Still she didn't speak, but just looked right through me as if I weren't there. The silence between us crackled and popped. I'd weathered many of my daughter's worst moods, but this time her behavior was new—and alarming. In the past when I'd asked if she felt in danger of killing herself, she'd always answered me straight up: "No." "Maybe, if I weren't so chicken." Or, "No, I just want it be over." And then we'd acted on her response; we'd kept her safe. Never before had she refused to answer the question.

I pushed back against my fear, reassuring myself that if—without creating a public scene—I could get Grace to agree to leave with me later on, I'd be able to convince her to go over to the hospital. And who knew? If she were able to settle down enough, perhaps we could avoid inpatient hospitalization—and the absolute loss of control it represented. Maybe, I rationalized as I slipped into denial, an intensive outpatient intervention could work for her. After all, who knew Grace better than I did? As her mother, couldn't I provide her with sufficient protection because I believed I did have the right resources? The fantasy that I could save my child pulled hard. But deep inside, I knew. I knew that I needed to get my daughter to a place where another professional would get her the help she needed.

"What time are you done here?" I asked, as she continued to stare past me. "I'll meet you at that little place next door. We'll grab a bite to eat."

She stiffened. "I'm closing tonight. And there's inventory after that." I opened my mouth, but she cut me off. "I'm *working*." Contempt blazed in her gaze. "I'm not meeting you anywhere."

I never drove out of the parking lot that afternoon. Once in the car, I confirmed with Roxanne that she'd cancelled all my patients. Too afraid to leave this unrecognizable version of my daughter unmonitored, I positioned my car two rows behind hers and just sat there. And waited. Then, fished around in the bottom of my cluttered purse for the old rosary of my mother's—my "emergency beads"—that I kept for times of trouble. I'd never felt a need to use it, though I'd carried it with me everywhere for years. Gripping it in one hand, I picked up my cell phone to call Evelyn, who answered on the first ring.

The relief I heard in her voice when I told her I had found Grace vanished when I described how our interaction had gone. Her tone sounded grave, and my mind became frozen by dread. She reiterated her concerns for Grace: how black my daughter's thoughts had become; how hopeless she felt; how unreachable she was emotionally. She repeated her worry that Grace's ability to make sound decisions was "off." And, as she had when she'd called me that morning, she punched the words "at high risk," underscoring how imperative it was that Grace be closely watched and not left alone.

As much as I knew that I needed Evelyn's guidance, inside I wanted to scream with every word she spoke. I wanted to tell her to stop. To please just shut up. My hands shook as I wrote down her private phone number. She said she would reach out to Grace when we finished our call. My voice quivering, I thanked her and flipped the phone closed.

The plan Evelyn proposed was one already underway: watch and wait; try to engage Grace when she left work for the day. And to stay in touch with her, as well, calling her mobile if necessary. After our discussion, I phoned Phil, despairing. Together we struggled—what else could I do? Then, as if I were channeling my mother, I put my lips to the beads that had been running through my fingers as I spoke, and begged God to keep my daughter safe.

For more than five hours I sat there, numbed by the cold and everything that was happening. I ran the car's engine to stay warm, but only for brief intervals so that I wouldn't run out of gas—perhaps anticipating, on an unconscious level, that I might have to tail Grace once she finally left work. It grew darker and darker. The windshield fogged from my breath and I was forced to crack a side window open from time to time. The noise of the world moving forward filtered in: Christmas shoppers drifted from store to store, and a Salvation Army brass band stationed nearby played holiday tunes. It all made me sick to my stomach.

Over and over again in my mind, I tried to piece together what had precipitated Grace's current crisis. Had she stopped taking her medication? She'd done that before—usually when she grew frustrated with how bad she felt and believed it wasn't working anymore. Or when she'd convinced herself that she ought to be able to handle her moods on her own.

Jesus, when was the last time you even asked her if she'd gotten her prescriptions refilled? Do you even know which medications she's taking anymore? I tried to block the mocking voice.

Maybe she was worried about graduation. About it being another difficult transition. *And of course you have a great track record helping her with transitions! Like when you helped her go from being an only child who'd always had her mother first, to dealing with a new male in her life, and a stepsister who had treated her with disdain?*

Sitting there in the car getting colder and colder, I agonized over why I hadn't been able to prevent everything that was happening now. But, unable to think straight, I had no real explanation for Grace's deep downward spiral. Nothing made sense to me. When I closed my eyes, I saw the empty look on Grace's face as I inquired about the classmate who'd killed himself. What had she *really* been thinking that day when we learned he'd gone missing? Had she already been contemplating suicide when we learned that this was the way he had died? I grasped the rosary tighter in my palm.

At six o'clock, Phil knocked on the window of the car. "Should I go in and try and talk to her?"

Ten minutes later he came back, his face ashen.

"Didn't go well," he reported, rubbing his cheek with his hand. "She called me your henchman and told me to leave."

Henchman. The word resounded in my mind, reminding me of another time. *Didn't you set up Phil to be a henchman on the day you got engaged, too? Haven't you just done the same thing again? Something else that backfired?*

Yet didn't the hours I'd just spent trying to keep my daughter safe and alive—while nevertheless tolerating her fury—prove that the two situations weren't the same? I had been the one to confront her this time. Or did such a distinction not matter anymore? Grace believed I had enlisted Phil to ensnare her into complying with Evelyn's and my plan.

"This is really bad, Phil." Foreboding overflowed the space I'd reserved for hope. "I think you should wait for me at home. I'm going to need you when we get there."

He took off, and sometime later, I glanced at the clock on the dashboard: 6:57. I looked up in time to see Grace leave the store, her coat flapping in the wind, and head toward her car. It wasn't anywhere near the 9:00 closing time. She'd lied to me. Grabbing at my key ring, and then my purse, I ran to the passenger side of her car, and slid in.

Grace slammed the steering wheel with her fists. "Get out!!"

"Can we just sit for a minute? Talk?" I asked, trying to find my breath. "I'm not trying to ambush you."

She said nothing. Just jammed the key into the ignition. Once out in traffic, she swerved from lane to lane.

"Slow down!" I said, clenching my jaw. "You're going to have an accident." No response. Without warning, she pulled into a different strip mall. My body jolted as she whipped into a space and hit the brakes.

"What are you doing?" I demanded as she reached for the door.

"I'm going to buy some headphones," she snapped.

Running after her would have been futile, and so, again, I waited. Fifteen minutes later, she stormed back to the car, empty-handed. By then, I had moved into the driver's seat.

Neither of us spoke as I began the drive home, my mind spinning about what could have happened when she was behind the wheel. She might have driven straight into a wall. Or another car. Or a pedestrian. But, by some miracle, no one had been touched and the car had suffered not even a scratch. But Grace wasn't going to be as lucky.

Once inside the house—powered by adrenaline and with all her judgment vanishing under an electrical charge—she began to pace. Back and forth, room to room, she moved like a cheetah stalking some kind of prey. She only stopped when her boyfriend appeared at the door—I suspected she had called him during her bogus search at the Best Buy. Quickly she let him in, and they headed toward the living room.

"Look, you guys are welcome to talk here." I offered, trying to figure out what to do next. "But Grace—you're in no shape to go anywhere. Please don't leave." I stared hard at the boyfriend to make my point. "If you do, I will call the police."

She began to sob then, hard, and I left them so that they could have some privacy. I eavesdropped from the kitchen. The two of them sat there together for a little while, but nothing calmed her down. After more minutes passed, she began begging him to leave.

"I don't want you here!" she cried. "We're done! Just leave and don't come back!" Confused and unnerved, he followed Grace to the foyer and then stared at the floor. More words then, her voice ever insistent that he just go. After arguing with her for a minute, he headed back to his truck.

For just a moment after she slammed the door closed, our roles reversed. Determined to keep my daughter safe, I now became the one who, like a long-legged cat, was ready to lunge. But at that point, she took me by surprise, springing forward and pushing me aside with a hard shove. As I nearly fell, she rushed past me and raced up the stairs. I regained my balance and sped after her—but I was not fast enough. Click. She locked the bathroom door.

"Grace! Open up!" I pounded my fists against the wood. "I swear to God, I'll break this door down!"

Silence from the other side.

I pounded harder.

"Terry!" Phil's voice came from behind me. "Move out of the way."

A loud noise and then suddenly the door was ajar. Had Phil kicked it open? Had she unlocked it?

"Let me by." Her voice was flat as a zombie's. "I'm going to my room."

I stepped backward into the hall. "Oh, Jesus," I cried as she moved past me, in slow motion now. "Oh, Jesus. What did you *do?*"

She held her arms angled outward, in front of her body, as if she were carrying a weighty box. The wide gashes on her wrists, however, were hardly imaginary. Or the bright red that ran from them.

Phil was already on the phone. "I need an ambulance." Dizzy, I stumbled into the bathroom to grab towels. There were splotches of blood on the floor. And pills of some kind scattered across the vanity counter—perhaps as many as a hundred. *What are they?* I wondered. Had Grace had time to take any? A few? A lot? Would she tell me?

"Sit over here." I guided her toward the top of the stairs, taking no chance of letting her sit near a door. Afraid to touch her for fear she would bolt, I handed her a cloth to press against her wounds rather than doing it myself. "Wrap it around tight, Grace," I urged. "Is it okay if I help?"

She didn't answer, but complied. She sat there looking perfectly calm and didn't say a word—as if the cutting had relieved her of her frenzy. A release of blood; a release of relentless and painful emotions. But perhaps, like me, she was also quiet because she was in shock. I stood behind her on the landing. Phil kept watch at the bottom of the stairs, looking out into the dark of the driveway beyond, waiting for the ambulance. No one spoke. The house was still, the silence pressing in on us.

∿

Except for the static of walkie-talkies that announced the arrival of the police and the EMTs, I heard nothing. It was as if all my auditory information had short-circuited, leaving me only the ability to see. Consequently, I would remember just the visual details of what followed: the doors of the ambulance thrown open wide; the pulsing lights of the squad cars that were parked out on the street; the white sheets of the gurney drawn tight and ready for my daughter. How impossibly sad and strange it was to see the outline of the stretcher silhouetted against the Christmas tree, which was so brightly decorated, like a holiday package. Two first responders helped Grace downstairs, one step at a time.

I insisted on going to the hospital without Phil, following the ambulance by myself. After all, that was how I had become accustomed to treating crises. I weathered them alone.

As my daughter disappeared into the maw of the ER, I drifted without purpose through the hallways of the hospital. I stared into the officious eyes of the social worker, my gaze telegraphing that I wanted her to disappear so that I could be left alone. Later, when the team had finished stitching Grace's wrists, I peered through the window of the isolation room, ready to cry but somehow avoiding breaking down. She lay flat on her back, her hair tangled around her face. Was she medicated into unconsciousness? Or had she simply passed out? Visible above a thin blanket were her arms; gauze bandages wrapped tightly around her wrists. I wondered just how much blood she had lost. I paced with agitation.

When there was no more pacing or peering or waiting to be done, I walked back out into the cold, having no place to go except home. With Phil off to bed once we'd run out of words, I was unable to sleep and unable to cry. I gathered up cleaning supplies. On my hands and knees, I scrubbed at the carpet outside the bathroom. Hard. And then harder. Suddenly I was desperate to erase the stains that turned to rust beneath my hands on the towels. Even if the carpet's ivory plush were ever to be restored, nothing would change. The sky would still be black. When morning came, the sun would still have collapsed in on itself. I would still feel the same pain, stamped on my soul.

An Arsenal of Love

"There is love in holding," he said.
"And there is love in letting go."

—Elizabeth Berg,
The Year of Pleasures

GRACE'S FIRST CALL FROM the hospital jarred me from the stupor into which I had fallen. When I'd called the psychiatric unit earlier that morning I had learned that she'd denied me permission to receive any information about her condition or to be on the approved list of her visitors; now I hoped, for an instant, that she had changed her mind. But the guttural fury in her voice signaled otherwise.

"Get me out of here! Get me out of here! Get me out of here!"

"I tried to check on you a little while ago but the nurses won't tell me anything." I tried to stay calm in spite of my distress. "Grace, I know you're upset—but the hospital won't release you until they're sure you'll be safe."

"Get me out of here. Now!"

"I don't have the power to do that. Just like I can't see you without your permission. You're twenty-one. An adult." My head pounded. "But look. You did make the right choice when you said you'd stay there voluntarily."

"They didn't explain it to me! I never meant to be forced!"

"Calm down. It only means that you're going to give the hospital a little bit of time to see what's up with you." I kept my tone measured and spoke with care. "I did let Evelyn know last night that you'd been admitted. I'm sure she'll be calling you and she'll also talk with the staff. Come up with a plan." My hands were trembling. "It's going to be okay."

"Stop! Stop! Stop! Get me out! I'm a prisoner in here!"

A sick feeling crawled over me as I imagined how scared my daughter must feel. Confined against her will, listening to the unit's door swinging shut behind all those who entered and left, and locking with a dead thud. An image flashed in my mind: the faces of the staff on the psychiatric ward where I'd trained decades before. Busy. Some looking as if they could not care less about a patient's fear. My stomach churned. Was anyone paying attention to Grace? Were they being kind to her?

"Honey, can you stop for one second and listen to me?" I looked out my bedroom window, my eyes fixed on the yard's barren trees. "If you give me a chance, maybe I can tell you something that might actually help." Though I was trying to alleviate her distress, I didn't really believe I'd be able to say anything she could hear at this point. Still, I had to try.

"Now!" she spat out. "There's exactly one phone in this place and people are walking by all the time." Panic drenched her voice. "So I don't want to hear one more fucking thing from you. Get. Me. Out!"

"Grace, this conversation is going nowhere," I said, finally pummeled by her continuing broadside and needing to be quit of it. "I don't want to add to your stress, so I'm getting off now. Let's talk again in a little while." And then I hung up on her, upset and shaky. Running on worry and feeling helpless to advocate for my daughter, I sank into a chair.

Grace phoned back a dozen more times in rapid succession, not waiting for me to speak. "Get me out!" she shouted each time, before cutting off the call. I called the nurses' station to report what she was doing; the phone ceased to ring, and I realized that they must have forced her to stop. At least for the moment.

I wondered then if Grace had in fact signed a voluntary admission form and whether it had been explained to her; if she had done so, she had most likely agreed to a period of hospitalization during which she would be assessed by psychiatrists and nurses alike, on a "locked" unit. I made a mental note to ask Evelyn if Grace's admission was voluntary this way, or whether she'd been placed on the ward using a different criterion: a seventy-two-hour "involuntary hold," which would keep her there for at least three days because she was judged to be a danger to herself. An instant later, I was overcome by a wave of dejection. What difference did it make if the hospitalization was voluntary or involuntary? She had no control over herself or her circumstances. And, in the long run, that was all that mattered.

I made two phone calls that morning after speaking with the nurses on the ward: first, to Roxanne, to update her on what had happened the night before, and to ask her to cancel all my appointments for the next several weeks; and then Flo, who was still at our mother's.

"You can tell Mom that Grace is terribly depressed and that she's in the hospital." The words came from some other part of me, a numb one—as if I were in a trance, as if I were fighting reality by letting a fog descend over my emotions. "But leave out the part about cutting her wrists. That'll only make her worry even more. Just let her know I'm okay. Just say I'm too exhausted to talk."

How many times had I heard my mother say she was "too exhausted to talk?" Probably thousands during my fifty-seven years. "Too exhausted" expressed how overwhelmed she felt, or how angry, or how much she wanted to hide. Or, even, all three simultaneously.

"Make sure she understands that I'm still reeling," I added then. "I don't want her to feel shut out."

Christmas came and then disappeared—the day itself a charcoal smudge in my memory. Weeks would pass before I would remember the carefully wrapped packages that I'd stacked in an extra closet and then forgotten about in all the turmoil. Remembering them later, I got those boxes out of the house and off to a charity as fast as I could, their presence too painful a reminder of the moment when our lives fell apart.

For those first four days after Grace's hospitalization, I remained sequestered in our master bedroom, waiting for the holidays to finish out, my interactions with nearly everyone nonexistent. Evelyn called to leave messages assuring me that she was in daily phone contact with Grace, and Phil hovered nearby to comfort me. Apart from that there were only the phone calls I made over and over to the insurance company to clarify and resolve coverage-related issues. I worked my way through the tiers of representatives and spent hours trying to explain that certain stipulations to Grace's coverage—which was excellent—did not apply in this case. The conversations were maddening and left me feeling frustrated—trying so hard to advocate for my daughter—just as I had when she was a little girl in need of surgery for her kidneys.

The morning after Christmas, I spoke with Evelyn—but only briefly. I'd been sitting by the window, an unread book in my lap, when my husband handed me a shawl and the phone; his expression was tender.

"I saw Grace yesterday." Evelyn's voice was calm and that reassured me. "And she's quite angry with me, too. You're not alone there," she added with a small laugh. "I've encouraged her to call you. And even if she won't see you, it might be good for you to drop off some of her stuff with the nurses. Clothes, a book, her bathrobe."

"Of course," I replied, choked up that I would be allowed to do something for my girl at last.

"I'll be following her closely once they discharge her," Evelyn continued, "which I'm guessing will probably happen by New Year's."

"She's been there four days now. It's killing me not to know what's going on."

"I'd have to say, she's so depressed, and so heavily medicated right now, I'm not sure how much she's really able to participate in her care."

"Has there been any coordination with Adler?" I asked, referring to Grace's psychopharmacologist.

"Well, as you know, that's hard when the patient's treatment team is not on staff at the hospital. But I've been talking with him. I'm not sure how much contact he's had yet with the attending psychiatrist there." She paused then, as if letting me absorb all that she'd said. "I know this must be very, very difficult."

I closed my eyes and pinched the bridge of my nose, hoping to press back my tears.

"I've spoken with a colleague of mine. She's very wise and I think you would like her." She lowered her voice. "She might be a good person for you to talk with."

I wrote down the therapist's name and number and tucked the piece of paper inside the book lying on my lap, somehow knowing that I'd be calling this woman shortly.

After gathering together what I guessed Grace would need from her bedroom—careful to choose things that were comfortable and soft to the touch—I called the unit to let them know that my daughter's therapist had recommended I drop off some of Grace's belongings. I also asked that they suggest Grace meet with me when I dropped them off. They remained noncommittal, and later, standing in the anteroom to the psychiatric ward, numb with pain, I was embarrassed by my daughter's latest refusal to see me. In silence, I watched an aide sort through the small duffle bag of my daughter's belongings. Minutes later, my cheeks hot, I went to the elevators with the emptied satchel and leather ties from my daughter's fleece-lined moccasins gripped tightly in my hand. "Sorry. Nothing that has laces," the aide had explained.

Later that same day, I finally did what I had been unable to manage in the previous four days. I phoned my mother.

"Oh, Terry!" Mom sounded short of breath. "I've been praying and praying! How's Grace doing? Is she out of the hospital?"

"I'm sorry I haven't called you myself, Mom." I bit at a ragged cuticle on my thumb. "This whole thing has been such a nightmare. I'm still trying to get a handle on when she'll be released. Looks like it will be in the next few days." Hearing the concern in my mother's voice made me wish I had reached out to her for comfort sooner. Or to comfort her.

"Maybe she's stressed out about school?" she suggested, obviously as desperate for a reason as I. In the background, a radio played loud enough so I could hear it. "Maybe all that studying is too much for her. Maybe she should be closer to home."

"I don't know, Mom," I said, suddenly overwhelmed again. "All that will have to be figured out." Outside, the weather had shifted; the yard was now cloaked in fog. "I just wanted to let you know I'm alright. And that I'll stop over when I can."

"Listen, Terry. You don't have to worry about me. Before Flossie left, she filled my refrigerator. My God, she bought enough food for a month." She took a wheezing breath.

"Are you okay? You sound like an old accordion."

"It gets dry in here but I have to keep the heat turned up."

"Well, it looks miserable outside, so whatever you do, don't go anywhere in the car." Sadness and worry filtered through my numbness; how lonely my mother must feel, so alone in her house since my father's move to a home two years earlier. And how increasingly precarious it was for her to navigate around the place she adamantly refused to leave. "I'd rather die than go to some damn old people's home and have a bunch of people who don't understand English bossing me around," she'd insist whenever I broached my concern for her safety. "Nobody's going to take away my freedom."

This attitude—while not surprising—was totally unlike that of my now ninety-three-year-old father. Opposed to the idea of a nursing home despite the fact that he'd already traded his cigarettes for an oxygen tank and was wheelchair-bound, Dad had initially clung tight to his belief that, as Mom's protector, he had to be physically present. On a deeper level, however, I knew that my father wanted to prove himself to be the reliable provider he'd always been. Going into a nursing facility would cut deep into his and Mom's limited savings, fueling her lifelong terror that she would be left penniless with nowhere to go. And she *had* balked—even at the idea of bringing in home healthcare services. Refusing the help even when I'd offered to pay. "I can't have strangers in my house!" she'd declared. "They make me too nervous. I can't stand having anybody poking around and touching my things."

"This is crazy, Dad," I'd finally said to him when we were alone one afternoon. Shuffling through the house, Mom's irritability about caring for her husband had taken on a more disturbing hue: she admonished Dad with regularity, her words like missiles of verbal abuse. "It's time for you to walk me through the money so we can handle it together. We'll make sure Mom has whatever she needs." I waited then, allowing time for the point to sink in before speaking more bluntly. "And if you think you're protecting her by staying here, you're wrong. You know she can't take care of you. Mom's overwhelmed—like she always was when we were young. And she's taking her stress out on you." I paused. "Just the way she did with us back then."

A short time later we moved him to a small Catholic nursing home, a transition that he handled with grace. And much changed for the better for him at that point. Well taken care of and treated with dignity, he was faring far better than Mom was, still home and now alone.

Through the phone, I wanted to offer my mother something that might soften her solitary state. Despite my depression about what was happening to Grace, I tried to sound optimistic and focus her attention elsewhere. "I'll call you tomorrow, okay? Maybe next week, if I have any energy, we'll go spend time with Daddy."

"Oh, Terry, that'll be too much for you," she insisted. "Anyway those girls there wait on him hand and foot." She let out another dry cough and I didn't like the sound of it, making a mental note to alert the community nurse who made free house calls to senior citizens.

～

Eight days after Grace was admitted to the psychiatric ward and three days before the year turned, the doctors released her without letting either Phil or me know ahead of time. An hour after she called announcing she was about to be discharged and needed a ride home,

I arrived at the hospital and was finally admitted onto the unit. There, I discovered no viable discharge plan had been made for any of us. At least, not in my opinion.

The discharge planner handed me a sheet of paper with the names of a few psychiatrists in the area who could be contacted for follow-up care. "Really?" I said, scornfully. "Does this mean that in eight days no one's bothered to coordinate with the doctor who's been prescribing my daughter her medications for the past four years?" I was enraged. How could we keep Grace safe now?

Unbelievably, matters got even worse once I arrived home with my groggy and disheveled daughter. I had barely enough time to wonder what medications she had been given before she announced that she was going to stay at her boyfriend's home—the same young man she'd banished from our house on the day of her breakdown.

"His mother says it's okay," she said, her tone dull and muted. Alarmed by how she looked and sounded, but hoping to avoid any further escalation of the tension between us, I did the only thing I could think of. I followed her upstairs, past the train of garland that still decorated the bannister but now looked so cheerless and out of place, and watched while she threw some clothes into a large plastic bag. I managed to wrangle from her the address and phone number of her boyfriend, and—once she had gone—left Evelyn a voice mail.

Then I went to the bathroom and threw up.

It took another week—a week during which I believed I would surely drown in my anxiety unless I found a pocket of air through which to breathe, a week before my mind grew clear enough that I could wake in the morning and not have the urge to vomit. It took that long for the family sheltering Grace with benevolence and compassion to realize how close she was to acting on her longing to die. "Andy says he's afraid he's going to wake up to find her dead in the bed," his mother shared at last. "She has all kinds of medication with her and he says she's been drinking. That she's out of it a lot."

Another round of crisis played out, but finally, in close coordination with Evelyn and the psychiatrist who had been managing her medication for years, Grace grudgingly agreed to enter an intensive, outpatient treatment program that specialized in working with severely depressed, college-age adults. For the first time in a long time, she would live at home in a way that mirrored nothing before. How fervently I wished it could have been under different circumstances, circumstances that represented "normalcy," like coming back to us before launching into her first, post-college job—rather than taking a medical leave from her final months of study.

But wishing was the least of it. I was terribly afraid for—and of—this alien version of my daughter, whose extreme irritability and restlessness defined her. Worst were the evenings after her long days in the treatment program. She stomped around the house until she finally succeeded in finding someone—her boyfriend or some "new friend"—to pick her up, at which point they would disappear for hours. Not even a record-setting snowstorm one frigid night deterred her from jumping into someone's car and traveling a long distance. Her judgment was abysmal.

I hovered in the background, watching, watching, ever careful to hide my fear; I knew it served no purpose and would only drive Grace further away. Most unsettling of all was the knowledge that I could not reach her, and that she could not hear any kind of reason. How hard it was to witness her fury with me.

"You think that everything you do, you're doing for *me*. But it's really all about *you*," she hissed, contempt in her eyes, her voice like the ice in a pond frozen over in deepest winter, its surface not to be shattered regardless of how fiercely I pounded on it. "I don't want *anything* you have to give me. I can't stand to even be around you."

It unnerved me to be the lone target of my daughter's verbal attacks, as she never went after Phil. How I wished I had the power to ease her pain. To help her find peace. But I understood then, for the first time perhaps, that I didn't have any weapon approaching that in my mother's arsenal of love. No more than I'd had such a weapon when I was a daughter, watching Mom from our dark living room doorway that night when I stood in thrall to my horror—helpless to stop her from muttering how much she hated her life and wished her children dead.

Now it was my daughter who smoldered with rage. However, I was no longer the devastated child, listening as her mother spewed her hate. Now I was the one with the power—and the responsibility. I was the mother called upon to bow her head under her child's animosity in these darkest of hours, with the hope, however distant, that soon some kind of rational thinking would return.

And I wondered, without ceasing, about the cause of her illness. How much of her mood disorder was chemically driven—or biologically based? How much was due to the job I'd done as a mother? I believed I'd provided her with steady support and a lot of attention and love, and I'd apologized for any poor decision I'd made in the past. But now I wondered if Grace and I had succeeded at all in being parent and child in appropriate ways. Were we still stuck in that same old mire of resentment that began when she was an early teen—in the animosity that only now was expressed fully in this anger whose words could fill an entire book with their poison?

Constantly mulling over what I should do and how I should behave toward her, I tiptoed around her moods; once again I was trying to figure out when to step in and when to let go. Sometimes, I tried to amuse her with light conversation; other times I insisted that she engage. I discussed all of this with the therapist that Evelyn had suggested I call for myself, and now it was Roslyn who listened, intent as she concentrated on all that I was sharing. In despair I asked: how was it possible that my daughter viewed me as a harpy who was smothering her, one from whom she could not escape?

Was Grace right? Was that who I'd become?

Our relationship had always been complex. The natural process every mother and daughter undergo as they cut the cords of an intimacy of emotion that exists from birth was complicated by my own early history, remarriage when she was at a vulnerable stage, and even more by the horror of her suicide attempt. I wondered: in my fear of losing her, had I lost sight of where the boundaries between us belonged? Or worse: had I only fooled myself into believing that I'd *ever* gotten this matter of boundaries right? After all, I'd been the single mother of an only child for such a long time—perhaps even, emotionally, before my divorce from the perpetually absent John. And before becoming a mother, I'd never had a model for a healthy bond between a mom and a young adult daughter. Was it possible, as Grace now seemed to want to believe, that I was the kind of mother who simply couldn't "let go?"

I sobbed my way through my therapy hours, dipping each week into a deep well of anxiety, sadness, and grief. Near the end of winter, with Grace a bit sturdier but no less furious with me, I finally had something to say.

"Listen, Grace," I began one night, as I slipped into a chair across from her in the kitchen.

I'd caught her off guard, and she glanced at me, puzzled. I wondered if she would get up and leave. "I'm not pretending to know what you need." I placed my palms flat on the table. "And maybe someday I'll discover that I really am your problem." I paused. "But here's the thing." I looked at her intently now. "Nobody has to die."

She blinked. I waited again, wanting my words to sink in. "Not you. Not me." Keeping my tone level, I used her continuing silence to keep on talking. "What I'm saying is, you don't have to wish me dead, or wait for me to drop from a heart attack to be free of me." I lowered my voice then, nearly to a whisper. "And you don't have to kill yourself to get relief from the pain."

Still she didn't speak. I pulled my hands back and folded them in my lap. "Or from whatever scares you about building your own life."

Her eyes drifted upward, as if she were chasing a thought.

"Look. I know I still have work of my own to do with my therapist." I kept my voice steady and pressed on. "I just want you to understand that you're surrounded by people who love you. People you can draw from for help. You don't have to go it alone." And then I stopped talking and just listened: the tick of the mantel clock; the breathing of the retriever-mix that rested at my feet, a dog that Grace had rescued from a shelter a few weeks before. "Do you understand what I'm saying? That this whole mother–daughter separation thing doesn't have to be driven by rage? Doesn't have to be lethal?"

"Yes," she said quietly, as she slid down in her chair. She lifted her head and her eyes had softened. I thanked her for listening. Then quietly walked out of the room.

One afternoon around that same time, looking for an escape from the tension with Grace and feeling badly that Mom had been stuck in the house through the cold winter months, I called her to make plans to see a movie. I still associated movie theaters as the places where my mother retreated when most angry and depressed during my childhood, but on this day, I simply wanted to indulge her. As always, my mother loved getting out for an afternoon, and she always welcomed an opportunity to see a new release. Unfortunately, my call that day took a quick turn south.

"Terry, that's great. But listen," she said, her voice firm. "The next time you're over, I want you to take me for my driver's test." She cleared her throat. "With all the cold, I've been a prisoner in this damn house. I just can't have my license expire."

Since January, I'd known this discussion was coming. Flo had taken her twice to try to get it renewed when she'd been in town over the holidays. And twice Mom had failed the road test.

"I hate to tell you this, Mom, because you're not going to be happy." I drew a deep breath. "I'm not going to go to the DMV with you."

"Why not?" she screeched into the phone. "You're coming over in my direction anyway!"

"I'm sorry, Mom—but you're not going to be able to drive anymore. It's too dangerous." And with that one sentence I denied my mother that which she coveted most: having wheels. To drive represented the last vestige of control in her life. Telling her hurt. "I promise," I compromised, "I'll take you wherever you need to go. I'll run all your errands for you. But I won't take you to renew your license."

Dead silence.

"Forget it, then," she said in a steely voice. "I'll go myself."

"You already failed twice, Mom," I said, in a tone that matched hers. "You'll be too nervous to drive—God forbid, you could even have an accident. And you'd be uninsured!"

"Listen. I'll drive without a goddamn license, if I have to!" she shrieked. "I've never had an accident! I'm losing my mind staring at the walls in this frickin' house!"

"Mom! You're ninety-frickin'-four!"

Back and forth we argued, the conversation going from rough to worse, until my mother unleashed a barrage of goddamns and other assorted blasphemies that would have impressed a sailor. Holding the phone away from my ear, I marveled at her life-long ability to string together curse words in a way that created such rhythmic flow.

"Now look what you've done!" she said when she'd run out of any further invectives. "Because of you, my soul is in hell!" And with that, she hung up on me.

Even with winter on the wane, the streets were still icy. I didn't trust that my mother would not make good on her threat to steal away in her twenty-four-year-old blue Taurus, and so I convinced Phil to accompany me to her house. We used my spare key to get into the garage where he disconnected the car's battery with élan.

Three days later, arriving at her house to take her to the movies as I had promised, I peeked first into the garage. Like someone checking for mice that might have invaded a pantry, I wanted to see if any trail of evidence indicated that Mom had gotten behind the wheel. I turned on the light and laughed for the first time in months. She'd tossed the heap of throw pillows she always used to get herself high enough in the driver's seat across the garage floor.

Mom never did confess that she'd tried to start the car and that it had been stubbornly silent. Occasionally, she grumbled about not being able to drive, but her protests were half-hearted. Perhaps the simplest explanation for her dropping the entire issue was spiritually driven. Maybe she didn't want to risk getting herself riled up after having "taken the Lord's name in vain" a record number of times. She was, after all, well into her nineties. Already in overtime, she nevertheless had a soul to protect. A soul she needed to keep out of the hell she believed in so fervently.

Going to the movies with her was pleasant that day. So much so that I suggested we do it again soon. But when we did a week or so later, the excursion didn't go nearly as smoothly. I was tired that afternoon, the strain of trying to manage my work and my personal life weighing me down. I'd just buckled Mom into the passenger seat of the car when she asked about Grace.

"Maybe a little better. But still very depressed," I reported, as I started the engine. "But that's not unusual. It'll take time."

"Do you think she really needed to be in that hospital?"

Startled and defensive, I responded in a sharp voice. "Yeah, Mom, I do. We didn't have any choice."

Minutes paused before she spoke again. "Well, I'll tell you. I don't get it." She pulled a stick of Juicy Fruit from the pocket of her purse. "What the hell does Grace have to be so depressed about, anyway?" Her fingers picked at the wrapper. "Jesus, Terry. She's got everything going for her. And she's got you running all over the place in your free time. When are you going to stop catering to her?"

I set my jaw and drew my lips into a tight line, but the words pushed out of my mouth anyway. "Okay, just stop right there!" I held up a finger in warning. "I don't want to hear one more word." Fury swelled. How dare she be angry with me for spending time with my daughter when she was so sick! This—after all the help I'd given *her*? We drove on in silence, my mother staring out the passenger window, her hands fidgeting in her lap. My anger simmered long after I'd dropped her back home.

Only when I was finally alone did I recognize that I was not her real target and the realization made me angrier than I already was. It was Grace with whom she was furious, Grace who had always reminded her of herself—a bright girl with talent and promise. It was Grace whom Mom had championed: attending her dance recitals and violin concerts; encouraging her to make full use of the chances she had to develop her gifts. Opportunities that she, Florence Crylen, had never been afforded in spite of how desperately she had wanted them. Now, Grace seemed weak. She'd become depressed and hadn't "toughed it out" in the way her grandmother would have.

Wasn't my anger really due to the fact that her attack on my daughter felt far worse than any anger directed at me ever could have? I wasn't used to her aiming at my Grace, so vulnerable, the one who was the child of my heart. And if my mother learned that her granddaughter had acted on an impulse that defied the laws of the church, her reaction would be far worse. And so, I never did tell my mother that Grace had slashed her wrists and tried to commit suicide. Although I'd come a long way in my pledge to avoid holding on to secrets, here was proof that old habits could be resurrected. This was a secret I had consciously chose to keep.

Spring came, then summer, and Grace began to make gains—though she was still fragile. With her depression under better control, by July she had decided to continue the treatment program she'd been in for nearly six months through summer's end, and then return to school to complete her final months of study before graduation in December. I was ecstatic.

And even Mom was holding her own pretty well. She'd made it through another cold winter, but with the midsummer weather so oppressively hot that year, she'd had little opportunity to enjoy time on her patio. Knowing how much she craved being outside in the warm weather months, I searched for time away from work, hoping to get her away. Take her out for a ride.

"Oh, Terry. What a surprise!" she said, one torrid afternoon toward the end of July, as I walked through the door and kissed the top of her head.

"Can you make it up out of that chair, Mom? I want to take you to lunch. How does that place next to the Hallmark's sound?"

"It'd be so nice to get out. Is this top okay?"

She bent over, slowly, and worked her swollen feet into a pair of open-toed canvas shoes. Then pushed herself out of her recliner and shuffled toward the four-wheel walker with its fold-up seat leaning against the wall.

"Grab my purse there, will you, Terry?"

"Where would you be without this purse that weighs more than you do?" I smiled at her as I joked. "Got your house keys? Your coupons? Your secret stash of cash?"

"Don't laugh. I never want to be left stranded," said the woman whose fear of abandonment had plagued her all her life.

Unfortunately, lunch could only be described as mediocre— unwittingly, I'd chosen a restaurant with nothing on the menu that her weak stomach could handle. Disappointed and a little worried that she hadn't eaten much, I then suggested we stop by the library so that she could pick up more of the audio books she so enjoyed.

Once in the parking lot, I helped her out of the car, putting my arms around her shoulders. "Wow, Mom! I'll bet it's over a hundred degrees. Why don't you let me give you a ride?" I gestured to the walker and opened up its seat.

But as we got up onto the sidewalk, the walker tipped backward suddenly. Mom fell onto the cement, hard. Anxiety flooded me as I bent to try and help her up.

"Oh!" she exclaimed, her eyes wide.

I made a quick decision to avoid moving her. "Just stay right there," I said firmly. Dialing 911 on my phone, I crouched down beside her.

That look in her eyes! What if she's having a heart attack? Do you even know what you're doing? Like the scared child I'd been when trying to care for my mother, I remained outwardly calm as I shielded my mother's body from those who stopped on the sidewalk to help. "No, we're okay. Please don't touch her."

"Terry, I can't breathe."

"They're on their way, Mama. The ambulance is on its way."

In the emergency room, Mom moaned loudly as staff moved her from the transport stretcher to the hospital gurney.

"She went down really hard," I blurted to the nurse. "Can't she get something right away for the pain?" Seeing my mother look so small and vulnerable, I could focus only on how much she was suffering. "How bad is it, Mom?"

"Terrible," she moaned. "Agony."

"Please don't make her wait," I begged. "You can see how fragile she is."

"Fifteen," Mom moaned when the nurse asked her to assign a one-to-ten number to the level of her discomfort. Quickly, an IV was set up. As I watched the fluids drip from their bags, I monitored her face, waiting for the frightened look in her eyes to abate. Then, pushing a chair flush to the bed where she lay without moving, I dropped my head into my hands and lost control.

"Mom, I'm so sorry," I sobbed. "I'm so sorry." I couldn't stop myself, even though I knew I should be strong for her. Maybe it was all too much—caring for her at the same time I was trying to care for Grace.

"Now, Terry," she said. "You listen to me." Her fingers tapped the crown of my head. "It was an accident." She stroked my hair. Which only made me cry even harder. Never before had she touched me in this way. "I mean it," she went on. "I don't want you ever to feel bad about this." Impossible as it seemed, given how badly injured I suspected her to be, her tone was as tender as it was insistent. My body went limp as I realized that my mother was reassuring me that I wasn't responsible for her pain.

Later, after an X-ray revealed a fractured left arm and two fractures on her spine, my mother waited until the ER doctor disappeared around the curtain of the makeshift room, x-rays in his hand. Only then did she gaze at the ceiling, and cry out with unexpected force.

"Sweet Jesus! I just want to die!"

I picked up her "good" hand, kissed it, and then patted her hair as she had patted mine such a short time before. Struck by how vehemently she'd spoken, her words like a plea to the heavens, I didn't rush to reassure her that she was not going to die. Instead, I vowed that I would do everything possible to ensure she was spared more suffering.

After a short stay in the hospital—during which time she repeatedly complained that the hospital staff "forgets I'm here when you're not around, Terry"—I arranged to have her moved into hospice care at the same Catholic nursing home in which my father lived; they were only rooms apart now, just down the hall from each other. Although Mom was totally bedridden, Dad was not. Generally mentally sharp, he could—with the help of an aide—use his wheelchair to go the short distance to visit Mom and offer her comfort. But heartbreakingly, perhaps in his excitement to have her near once again, my father seemed unable to comprehend the dire nature of her injuries. "Terry, when will she be able to have lunch with me in the dining room?" he asked, over and over.

Elderly nuns moved past her doorway, also residents of the home—nuns who undoubtedly must have reminded my mother of those long-ago enemies in their black-and-white habits. One by one, they wheeled or walked toward their destination: dinner, the chapel, the tranquil garden out back. Some had tufts of white hair poking out of their shoulder-length veils. Often, they would pause at the entrance to my mother's room and singsong a greeting to her. Sometimes they called her by name—"Hello, Florence." Other times it was "Peace be with you, dear." But always they reassured her, telling her that she was in their prayers.

If she was awake, Mom would unfailingly answer them. Her eyes half-closed, she offered up a little wave, her mouth curved upward. Not unlike how I remember Grandma Healy's smile when she said goodbye to us after our afternoon's excursions. My mother was transformed each time these scenes with the sisters played out. The lines in her face softened; she breathed easier. Every promise of prayer seemed like an anointing, a vocal laying on of hands. Her fingers, even the ones that poked out of her cast, relaxed over the folds of her blanket. The war had ended. My mother was being welcomed home.

I'd been keeping a close vigil in the days since the emergency room, monitoring her alertness and her pain, but now, because she was receiving morphine more freely through hospice care, Mom was physically comfortable. And still lucid, too. We talked quietly whenever she wasn't dozing—snippets of conversation that included her mention of the small kindnesses and pleasures for which she was grateful. Like how gentle the ambulance attendants had been when transporting her to the nursing home. And how much she enjoyed the tiny sips of coffee that she could manage with a straw. Appreciative comments that made me both smile and want to cry.

She had questions, too. She wanted to know who was caring for her beloved and overweight Pomeranian (a dog with whom Flo had surprised my parents when they were in their early eighties; I had chastised my sister for this poor choice of a gift, given how old they were, but the dog had become Mom's devoted companion). Whether I had remembered to turn off the air conditioning in her house to keep costs down. "And what about my purse?" she'd asked more than once. "Did you put it someplace safe?"

Each day, she had new questions, questions that had to be checked off her mental list of worries. Always, I reassured her that she need not concern herself about them, my voice rising and falling as if I were crooning a cradle tune. After a while, she'd close her eyes, like an innocent being carried off into slumber on the wave of a mother's song.

There was one point, however, after she'd been at the nursing home for several days, when I asked her a direct question.

"So, Mom. Are you really done, or are you thinking that maybe you want to fight this one out?"

She paused before answering me, a serious look on her face. "How long would it take?" she whispered.

What did she mean by "it?" Was she asking me how long it would take to die? Sadness enveloped me. I didn't know to which part of my question she was responding—the dying or the gaining enough strength to fight. Whichever part it was, I realized that I didn't want to know the answer. I did not want to lose her.

"I don't know, Mom," I whispered back. "But you don't have to decide today."

Six days after Mom's admission to the home, Grace and I were scheduled to go out of town with Phil for her stepsister's wedding. My daughter had—despite her continued estrangement from Sarah—nevertheless agreed to play her violin during the service. And although a similar distance separated Sarah and me, I knew that my presence at her marriage was important to Phil. But I also could tell that this wouldn't be an easy trip for Grace and, wanting to be supportive, I asked her if it would be helpful to her if I came. She said yes. Things were improving between us, and so the decision was an easy one. To be there for my daughter took top priority.

"Now don't you go anywhere on me, Mom," I'd said to my mother on the evening before the wedding; I was picking up my purse and getting ready to leave her room. Then, leaning in close, I brushed her still beautiful white hair with my hand as I kissed her forehead. Her skin was warm against my lips. "Flo's plane lands in another half hour, and she'll come straight here from the airport. I'll be checking in with her tomorrow to see how you're doing." I smiled from the doorway. "And I'll be back here first thing Sunday morning. I love you." She'd nodded and waved off me and my concerns.

Some sixteen hours later, and only ten days after the accident on the library sidewalk—for which I still felt responsible—congestive heart failure took my mother from me for good. Despite all the hardship and the distance, despite her lifelong obsession, she did not die as she had so feared: alone. Three of her other children and her husband of seventy-two years were gathered in the room filled with the bright plants and flowers and family pictures I'd brought from her home hours before her transfer from the hospital. She died surrounded by her family.

But on that Saturday afternoon, I was not beside her, and my mother rode onward into death without me.

∾

The communal walk from the nursing home chapel where we'd held Mom's service to the cemetery was short. Grace paid tribute to her grandmother with a violin solo. Sitting tall in his wheelchair at the graveside, his eyes puddled with grief, my father leaned toward me. "It's pretty here, Terry. Nice trees. Very peaceful."

As my mother's casket was lowered into the ground, I reached for my daughter's hand. This time, she did not resist. I wrapped my fingers around hers and squeezed them lightly. She squeezed mine back and warmth crept over me, despite my sorrow. For those few moments, the enormity of our shared loss erased the distance between us. I released Grace's hand then, wanting to do so before she had the chance to withdraw from my grasp. When the recitation of prayers for my mother's soul ended, I reached into the basket of flowers at the foot of her grave and chose a pearl-colored rose—its stem long and sturdy, the thorns snipped away. The fragrance of the blossom enveloped me like a balm. I breathed it in. And then I let my mother go.

Different Time, Different Station

The difference between hope and despair is a different way of telling stories from the same facts.

—Alain de Botton
The Consolations of Philosophy

LOSING MY MOTHER WAS like a bruise to the heart. But my sadness, as tender as it was, did not approach the all-encompassing grief I'd felt as a child reaching out for a mother who did not—who could not—reach back. Sorrow pooled deep after she died, but the little-girl anguish, the long-ago loneliness that had once seemed powerful enough to rob me of breath was absent. I waited, half-expecting to feel that crush against my breastbone, but it did not come.

In a practical sense, my belief that my mother had not suffered in those final days of her life attenuated and relieved my grief. She'd told me she was physically comfortable, and in her eyes, I saw no shadow of pain. The knowledge that she had not been abandoned, or "left to rot in a corner," as she had so often described her fear of aging, gave me solace. Circled by family, embraced by her faith, my mother had not died alone. And while happiness seemed to have eluded her except for a fleeting period when she spun youthful dreams on a ballroom dance floor, I imagined that my mother, had she been able to weigh in on the matter, would have pronounced her death "a good one."

But grieving her loss turned out to be easier than grieving the fact that I had not had the emotionally available mother I'd wished for; only upon her passing away did I realize that sometimes fantasies die last. I had been a mother to my mother for most of my life, with few opportunities to be the daughter who received her mother's comfort and support—opportunities that only came later in our lives. Yet, the finality of it all didn't hit me until weeks after she was gone; the reality of her death forced a thought I couldn't shake: no more chances; no more chances for love.

On a late summer day, I sat on the steps of our backyard deck reveling in the warm rays of the summer sun. It was then that I recognized the inner voice of my younger self. *It can never happen now! She's dead! And she died without saying the words. The actual words!* Staring out toward a lilac bush, I remembered once again the little girl who had imagined she could make her real mother over in the image of her pretend Radio Mom. A mother who, if the daughter were patient enough, would say "I love you," a smile on her lips as the words echoed in the air. Wasn't this, on some level, what I still wanted and now could never have?

Rationally, I no longer doubted that my mother had loved me as best as she could. One of her last notes to me had read "you are such a blessing to me. Love, Mom." But sadness about my unrealized wish—the ache of never having heard her say the words aloud—settled around me. The remnants of my fantasy that Mom would one day become fluent in a language so foreign to her had nowhere to go. As I had with her physical being, I now had to lay to rest that hope of a verbal expression of her love.

I sat with a host of emotions that afternoon. Afterward, I got up and went back into the house to be with Grace and Phil, recognizing peace within myself. Peace that came from knowledge: despite having been cheated as a daughter, I had found a path to loving my mother—and with compassion. All had not been lost, I reminded myself. In the end, *I* was not lost.

This awareness of being lonely—but not lost—was one that I strove to embrace over the following years. And sometimes, in those early months after her death, as I sifted through the good memories I had of my mother, I occasionally tested the thickness of the scars along my daughter skin and felt grateful that the mother-wounds, which had once been so raw, no longer stung. Some scars had faded; some, I expected, would always remain tender. But healing had occurred—and was still occurring. This, too, was a comforting insight. Suffering *could* be ameliorated. Pain didn't have to be the final emotion.

As summer waned, Grace prepared to return to classes for her final semester before college graduation. With our relationship a bit reconciled, and before she headed back to school, she invited me, along with her therapist, to attend her last group session at the outpatient treatment center. There, at a small reception, she was celebrated by her therapy team and fellow group members and seemed lighter in mood. More relaxed. Those qualities I hadn't seen in her in a very long time.

She gracefully accepted compliments about the progress she'd made and her eyes grew wet as she hugged peers and made her goodbyes. As I stood in the background, joy suffused me until a strange sensation descended. I suddenly recalled the last time I'd witnessed Grace being singled out for her accomplishments—it had been after that performance in her college's production of the Tennessee William's play. A weight settled on my chest, knocking away the swell of pride that had started to grow there, and my body grew suddenly hot. Was there more going on beneath her shy smile? Was her laughter just part of some act she felt compelled to perform, as it had been that autumn evening, some ten months before?

I forced myself to challenge the worry—something I was practicing in my therapy as a way to counter remembered trauma. "That was then, this is now," I thought to myself as I did the rhythmic breathing I often used to calm myself. "She's stayed with the program the entire seven months. She's done well." I made a conscious effort to remain present and enjoy the pleasure the day brought.

And then, just as I'd done on the night of her college performance, I reached for her, and gave her a long hug. She hugged me back, and, in that quick moment, illusions about the future fled. How difficult the process of releasing my daughter into her own life would be, especially as her health would always be of concern to me. I would try to accept her struggles, but it would be difficult. Still, breathing slowly and staying in the moment, with hope in my heart for whatever step she would take next—this I could do.

More years would pass before I could glance into my mind's rear-view mirror and realize how, through so much of my life, I had been suffocated and driven by fear. As adept as I'd become in learning how to mother myself and hum my own lullabies, I now understood how lonely it is to be one's own mother. It provides a song that can only echo through your heart alone because there is no answering harmony: no one else sings it with you. I could see, for the first time, that the flame of being heard and understood burns low if it goes unrecognized.

I've spent a professional lifetime listening to other people's stories, but beyond working on myself in therapy, I've done little to share my own—except for this one story which I've taken on the risk to write, hoping other women will identify with it. In reflecting on the curious child I'd once been, I remember: the little girl wanting to take chances and eager to spirit herself away from the stoop, the one eager to connect with the world and all its mysteries and challenges. And while my younger self's search for Radio Mom was finally abandoned, what eventually emerged in its place was an important discovery. Radio Mom was not merely a fantasy; unconsciously, she was a role model as well. She taught me to work hard to be as much of a broadcaster and receiver of love as I had imagined she would have been herself.

Yet, having focused so much on my life on mothering—mothering others, mothering my mother, mothering myself—perhaps it is time, at last, for me to relinquish the vestiges of the need to go solo. No longer lost, no longer lonely, I want to be part of a chorus of voices.

Now, my own voice sounds in my ears—loud and clear—as I make my way through the memories of these years. I face a different journey now, and this time I make it with others by my side as I sing. I hear applause as I make this step forward. It is Radio Mom who cheers me on and, perhaps in some subtle way, my own mother, too.

Chapter Epigraph Sources

Introduction

Anne Lamott, "Why I Hate Mother's Day:" This article first appeared in Salon.com, at *http://www.Salon.com* on May 8, 2010. An online version remains in the Salon archives. Reprinted with permission.

Chapter One: My Radio Family

Joyce Peseroff, *Eastern Mountain Time.* Copyright © 2006 by Joyce Peseroff. Lines from "Museum of Childhood" reprinted with the permission of Carnegie Mellon University Press.

Chapter Two: Devil and the Pitchfork

Anna Quindlen, Excerpt from STILL LIFE WITH BREAD CRUMBS: A NOVEL by Anna Quindlen, copyright © 2014 by Anna Quindlen. Used by permission of Random House, an imprint and division of Penguin Random House LLC. All rights reserved.

Chapter Three: Sticks and Stones

Ruth Stone, *Simplicity.* Copyright © 1995 by Ruth Stone. Lines from "The Wound" reprinted with the permission of Paris Press, at Wesleyan University.

Chapter Four: Liar, Liar, Pants on Fire

Malachy McCourt, Excerpt from *Death Need Not be Fatal* by Malachy McCourt, Copyright © 2017. Reprinted by permission of Center Street, an imprint of Hachette Book Group, Inc.

Chapter Five: Odd Girl Out

Mary Pipher, Excerpt from *Reviving Ophelia: Saving the Selves of Adolescent Girls,* Copyright © 2005. Reprinted by permission of Penguin Random House.

Chapter Six: Outside the Lines
Ann Hood, Excerpt from *The Obituary Writer*, Copyright © 2013. Reprinted by permission of W.W. Norton Company.

Chapter Seven: Flying at Low Altitude
D.W. Winnicott, Excerpt from "Communicating and Not Communicating Leading to a Study of Certain Opposites," in *Maturational Processes and the Facilitating Environment: Studies in the Theory of Emotional Development,* Copyright © 1965. Reprinted by permission of The Marsh Agency, Ltd.

Chapter Eight: Show Time
Clarissa Pinkola Estes, Excerpt from WOMEN WHO RUN WITH THE WOLVES by Clarissa Pinkola Estés, Ph.D., copyright © 1992, 1995 by Clarissa Pinkola Estés, Ph.D. Used by permission of Ballantine Books, an imprint of Random House, a division of Penguin Random House LLC. All rights reserved.

Chapter Nine: An Unsafe Neighborhood
Annie G. Rogers, Ph.D. Excerpt from THE UNSAYABLE: THE HIDDEN LANGUAGE OF TRAUMA by Annie G. Rogers, Ph.D., copyright © 2006 by Annie G. Rogers, Ph.D.. Used by permission of Random House, an imprint and division of Penguin Random House LLC. All rights reserved.

Chapter Ten: Acts of Balance
Maggie O'Farrell, Excerpt from I AM, I AM, I AM: SEVENTEEN BRUSHES WITH DEATH by Maggie O'Farrell, copyright © 2017 by Maggie O'Farrell. Used by permission of Alfred A. Knopf, an imprint of the Knopf Doubleday Publishing Group, a division of Penguin Random House LLC. All rights reserved.

Chapter Eleven: Missing in Action
Pablo Neruda, Excerpt from "Sonnet XCIV" in English translation provided by Gustav Escobada, in *The 100 Sonnets: English and Spanish Bilingual Edition,* copyright © 2014 by Pablo Neruda. Used by permission of Agencia Literaria Carmen Balcells, S.A., representatives for the Neruda Foundation.

Acknowledgments

It is with gratitude that I thank:

Brooke Warner, publisher at She Writes Press, for her unstinting support for my book, and to Samantha Strom and Lauren Wise, SWP editorial project managers, and Julie Metz, SWP cover designer, for their guidance through the publishing process.

The members of my Madison writing tribe, who welcomed me into their fold and spurred me on, with special thanks to Julie Tallard-Johnson; Linda Sonntag; Colleen Sims; Anne Liesendahl; and Madeleine Uranek.

Edward Rossini, Ph.D., mensch, pal, and unwavering cheerleader.

My siblings, Patty, Flo, Paul, Mike, Rob, Tom (and Jeanie, in spirit), for supporting my desire to explore the experiences that our mother and I had shared—and those that she and I did not—as well as all the emotions that accompanied them.

Roxanne Levin, sister of the heart, whose friendship has enriched my life beyond measure.

Linda Gray Sexton, Radio Mom extraordinaire, whose steadfast support made it possible for me to realize my "third act" dream.

My husband, Phil, for his abiding love and generosity of spirit, and his unerring ability to spy the silver lining, no matter how dark the cloud.

And especially, Grace, my "BBG," for trusting me to tell my story without taking over hers.

About the Author

Terry Crylen's thirty-five years in the mental health field, thirty of them in private practice as a Ph.D. Licensed Clinical Psychologist, served to enrich her understanding and appreciation for the emotional power of the mother–daughter relationship. Terry's solid credentials and a wealth of experience represent the foundation upon which *In Pursuit of Radio Mom* rests.

As a graduate of Northwestern University, Crylen's career in mental health focused largely on working with adolescent girls and adult women presenting with clinical depression, anxiety, and complex mood disorders. She also collaborated closely with other health professionals in the treatment of substance abuse and eating disturbances. Additionally, she worked with scores of parents, teachers, pediatricians, as well as psychiatrists for children and adolescents, to address patients' academic, social and behavioral issues.

A life-long Chicagoan, Crylen is committed to supporting

community efforts aimed at creating opportunities for the city's economically disadvantaged youth, and is an ardent supporter of the arts. Along with her husband, Phil, Terry is also a "frequent flyer," devoted to maintaining strong ties with family––most of whom are scattered across the US. When not on the road, or writing, she can be found hanging out with four-legged friends or with her nose in a good book.

SELECTED TITLES FROM SHE WRITES PRESS

She Writes Press is an independent publishing company founded to serve women writers everywhere. Visit us at www.shewritespress.com.

Twice a Daughter: A Search for Identity, Family, and Belonging by Julie McGue. $16.95, 978-1-64742-050-5
When adopted twin Julie faces several serious health issues at age forty-eight, she sets out to find her birth parents and finally gets the family medical history she's lacking—and she ends up on a years-long quest that ultimately reveals much more than she bargained for.

The Girl in the Red Boots: Making Peace with My Mother by Judith Ruskay Rabinor, PhD. $16.95, 978-1-64742-040-6
After confronting a childhood trauma that had resonated throughout her life, psychologist Dr. Judy Rabinor, an eating disorder expert, converted her pain into a gift and became a wounded healer—a journey that taught her it's never too late to let go of hurts and disappointments and develop compassion for yourself, and even for your mother.

At the Narrow Waist of the World: A Memoir by Marlena Maduro Baraf. $16.95, 978-1-63152-588-9
In this lush and vivid coming-of-age memoir about a mother's mental illness and the healing power of a loving Jewish and Hispanic extended family, young Marlena must pull away from her mother, leave her Panama home, and navigate the transition to an American world.

Boot Language: A Memoir by Vanya Erickson. $16.95, 978-1-63152-4465-3
In order to survive her childhood, Vanya Erickson was forced to become fluent in two languages: that of her Christian Scientist mother, who spoke only honeyed versions of the truth, and that of her rancher father, whose words were hard as the scrape of his boot heels and stung like the back of his hand.

Bowing to Elephants: Tales of a Travel Junkie by Mag Dimond $16.95, 978-1-63152-596-4
Mag Dimond, an unloved girl from San Francisco, becomes a travel junkie to avoid the fate of her narcissistic, alcoholic mother—but everywhere she goes, she's haunted by memories of her mother's neglect, and by a hunger to find out who she is, until she finds peace and her authentic self in the refuge of Buddhist practice.